Investment Risk Management

Wiley Finance Series

Investment Risk Management

Yen Yee Chong

John Wiley & Sons, Ltd

Other Wiley Editorial Offices

John Wiley & Sons Inc., 111 River Street, Hoboken, NJ 07030, USA

Jossey-Bass, 989 Market Street, San Francisco, CA 94103-1741, USA

Wiley-VCH Verlag GmbH, Boschstr. 12, D-69469 Weinheim, Germany

John Wiley & Sons Australia Ltd, 33 Park Road, Milton, Queensland 4064, Australia

John Wiley & Sons (Asia) Pte Ltd, 2 Clementi Loop #02-01, Jin Xing Distripark, Singapore 129809

John Wiley & Sons Canada Ltd, 22 Worcester Road, Etobicoke, Ontario, Canada M9W 1L1

Wiley also publishes its books in a variety of electronic formats. Some content that appears
in print may not be available in electronic books.

Library of Congress Cataloging-in-Publication Data
Chong, Yen Yee.
   Investment risk management / Yen Yee Chong.
      p.   cm.
   Includes bibliographical references and index.
   ISBN 0-470-84951-7 (cloth : alk. paper)
    1. Investment analysis.   2. Risk management.   I. Title.
HG4529 .C47 2004
658.15'5–dc22   2003021828

British Library Cataloguing in Publication Data

A catalogue record for this book is available from the British Library

ISBN 0-470-84951-7

Typeset in 10/12pt Times by TechBooks, New Delhi, India
Printed and bound in Great Britain by The Cromwell Press, Trowbridge, Wiltshire
This book is printed on acid-free paper responsibly manufactured from sustainable forestry
in which at least two trees are planted for each one used for paper production.

Contents

1

Introduction to Investment Risk

A walk in the investment maze faces millions every day in our global trading community. There are countless investment opportunities right under our noses. Some are good, others smell instinctively bad. But, how are we to know if the whiff of the business opportunity is really "off", or does our nose fail us? The scent of prestige used to be a leading indicator for investors. Yet, there have been spectacular failures at Andersen, Enron, Global Crossing, Tyco, Worldcom, Marconi, Equitable Life, Swissair and Sumitomo. These show that the value of a "big name" firm can be dubious. What have we really bought into?

Management theory, backed up by advanced information technology, would like to come closer to guaranteeing a sound investment choice. Investment experts bring the risk and return together. But, the danger is that final selection is still based upon prestige and not value. It is worse when this value is exposed as fraudulent. An analytical survey of fraud in the USA found that firms were losing about 6 % of their revenues to occupational fraud and staff abuse.[1] This was estimated to be worth $400 billion. Furthermore, even good companies suffer from strategic misdirection by the executives, and their investors may find themselves on the sidelines watching the ship go down. We can be average at investing, and if the boat is sinking we are even worse at influencing the decisions of large corporations. H. Ross Perot said that trying to change the plans of the General Motors leaders was like: "Teaching an elephant to dance."

DREAM VERSUS RUDE AWAKENING

Modern business theory has, undoubtedly, left us richer to manage our investments. Pricing theories and various portfolio models have provided a foundation for building future wealth. Later and more sophisticated theories have incorporated a discount for that omnipresent element in all business activities – risk.

No enterprise is immune to the dangers that constitute risk. Yet, risk is in itself a good driving force to promote greater or more productive effort – the stock market feeds off two key motivators: fear and greed.

Greed is a unidimensional factor that eggs us on to increase profits. There is no law that defines greed as an intrinsic criminal offence; CEOs and directors have been quick to extract as much pay and benefits from a company before they leave. Yet, excess greed comes before a fall. They should come to fear regulator and shareholder activists' counter-attacks. Fear is the expression that we are about to suffer damage in some manner, primarily financial loss on the markets – we call the damage a potential hazard. Excess fear leads to stasis, and eventual business ruin. Risk is an ever-present factor in any enterprise, and profit is regarded as a proper reward for bearing the risk in the first place. The notion of a risk-reward ratio comes in, and the concept of "acceptable level of risk" is a natural result.

---

[1] Association of Certified Fraud Examiners, *Fraud Survey of 2608 Companies*, 1996.

Risk management is the modern discipline that answered the call to handle business risk; the prime example being company failure. Many of the failures listed above cannot be attributed to criminal acts – corporate fraud and CEO theft reflect sentiment that is fine for the sensationalistic press, less so for the court room. Furthermore, a company director is rarely brought to court for losing control of a company. It is extremely unlikely that they would have the personal assets to come close to refunding their shareholders in full. Insurance premiums are rising, and there is no guarantee that pay-outs are increasing pro rata; you get an insurance company's assessment of damage, not your costs of replacement. In view of these shortcomings, traditional legal and insurance avenues of redress are not to be leant on as a crutch. A new look at risk management is required.

This book targets those risk factors that threaten a loss in our portfolio value or investment. We adopt a view of business investment as a closed project. This enables us to use a more disciplined analysis of what governs enterprise success, and that involves project management. We focus upon what constitutes investment risk; how organisations handle investment risk; how we can manage investment risk better. Briefly speaking, we can bring sound engineering and actuarial tools to examine risk and risk management in depth. Forensic accounting is needed for a deeper investigation of a company over its statistics and corporate personalities. These views are, oddly, absent in many business books on risk management. These financial engineering methods are useful for the banking and fund management sector.

Everyone harbours a dream, and high profits without risk are the ideal in the financial world. Saving is the obverse of consumption and real-life pressures come to the fore to make achieving this dream more problematical. Returns are dropping on average, as the recent falls in the global stock exchanges have shown. Furthermore, the world's population is continuing to age, certainly so in the major developed nations. Pension funds are now reducing their benefits and/or finding themselves under-capitalised. So, where is the dream now?

The changing demographics mean that, per capita, fewer people of working age are supporting more retired folk. Pensions form the biggest average holding by value of any household, more expensive than their personal house. Add up all these pensions and they form the largest fund of private households in most Western countries. Pension fund managers and institutional investors now exert a larger block vote upon corporations than the majority of private investors. For example, CalPers and Teachers TIAA-CREF are large funds in the order of $148 and $270 billion, respectively. They are influential in the field of corporate governance – one example being their near-success in scotching the HP–Compaq merger.[2]

Sadly, people often devote more attention to their house and all its accoutrements, rather than choosing their investment. They pore over home furnishings or kitchen equipment, but their choice of pensions comes last. Some CEOs, like Dennis Kozlowski of Tyco, preferred to use company funds to help deck out his apartment in style. It is no surprise that the public patience with modern corporate leaders is wearing thin. The CEOs' avowed duty to shareholders is now plainly exhibiting a tenuous link to reality.

People are beginning to experience real disappointment when their pension returns are given upon retirement. A Robert Maxwell comes along occasionally to rob a pension fund, or an Equitable Life fund catastrophe occurs to destroy public confidence in the future. But these crooks are in the minority. Can the public prosecutors ever prove conclusively that there was any criminal activity within the Tyco, Marconi or ABB losses? Given this doubt or mistrust,

---

[2] www.Calpers.ca.org, 2002.

should the public pull all their money out of pensions and invest it elsewhere? If so, where? This disillusioned attitude alone would lead to a strain on the pensions system, particularly that managed by the professionals.

It is said that wars are fought over oil; yet, the 21st century could see the real investor battling over corporate profits, and the pension funds will figure largely. The changing demographics of the larger older population stresses pension funds to provide for the retired. There will be a stark separation of expectations and reality as people struggle with the net sums left to survive on. The new defined contributions plans and the closing of some pension funds to new entrants further splits the retired world into the haves and the have-nots.

Yet, investment funds such as Fidelity Investments – the world's biggest fund, will definitely continue to be numbered among the "haves". Furthermore, with nearly $900 billion in assets under management, such funds will move stock markets around the world through their sheer size and influence. Investment funds will continue to exercise significant authority upon how money is invested.

More recently, some funds have become vocal advocates for socially responsible investment, such as the Coalition for Environmentally Responsible Economies (CERES)[3] with more than $300 billion in assets. It is not just a mere focus upon corporate profits, but an explicit drive for accurate institutional reporting. These are to be conducted under stricter ethical guidelines on environmental, economic and social grounds.[4]

Recent years have not been entirely kind to funds. Fund managers could have lulled themselves into projecting glowing consistent returns of 10+ % p.a. on the stock market. Now, a long-term average of 4 % to 6 % p.a. could seem more probable. We have to link reality to a suitable investment risk vision. Furthermore, a fall of −25 % was not only realistic, but a sad result in many stock exchanges during 2002.

We are faced with the snowballing prospect of client and business pressures to "beat the market" in finding returns to investment. Over-eagerness is an enemy of caution, and that can only lead to added danger or "unreasonable risk". We look to restore a balance between risk and return within this book.

BOOK STRUCTURE

This book looks at the uneasy marriage between investment and risk. Given the importance and increasing role of funds within the markets, there is an emphasis upon institutional investors. We have aimed this book towards those who work in the banking, fund management and insurance sectors. It does not take a pure accounting, engineering, IT, banking legal, or insurance treatment of risk – such a limited stand would probably impoverish profitable analysis. There is input from the actuarial and the forensic accounting professions, and methodologies from the project management discipline.

This is a synthetic view of risk management, also looking at the organisations that operate in the financial sector. The manner in which people work together to reduce risk is analysed in *organic* risk management. Previous studies of risk management have concentrated too much on the mechanics and numbers – this is not a healthy fixation.

---

[3] www.CERES.org.

[4] "The global 100 investors: the most influential investors on the planet." Lori Calabro and Alix Nyberg, *CFO Magazine*, 25 June, 2002.

This has tended to cover a multitude of reasons for risk or business hazard. The dangers of operational risk, and proposed solutions, will be detailed in later chapters. This introduction to the category of risk known as *operational risk* is within Chapter 1.

We look at the concept of risk, and the undeniable link it has to return in Chapter 2 "The Beginning of Risk".

The basic union between risk and return is detailed in the summary of results borne out in the early study of portfolio management within Chapter 3 "Investing under Risk".

The divorce between reality and theory has worsened under recent corporate failures. Shining the occasional spotlight on previous business cases helps the reader to understand the course of investment history in Chapter 4 "Investing under Attack".

Explanation of the leading trends in investment theory and financial regulation offer the benefit of making better-informed decisions based upon an investment methodology. These are examined in Chapter 5 "Investing under Investigation".

So, learning danger signs from past failures offers a profitable business warning radar for professional investors. These are outlined in Chapter 6 "Risk Warning Signs".

Technology has played a large part in the development of risk management as a modern business discipline. We examine some of the state-of-the-art financial techniques and their associated IT-based risk management systems in Chapter 7 "The Promise of Risk Management Systems".

Yet, technology never solved all our business problems. There is some prospect that de-mystifying current investment dogma will offer a better and balanced return in the future. We present an overall view of realistic risks in Chapter 8 "Realistic Risks".

Over-simplification of some business ideologies led us into a false lead of risk management. One symptom was the classic "one-size-fits-all" business response.

Financial leaders have reworked business theory and regulations into a more appropriate cogent investment strategy. One such development is the release of the new banking regulations for banks around the world known as the "Basel II" guidelines. Their new views on banking risks are outlined in Chapter 9 "Risk-managed Banking and Basel II".

The evolving paradigms on investment risk have led to new ideas on modelling risk. These are summarised in Chapter 10 "Future-Proofing against Risk".

Visiting the past has shown us the potential graveyard of many previous, proud companies and investment dreams. Even a current examination of the current state of investment risk management demonstrates the splintered thinking of the business community. The business orthodoxy is hide-bound by mechanistic theory; we require treatment of corporations more like living beings requiring "organic" risk management. These can, and should be, joined up by integrated risk management detailed in Chapter 11 "Integrated Risk Management".

Whether we engage in simple personal investments, or much larger and more complex corporate business decisions, we can all benefit from risk management to preserve the value of our investments. These are summarised in Chapter 12 "Summary and Conclusions".

2

The Beginning of Risk

We look at what risk entails at the beginning. These hazards are linked to the actual result, but humans tend to focus on the danger only when it materialises. The fear of investment failure has led to risk management emerging as a more visible business skill and discipline. We introduce risk management within an investment project management methodology. The three investment risks: credit, market and operational are defined.

Recent financial disasters are listed as case studies. There is a greater need to find true information about companies and their leaders getting beyond their reputation. These form part of our warning system in our risk management methodology.

RISK AND BUSINESS

Profits are created through business activity, with bread often used as slang for money. Risk and business come together more often than a peanut butter and banana sandwich. Yet, risk is the banana skin upon which many businesses slip. Look at the recent crashes of those considered as "safe investment vehicles". As if the collapses at Enron, Andersens, Worldcom and Equitable Life were not enough, these came on the public crashes of dot-coms. A lot of banana skin, but no bread for those poor investors.

Thus, it is surprising to some that the financial sector, while claiming to be well risk-managed professions, continues to experience losses on a significant scale. The increasing public opinion is that Wall Street (or the City of London) is a road that leads from a shark-filled pool at one end, to a graveyard at the other. Maybe, we have to get used to conducting risk management for ourselves to ward off attack. Investing is becoming akin to swimming with sharks.

CASE STUDY: THE SHARK AND ITS RISK

This type of natural risk is feared on the shores of the USA, Africa and Australia. The attack can kill in seconds in the larger and more deadly species. Within other countries, it is considered a delicacy; gourmands in Asia relish eating sharks' fin soup as an appetising dish. So, the jaws of this shark are potentially fatal, while the other parts are very tasty. Risk is a different among people according to their cultural risk appetites. Others prefer just to avoid the fatal risk completely.

1. The potential death from a shark attack is a "hazard" phenomenon in the first line of risk analysis.
2. The intrusion into its path is the second element or "risk catalyst" in a shark attack. Within the process, the victim is open to injury through "risk exposure".

3. The third element is the "risk result" or event. Death is rare within the total population, so it can be termed a *low-frequency, high-impact risk*.

However, for interested observers, in truth, the real statistics for shark-attack fatalities are not generally very high. The shark attack is a potential risk for all swimmers in tropical marine waters, but bees, wasps and snakes are responsible for far more deaths. The annual likelihood of death from lightning is 30 times greater than a shark attack in the USA. Statistics point to far higher chances of dying from drowning or cardiac arrest than from any shark attack. Many more people are killed driving to and from the beach than by sharks.[1]

One characteristic danger sign of many sharks is that it is a relatively fast-moving aquatic with a prominent dorsal fin. There are some familiar warning signs for investors too. Yet, substandard companies that lose your money or suspect business counter-parties do not necessarily exhibit such glaring warnings. Nevertheless, we can establish a corporate risk profile to sway us from investment-risk sharks.

Corporate victims from bankruptcy or share price collapse are more frequent. A careful observation of the whole investment market distribution of probabilities, outcomes and their utilities, is necessary to profile the risks from suffering such a bad attack. Just as an intuitive view of this shark-risk profile is strongly biased to overestimating the downside risk and the final risk event (death), the rarity of company bankruptcy attack has had a perceived lower risk or probability.

Most non-financial industries characterise risks as hazards. Yet, the end result need not be a loss event; in fact, there are several event results where there is a happier and more profitable event. There is a one-in-a-million risk that you will win the jackpot lottery prize. Then, we can apply mathematical and computer techniques to derive analytical results.

Defining a risk event, and categorising it in the frequency-impact risk matrix is one start for analysing risk. Then we can see how a loss occurs. A loss, then, is a three-step process, starting by a hazard, with the help of contributing factor or catalyst, a risk event itself, and with it a concomitant loss or result (see Figure 2.1).

The chances of this hazard resulting are conceivably higher when there are deep individual and political connections involved.

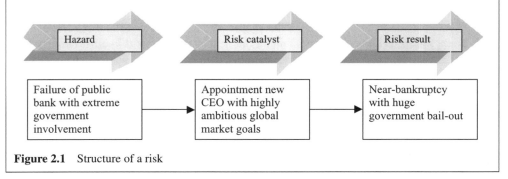

Hazard	Risk catalyst	Risk result
Failure of public bank with extreme government involvement	Appointment new CEO with highly ambitious global market goals	Near-bankruptcy with huge government bail-out

Figure 2.1   Structure of a risk

[1] Florida Museum of Natural History, 2002.

CASE STUDY: THE RUIN OF CRÉDIT LYONNAIS (CL)

This was a proud bank that expanded rapidly from 1987 onwards. New drives then aimed to take CL to a global scale that would rival the major US investment banks. The ambitious growth was fuelled by hubris and additional funds from the French government. A business culture locked in the depths of the Paris Elysée sought to be as skilled and powerful as the top global US financial players. This goal was a goal that pushed CL towards bankruptcy.

The catastrophic moves inadvertently linked strategic risk with a lax risk management function. Middle office risk management played no significant part when political power and individual ambitions were supremely dominant. The bank nearly went bankrupt after 1993; its bail-out estimated variously in the region of $25 billion.[2]

However, spectacular corporate implosions need not be attributed to political chicanery or dot-coms. SwissAir and Equitable Life are examples of highly respected companies that had the gloss taken off in no uncertain terms. Investors should take the responsibility to arm themselves with the required company information to beware the hazards that lurk under the label of "operational risk".

Sources of historical data could prove beneficial for potential investors. We have to go outside the usual ambit of corporate profits or financial losses quoted in the newspapers and online media. We need analysis to determine actual company performance, as distinct from company PR and spin.

Take the once-respected engineering firm, ABB.

CASE STUDY: ABB ENGINEERING

A glorious reign for Percy Barnevik seemed to good to be true. He was reckoned to be Europe's top CEO for quite some time. The ABB share price fell 80 % from its peak share price of over 50 SFr in 1999. It has lost 96 % of its peak value into 2002 (Figure 2.2). Then, he and his colleague were meant to take $136 million in a pension pay-off. The directors prosper and the company suffers. There was a mini-revolt among many investors. Barnevik ended up with less. The ABB bonds had become graded by Moody's in 2002 as junk.

Ironically, the shares of ABB rose significantly in 2003 once it had agreed a rescue plan for its US subsidiary Combustion Engineering (CE), amidst its rising asbestos legal claims.[3] The extent of damages in the 1950s reappearing as a hazard 50 years later shows that our risk horizon can be too short. A loss database or a risk register has to be compiled that details such hidden legal risks.

In fact ABB survives, but its reputation is slightly tarnished. Some newspapers will look upon this episode unkindly, especially as they were probably among those that put a halo upon Barnevik's head as the most-respected European CEO. There is no suggestion that ABB was pushed among the junk of many tech shares that went bankrupt. Actually, the ABB share price recovered partly as investors began to separate perceived reputation from real company worth.

---

[2] See "A new scandal at Crédit Lyonnais", *Economist*, 11 January 2001 and "Crédit Lyonnais", *Erisk case study*, March 2002.
[3] "ABB shares rise on asbestos claims deal", *Financial Times*, 17 January 2003.

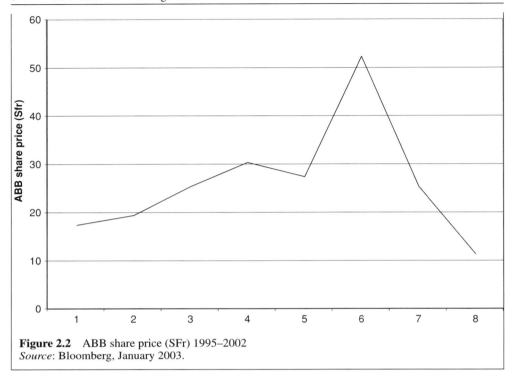

Figure 2.2   ABB share price (SFr) 1995–2002
Source: Bloomberg, January 2003.

What we have witnessed are the countless dot-com scams that were publicised following the extensive media coverage and US lawsuits. The dot-com shares were being "pumped and dumped" by reputable brokers and investment banks. The UK Financial Services Authority (FSA) has somewhat belatedly taken measures against "spinning", but it is unlikely that investors who have lost from the popular IPOs will recover much of their original assets. It seems the regulatory authorities can seek to prevent future financial malfeasance, but cannot recover compensation for investors, especially when another pump-and-dump scam occurs.[4] It is more like "bread yesterday, bread today, but never bread tomorrow" for the investor.

Investors' confidence has fallen to epic lows, and continued dissatisfaction is expressed by investor disillusionment in company management following recent corporate accounting scandals.[5] The regulator is called in to monitor the business environment, but a lot of this seems to be after the crash. We live and breathe in a market where having financial regulators around means in no way that investment risk is dead. A common recurring problem arises when the public buys seemingly riskless or "safe" investments from licensed financial companies. Risk perception has become separated from actual risk.

The next crisis is going to be borne by unaware consumers again, and they need protection. That is what laws and financial regulations are for; but the true success of any code is that companies and individuals:

---

[4] FSA press release, www.FSA.gov.UK, FSA/PN/102/2002, 23 October 2002.
[5] "Private share ownership in Britain 2002", www.Proshare.org.uk, 23 September 2002.

Table 2.1   US white-collar crime[1]

	% cleared	% arrests	Number of business victims	Financial institutions – number of victims
Fraud	33.12	79.52	47 907	2989
Bribery	61.78	93.22	16	0
Counterfeiting/Forgery	29.83	88.70	55 676	5310
Embezzlement	38.37	86.74	17 627	182

[1] "Measurement of white-collar crime using uniform crime reporting (UCR) data", Cynthia Barnett, *FBI statistics*, 2001.

- follow these regulations;
- be punished for contravening these regulations;
- suffering loss from illegal business activity can seek to obtain some form of compensation.

Numerous headlines in the news show the get-outs. Bernie Cornfeld of "Fund of Funds" infamy fled to the Bahamas. BCCI lost billions for account-holders. No one from Andersen or Enron has yet been jailed for their part in the scandal. Asil Nadir of the failed Polly Peck fled to Cyprus and was never extradited. Ernest Saunders had his trial stopped for his Alzheimer's disease, from which he recovered. Peter Young of DMG was deemed mentally unfit after appearing for trial wearing a woman's dress. These cases took a lot of time and money to come to court. In most examples, shareholders got little compensation or next to nothing. Both punishment and financial redress are missing. Naturally, public dissatisfaction with the legal system continues.

How are you going to protect yourself in the financial markets? The most public view of regulation is to guard yourself against numerous forms of investment fraud or con-tricks.

Investment scams

The plain truth is that white-collar crime pays well, it is the fastest-growing business, and there is little risk of being put away. See Table 2.1.

Securities and commodities fraud in the USA was reported as $40 billion per year in 2001. So it is worth keeping an eye out for this risk hazard.[6]

Banking risk and sharks

Yet, there is not a single government or agency on this planet that can legislate against risk completely.

> Taking "appropriate measures . . . to prevent financial crime" does not mean that financial services companies should have to spend enormous sums on reducing financial crime to zero. That is not possible.[7]

Financial regulatory authorities tend to be underfunded and understaffed. Often, even if punished, only minimal fines are meted out for the guilty parties, and few lawsuits are launched every year compared to the number of customer complaints. Worse still, the downsizing trend means that financial regulators and banks will be less well-equipped to police the risk arena.

[6] "Securities and commodities fraud", www.fbi.gov 2002.
[7] "The reduction of financial crime", House of Commons Standing Committee, 15 July 1999.

The ratio of internal audit staff to total staff in some institutions today can be as low as 60 % of what it was about five years ago and banks are bigger, trading more complex instruments, and money is moving faster around the system.[8]

So, within the financial markets the odds of detection and punishment are both relatively low for:

- being caught; and
- being punished.

RISK MANAGEMENT AS A DISCIPLINE

The idea of risk management is certainly not a new one; it is certainly as old as that great risk mitigation practice – building an ark. The business theme is the same, believe that the risk event can strike us, act constructively to mitigate or lessen the damage when it strikes us.

1. There is the first school of investment risk management – the *fatalistic* business philosphy; you are inevitably going to be hit by a risk event, so better be covered. Bear the load yourself – retaining the risk under self-insurance. Risk management means keeping a contingency fund for your company.
2. This is can be the second paradigm of investment risk management – the *technological* school. We are mathematically and technically developed in our understanding of risk event, so we can avoid or mitigate risk through smart moves in advance.

Risk management is the study and practice that offers some answers for choices in the financial markets. Many of these models are mathematically based, aided by sophisticated computers and telecoms. Given all the collected brains, university degrees, sophisticated mathematical models, powerful computers and market reports, we should feel pretty reassured.

Yet, why do some companies continue to make such appalling business decisions? One possible answer is that the investor passes the money, and management mandate, over to the CEO to run the company. But, does it mean that Buffett is asleep at the wheel? No. Company directors are going to make money for you if properly monitored and goaded; inevitably, they slip up now and then, so prod them when needed.

3. This is maybe the third school of investment risk management – the *watcher* school. Another view is that the huge amount and complexity of numbers and accounts cloud the central issues, we just have to watch our staff and business partners. Technology in a global economy enabled Nick Leeson of Barings or John Rusnak of the AIB in USA get away with "rogue trading". All were human-based errors and they should have been monitored closely.
4. This is the *organic risk management* school – there is a need to link up separate initiatives in order to deal with various risk events and the actions of human beings, so better integrate all these developments for "joined-up" thinking. Thus, there is little understanding of how human staff behave or adequate integration of high-technology. Integrating all the risk management technology, plus knowledge of investor behaviour leads us forward. Recent developments in banking, insurance, law, accountancy, IT, project management and forensic accountancy will provide us stronger holistic organic risk management.

---

[8] "Operational risk", Middle Office, spring 1999.

Process initiation
    Define objectives and the scope of what we are trying to achieve
    Estimate what staff, skill mix, budget and time required
Risk analysis
    Identify the risks that face us, now and later
    Study and estimate the probabilities of these hazards occurring
    Estimate the impact (profit or damage) associated with these hazards
    Collate these choices in a matrix for evaluation
    Recommend best decisions available under various conditions
Risk management
    Devise risk management plan
    Assign key staff for completion of project
    Allocate risk management budget
    Implement risk management IT systems
    Run investment risk model
    Execute risk management decisions:
        ignore risks (prepare to bear all burden yourself)
        mitigate risks (lessen damage e.g. write a hedging contract)
        transfer risk to insurer
        sell off risk operation to an external party
    Take on partners and business counterparties
    Monitor and amend risk management plan where necessary
Project close-down
    Review progress
    Log experiences in a risk register or loss database
    Recommend follow-up actions

Figure 2.3   Risk management of an investment project

The last school puts business processes and actions within a methodology. This can be outlined within an investment project as shown in Figure 2.3.

Humans and risk

Whatever view we take, given the size and complexity of managing companies, we rely upon "experts" to keep a watch out. So, risk hovers around even the most "respectable" company to its very core. Thus, we have entered into the grey forest of artistic accounting and interpretation. The inability of some notable corporations to state the true health of their accounts is a worry that we must address. The Andersen–Enron case demonstrates some of the ground for confusion.

We have tended to focus too much upon auditors and analysts' lack of common sense or ethics. Numbers and balance sheets are not even half the corporate and investment problem – they are just a common symptom. We need to thrust our noses purposefully into companies, past the financial details, and into the corporate reality of how human staff operate. We investigate two cases of retail store theft.

---

[9] Centre for Retail Research, UK, 2002.

CASE STUDY: HIGH-STREET RETAIL STORE LOSSES[9]

UK high-street stores lose more goods to shoplifting than any other EU country, an asset loss worth approximately £4 billion. This is about 2 % of annual turnover, against Germany 1.19 %. A lot of this loss is an "inside" job – UK company staff are responsible for 28 % of the merchandise stolen. We can see that banks often lose some of their annual turnover likewise, and a part can be considered an "insider job" too.

The costs of security control and surveillance is somewhat negated by the inability of the UK justice system to deal with the large numbers of store thieves. Nationally, 675 000 thieves were arrested in 1999, but fewer than 10 % make a court appearance. Of these, only 4000 are given a prison sentence. Threat of imprisonment can become viewed as empty.

We have included an example of shoplifting and theft, but we have not expressed the significance of fraud. Businesses acknowledge the negative impact of fraud, which costs UK companies and public agencies around £15 billion per year. The costs of prevention and investigation add a further £1.8 billion to the total.[10] The summary of personnel checks, corporate research and the formation of a loss database now become seen as a necessity for sound business in the light of the potential damage suffered. A loss database under Basel II could be part of the answer to documenting a bank's equivalent of pilfering or leakage.

It is interesting to know how many banks and investment funds do not conduct such basic exercises. It is not just risk management, it is the concept of business pure and simple. As we have seen, banking fraud and poor trading supervision can enable staff to lose millions. Worse still, our experience in banking risk management has shown that the omission of such sound business monitoring can be costlier, if not deadly.

CASE STUDY: ALLIED IRISH BANK (AIB)[11]

John Rusnak was sentenced to $7\frac{1}{2}$ years in prison. He traded foreign currency for Allfirst, the US arm of Allied Irish Bank. He pleaded guilty causing losses of $691 million in a trading fraud to make hundreds of thousands of dollars in bonuses.

Former US comptroller of the currency, Eugene Ludwig, conducted an investigation that cited Mr Rusnak for fraud, but he also criticised AIB for creating the conditions for this fraud to continue for such a long time. AIB's lax management and weak corporate controls sowed the seeds of down that eventually grew into one of the largest banking scams since the rogue trading of Nick Leeson that led to the collapse of Barings.

Such operational errors also occur in Western banks to an alarming degree. They will continue to do so as long as banks and investment funds have business operations and practices that are vulnerable to suffer extensive loss. These companies are vulnerable because their risk culture is sloppy and has atrophied, just like the risk sensors that help us avoid being bitten by snakes. The problem with some banks is that: *once bitten, not really any shier.*

---

[10] Department of Trade and Industry, www.DTI.gov.uk, 2002.
[11] "Jail for £430 m rogue trader", *Economist*, 17 January 2003.

The state of the investment game

Much of the financial industry story has been built upon foundations of professional investment management and accounting. Risk management as a discipline took off in recent years within the banking and investment funds sector. Front-office sales are backed by in-house investment analysis and efficient regulation. These generate huge amounts of information and analyses. A truck-load of data and associated computer processing techniques have been created.

Lately, the financial "experts" have tended to jump on the bandwagon and subject the corporate numerical data to intensive analysis. Much in vogue is the variety of mathematically based modelling techniques. These models include computing variables for Value-at-Risk (VaR), Asset-Liquidity Management, Asset-Liability Management, CAMEL and Capital Adequacy Ratios and so on. These techniques are believed by many to offer adequate protection for the investors.

But, we feel that there is something missing to the aggregate financial expertise in the market. The mathematically based causal modelling can lead us to ignore some human-based risks. This is where organic risk management can help us. The loss database is just one possible tool for compiling a list of human-based risks.

These are potentially damaging corporate actions that are difficult to detect from balance-sheets and numerical data. The Enron–Andersen catastrophe showed that mathematics and the number-crunching have limited use outside the bounds of competence, ethics and common sense. We are faced with a myriad of risks.

RISK TYPES

Risk is the possibility of an event happening. Risk is often associated with negative outcomes; although there are some beneficial possibilities too, people generally connote risk with loss or damage. We normally take the insurance and everyday life custom of linking risk automatically with an unpleasant event. It is necessary to consider to recap on our views of risk within a multi-step process:

- hazard – the risk of an outcome or event;
- danger or risk catalyst that allowed this risk to occur;
- impact of the event upon your group;
- risk management – the process in which you can limit or avoid the potential damage.

There are four risk types that we wish to examine in depth within this book.

1. Reputation risk
2. Market risk
3. Credit risk
4. Operational risk

These last three are the same major risk types outlined in the latest Basel II banking regulations.[12]

---

[12] "New capital accord – an explanatory note", Basel Committee on Banking Supervision, January 2001.

Reputation risk

The time-worn way to avoid risk was the tactic of keeping silent ("there is no danger, keep shtum"), or hiring a big name with a good reputation to reduce your investment risk.

Thus, taking on the services of the top Wall Street or London City investment banks, lawyers, accountants and specialists was a sure way or reducing risk because they were "safe" business partners. One of the drawbacks of this method is that we are relying on heuristics that are either unfounded or out of date. The rule of thumb: "prestigious reputation = great service".

CASE STUDY: EQUITABLE LIFE

The notion that a large, old and well-established firm means a "good risk" took a bit of a knock after the Queen's bank (Barings) of England went down after the Leeson disaster. History repeats itself when we are faced with a respected company founded in the 18th century facing a struggle for survival. It seems to have been a case of damage by acting in a risk-ignorant and not by intention or criminal act. Damage limitation provided by the UK life insurance company Equitable Life shows us where risk management often comes in after a risk hazard surfaces, not before.

1. The damage from the mis-selling scandal was quite severe, many funds found culpable of selling inappropriate pensions to the public.
2. Most funds were enamoured of the guaranteed annual repayment whereby the funds essentially bet that they could assure the policy-holder of a fixed amount each year upon retirement.

The stock-market slump threatened their ability to pay out to customers, plus it jeopardised the capital adequacy base.

The new management went on a damage-limitation exercise. This eventually succeeded in keeping the company afloat, despite hard knocks to its former prestige. It is a process of reputation risk recovery, which could not have been conducted by a low-level risk management exercise. In this case, top management:

- recognised the hazards;
- evaluated the impact of the risks;
- allocated vast resources to damage control;
- set about retrieving reputation and clients' trust;
- put in procedures to limit further similar damage in the future.

A better use of communication and efficient PR could have triumphed over mechanistic risk management. Equitable Life was under such financial pressure that it dropped 50 000 pensioners from its schemes. Pay-outs fall, the number of lives insured decreases and the number of satisfied policy-holders has shrivelled to almost zero. If only they had known beforehand. Equitable Life struggles on, but survives. We can just regret that these damage-limitation measures were not done before, but post facto (see Figure 2.4).[13]

---

[13] *Financial Times*, 16 November 2002.

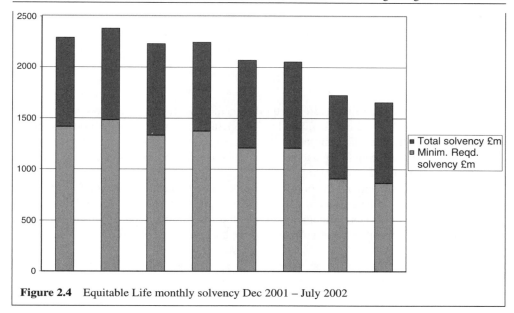

Figure 2.4   Equitable Life monthly solvency Dec 2001 – July 2002

Credit risk

Credit risk is the ancient hazard of suffering loss because of not being able to extract the promised return from a business partner. We also include counterparty and country risk within this category. Various examples exist: sovereign risk on issue of bonds and debt default such as the Russian economic crisis of 1998, or the Argentinian debt crisis in 2002.

Few banks only lend to one sector but actively diversify their portfolio. A modern bank (Commerzbank, 2001) shows how it makes arrangements for the projected level of domestic bad debt. See Figure 2.5.

Market risk

Market risk is the loss in value of the bank or fund's portfolio caused by changes in price (or price-related) factors. Currency rate, interest rate, equity price levels, volatility levels are changes or risks that come under this heading. A bond-dealing desk taking positions is a typical

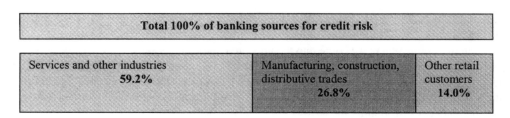

Figure 2.5   Credit risk
Source: "Provisioning for borrower risks by customer group – 'Commerzbank in 2000'," Annual report, 2001.

example of a portfolio under market risk. The large foreign exchange market trading feeds of these risks for good and bad where those who estimate the market risk well benefit, whilst those who calculate market risk wrongly generally fail.

Operational risk

This is a wide-embracing term that refers to the danger of losses from business system or process failure. This can include mechanical and human operations, faults in procedural design and system function. The Basel Committee on Banking Supervision adopts a narrower definition: "... the risk of loss resulting from inadequate or failed internal processes, people and systems or from external events."[14]

It includes legal risk and all errors from trading and settlement not previously covered in the above categories, to the criminal/fraudulent actions, up to the IT and system failures from human and external changes. Strategic, systemic and reputational risks are excluded. These are the categories of risk that are often said to be the hardest to model and predict – the human side.

When we have redesigned bank business processes, created dealing operations, or inspected fund managers, we work in a complex network of people and their varying skills. Some of these skills and experience are not really definable in numerical terms, but involve an element of intuition. Thus, investment risk management is an art, and not a science in many ways.

Risk management used to be a staid and reactive exercise, where the auditors would be called in after a company crashed or suffered loss. Now, it has become a specialist field in its own right encompassing several disciplines geared towards a proactive stance to mitigate against risk consequences.

Formerly, risk management was just like an optional feature that you could choose to buy later. Lately, risk management is becoming an inherent part of the processes of wealth creation and a sought-after skill. We include some of the essential skills for modern risk management.

The variety of risk is so wide, and potential damage so deep, that risk management has become high profile in itself. See Figure 2.6. Directors are less able to pay lip-service to operational risk because of the high impact when the hazards happen. Compliance was such a boring and low-key event that companies devoted fewer resources to it. Now the regulators are devising stricter rules, and the public wants to see that these are met by the company, that directors do not wish to face the reputation risk of being known as inept or hiding something disastrous when it comes to complying with the disclosure regulations.

Risk management skills often involve a combination of financial training and an intuitive sense to sniff out suspect investment opportunities or partners. It has a strong mathematical foundation, but recently, some of this modelling has demonstrated weak underpinning. So, we come back to having a good "nose" for business – intuition and experience, instead of paper qualifications.

Then, we define where we come into the grey area that calls for the artistic gift of subjective interpretation. The Andersen–Enron–WorldCom (AEW) cases demonstrate where confusion led to crooked chicanery. Then, we define where we come into the nebulous area that calls for the artistic gift of subjective interpretation. Yet, we can hover above the company risk horizon and see dangers surrounding us.

---

[14] "Sound practices for the management and supervision of operational risk", Basel Committee for Banking Supervision, www.BIS.org, July 2002.

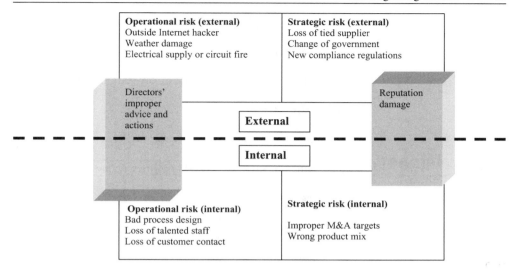

Operational risk (external)
Outside Internet hacker
Weather damage
Electrical supply or circuit fire

Strategic risk (external)
Loss of tied supplier
Change of government
New compliance regulations

Directors'
improper
advice and
actions

Reputation
damage

External

Internal

Operational risk (internal)
Bad process design
Loss of talented staff
Loss of customer contact

Strategic risk (internal)

Improper M&A targets
Wrong product mix

Figure 2.6   Risks inside and outside the corporation

The concept of an AEW risk-alert system would work in the same way as an AEW (airborne early warning) radar detects potential enemy action. It is tempting to point the finger at Andersen's accounting arm and try to fix the fault just there. Risk management is truly concerned with the fundamental source of errors and lack of control in modern corporate business, not just the symptom. The post-Enron quick-fixes and assurances must offer superficial comfort. We offer a view on the investor's AEW corporate risk-alert system in Chapter 6.

RISK AND DAMAGE

The fact is that although financial regulatory procedures for protecting the investor are well documented, financial redress and net loss are less well recorded. This means that even when the stock exchange and the regulatory organisations have given a good-housekeeping seal of approval to large numbers of listed companies, some records of company operations and the more truthful balance sheets take an opposite view. The imperfect relay of information, or interpretation by the investors, shows a divorce between extant risk and likely damage.

The finance industry wallowed in a "If it ain't broke, don't fix it" mentality for decades. Mistakes were made partly because of lack of proper execution in planning for extreme events, matched to negative impact. Every business builds a risk register with relative probability and associated impact. See Figure 2.7.

The different risk impacts and frequencies need to be dealt with by different people with various risk management skills. This varies from company to company, and from risk culture to risk culture. Where losses occur, these should be recorded in the loss database.

Insurance and fund managers form a highly organised risk-seeking profession that aims to share these risks for profit. It tries not to take on too much risk, or even too much risk that it does not understand. Otherwise, it stands the risk of dying as a business.

Insurance, even with its avowed expertise in risk management, is just as likely to face insolvency, as the crashes in their stock-market portfolios have revealed. Because banks, insurance companies and pension funds have a large slice of the entire stock market capitalisation,

	Low-frequency, high-impact risk Catastrophes to building safety – fires, electric power-outs, floods, etc.	***High-frequency, high-impact risk*** Loss of key staff to competitor. Death of CEO.
impact	***Low-frequency, low-impact risk*** Lateness in share registrar delivery. Lateness in filling month compliance report.	***High–frequency, low-impact risk.*** Lateness because of transportation problems. IT minor system crashes.
		frequency

Figure 2.7 The risk register (frequency vs. impact)

corporate inadequacy can force a sell-off of shares in their portfolios. This can create a systemic or pro-cyclical risk where continued selling destroys the stock-market value.[15] See Figure 2.8.

The threat of stock-market crash or some terrorist activity after September 11th may seem so uninsurable that some clients opt-out or go for self-insurance (bear the risk burden yourself). Otherwise, pay higher insurance premiums. A large corporation can retain a large risk because of the size and strength of its balance sheets.

Risk retention or self-insurance is troubling the insurance industry. Insurers' efforts to cope with loss of business have tried to offer alternative products or to cut premiums – both carry considerable risk. Cutting premiums or guaranteeing the pay-outs endangers the very same insurance companies that are meant to protect investors. Risk retention is also a prospect that troubles some investors – there is a tacit admission that they take a bet on an extremely low-frequency, high-impact risk. This means that their company can go bust, with little compensation for the investor. Business looks more like a gamble at the horse races.

Viable alternatives

There are loop-holes when we seek to protect ourselves through the financial regulators, the legal system, accounting or insurance. The validity of auditing and due diligence can be called into question. Rushed business diagnoses are superficial, and their foundations for defining a business conclusion are clearly limited.

---

[15] "New capital accord – an explanatory note", Basel Committee on Banking Supervision, January 2001.

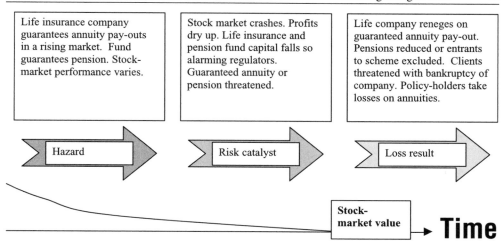

Figure 2.8   Risk in a life insurance company or pension fund

These severely reduce the effectiveness of traditional risk management avenues. The growing feeling among investors is that prevention is better, and cheaper, than a cure.

Accumulating a pool of corporate information might come in very useful. These avenues are explored in further depth in the following chapters. Some are:

- Traditional sources of corporate news in current events coverage.
- Prior company case studies and relevant industrial experiences from media sources logged in a "risk register".
- A deeper investigation of performance track-record of key company staff, counter-parties and business partners under detective and forensic accounting initiatives.
- Additional company reports filed under the Basel II new banking regulations.
- Procedure for early warning (AEW).

Those who have suffered enough from previous investments understand that reputation risk means perceived corporate value becomes rapidly uncoupled from real worth. We can now attempt to detect and discard undesirable business elements from our future plans using these data sources. One of the ways we can help to achieve this is to use an investment risk methodology. This is outlined in succeeding chapters within a view of a methodology for an investor's closed-end project, i.e. a launch and a desired end. So, when it comes to investing or building a portfolio, the increasing feeling is to do everything yourself.

3

Investing under Risk

We open with the need for rational investment analysis. Modern portfolio roots under CAPM are outlined, while an overview of VaR is explained. Position keeping and trading control are studied. The corporate governance structures for fund managers are evaluated. We analyse the value and differences between active and passive fund managers.

We look at elementary human behaviour when faced with enumerating probabilistic chances and using this knowledge relating to associated profitable outcomes. We see that human powers of calculation and common sense leave something to be desired.

The professionals use a myriad of financial modelling tools and portfolio models to form the basis of an informed decision. The efficient portfolio theory is reviewed in brief detail. It is thought that we can design portfolios to suit the investor's risk-return appetite perfectly.

We look briefly at Value-at-Risk (VaR) and Monte Carlo simulation. These techniques are widely used by most investment companies. We focus on some of the drawbacks and limitations of these techniques. One question is that since we are equipped with extensive financial theory, then why are so many mistakes and financial losses made? Some of these investment decisions are based upon faulty information or dubious assumptions.

Process problems and trading mistakes exist within any investment company, and the treasury exists to monitor and control these hazards. The importance of the treasury role is critical to police internal business procedures and staff. The treasury will also be aware of some of the main techniques used in risk management.

One of the main flaws is to concentrate on the theory and a view of a well-ordered world. This confusion means that there is a role for the professional investment adviser to assist the lay-person. But it can develop a naïve view of some professionals being intrinsically prestigious. The real world is more messy and complex than that and such deferential respect poses a reputation risk. An urbane view is needed of what interests professionals possess as stakeholders and what they deliver. Not understanding investment professional behaviour is a risk in itself. The extent of rogue trading and other self-interests also present a danger for the investment company.

We examine performance delivery and management control issues in fund management. We look at the benefits of active fund management against passive fund management. We need a more stringent and more realistic method of risk management that is concurrent with the modern markets and the various roles played by its human parties.

HUMAN BEHAVIOUR AND INVESTMENT CHOICE

Many studies use gambling examples to conclude that people are less efficient than computers in estimating probabilities in relation to expected gains or utility. That is, people are essentially subjective, with fallible memories and judgement.[1]

---

[1] "Artificial intelligence and stockmarket success", R.S. Clarkson, Institute of Actuaries, 11 May 1999.

- People cannot predict probability or severity of events with consistency. In the financial world, this leads to either bias of "things won't be that bad", or, the risk-averse "I fear the $100 loss more than I want the $200 gain". This is sometimes referred to as the "loss aversion" principle.
- The law of small numbers means that insignificant or unrepresentative samples of events can lead to an imbalance in opinion. Advertising and media coverage can be partly held responsible for an irrational tendency to purchase slim chances of getting rich. US, UK and Spanish optimistic folk buy their national lottery tickets in the extreme hope of winning.
- People are less accurate in their view of randomness, e.g. in gauging whether dice or cards are biased. Mental accounting and character judgement are clouded by non-financial influences.
- Assessment of real probability is hampered by emotion. Recollection of more emotive or recent events blurs possible from probable. The mass-buying hysteria in the dot-com craze and other investment bubbles is compatible with such experiences.
- People cannot construct probability or preference models consistently because any complex data collation exercise demands a more stringent methodology.

So, academic theories of estimated probabilities and expected utility and profit are of dubious worth because investors are both fallible and irrational.[2] The very tendencies of the same professional folk who manage investments and design risk management systems may be compromised by this same inherent bias.

Nevertheless, a lot of work has been done dealing with risk and return to move us away from our incorrect probabilistic judgement in the inexact science of portfolio management.

PORTFOLIO MANAGEMENT

We are constantly looking for a better portfolio with an improved calculus of risk versus return. It is often thought that we can build optimal portfolios with the data given.

Much of the bedrock was formed in the seminal work by Harry Markowitz in 1952.[3] We first started by assuming that capital markets have full competition, and we have participation of rational, well-informed investors. This market is known as "efficient". All securities are known and understood so that return increases with risk. Risk is measured in a manner based upon market price sensitivity called beta (β).

This means that an asset's beta is 1.00 when it fully reflects the movements of a benchmark, i.e. they move in tandem. This gives us a picture of market risk, so that a beta significantly above 1.00 means that the asset amplifies the market's movements. This volatility is traditionally viewed as risky.

We can thus put in stocks or bonds with a negative covariance or beta of -1.00 to protect the net value of the portfolio. This is the familiar technique of hedging to lock in your current value of asset. You can amalgamate a set of financial instruments of defined betas to build a desired portfolio. The investors can use their full knowledge in the transparent market to construct "efficient" portfolios to maximise return for risk.

Thus, we can derive an optimal risk-return point for each investor. Establishing an optimum risk-return point on the preference curve gives us the "best investment" for the market player.

This theory is known as the capital asset pricing model (CAPM), and it forms the bedrock of much investment theory. It is used in many universities and financial institutions for creating an "efficient portfolio". See Figure 3.1.

---

[2] For example refer to "Anomalies: risk aversion", M. Rabin and R. Thaler, *Journal of Economic Perspectives*, vol.15, no.1, 2001.
[3] "Portfolio selection", H. Markowitz, *Journal of Finance*, March 1952.

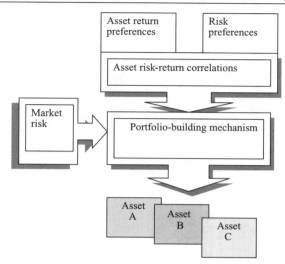

Figure 3.1   The CAPM portfolio-building model

The real world is a changing, dynamic environment. There is an accepted risk-return trade-off, and knowing this empowers you to invest fairly. See Figure 3.2.

However, the market constantly develops newer and more sophisticated models and investment vehicles. This requires a commensurate change in the investment strategy. The old CAPM notion of standard investors ("we are all the same, we all have perfect knowledge") looks a bit questionable now. Nevertheless, you can build safer portfolios by combining different assets.

The basic asset A and asset B portfolio model shows that you can reduce risk, the variance of the portfolio, by mixing assets to optimum point Y. You lose some expected return *r* %, but the benefit is lowering the risk from the extremes at points X or Z where variance is much more.

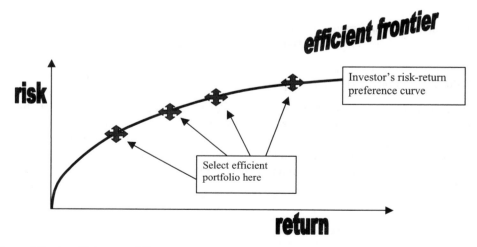

Figure 3.2   An efficient portfolio

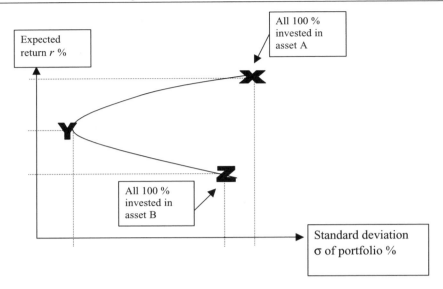

Figure 3.3   Two-asset choice portfolio

This reduction in the market risk is significantly higher than the lower return.[4] This forms the basis for the gospel of diversification. See Figure 3.3.

Moreover, there are even more complex "exotic" products introduced every day. The idea that our standard "vanilla" assets can be easily modelled to keep the market happy does not bear with modern highly leveraged financial instruments or derivatives. These new products and offerings do not have the properties of transparency and exchangeability often assumed in efficient portfolio theory.

We have seen that with CAPM and associated techniques, a view of an optimum portfolio can be used as a design blueprint. Now, with modern pricing and mathematical modelling we can push out the knowledge "envelope" of investment theory. More factors can be designed to make the models inherently more realistic than the former CAPM and efficient portfolio theory.

There are some fundamental behavioural issues that have to be added here when it comes to building a portfolio. There are two contrasting motives:

- Maximise potential return.
- Reduce or minimise risk to an acceptable level.

These can be augmented by other behavioural factors to model the investor's best choices. Thus, we can incorporate risk appetite – otherwise called risk tolerance (Tc); a discounted return variable known as the client's utility (Uc). These are used in conjunction with the expected return of the portfolio (Ep), and the variance of return of the portfolio (Vp).[5]

Therefore, we can derive an indifference curve for the investor as:

$$Ep = Uc - (Vp/Tc)$$

[4] For example, refer to *Principles of Corporate Finance*, ch.8, R.A. Brealey and S.C. Myers, McGraw-Hill, 2002.
[5] *Investments*, 6th ed., W. Sharpe, G. Alexander and J. Bailey, Prentice Hall, 1999.

Risk factor:

$$Rf = (Vp/Tc)$$

Investor utility:

$$Uc = Ep - Rf$$

Using such a basic equation, we can construct a model more compatible with the real world that postulates two risk appetites, one for the conservative investor (**A**), and another who is more aggressive and willing to risk his money (**B**).

Portfolio A

Conservative risk tolerance	40
Portfolio variance (Vp)	225
Risk factor (Rf)	5.625
Expected return (Ep)	8 %
Utility (Uc)	2.375 %

Portfolio B

Aggressive risk tolerance	100
Portfolio variance (Vp)	1600
Risk factor (Rf)	16
Expected return (Ep)	22 %
Utility (Uc)	6 %

An adventurous investor has a high risk appetite, one that entails high expected return with increased portfolio volatility. The conservative investor is more willing to experience wild fluctuations, and is happy to expect a lower return. It seems that we can please the customer perfectly.

There are some strong assumptions used over the real-time setting of risk-return preferences, plus the continuous computation of volatility and variances for the shares. We need to have access to a database of stocks and their variance and standard deviations. Yet, there are too many stocks in the market indices to be able to build a real-time portfolio using complete market data. Therefore, we usually take short-cut measures to derive probability curves.

An amalgamation of the assets gives a spectrum of risk weights for various combinations. See Figure 3.4.

We have the basic tools for constructing a portfolio, but we now need techniques for spotlighting the risk inherent in our portfolio choices.

Value-at-Risk (VaR)

Value-at-Risk (VaR) has been accepted by many banks and funds as a surrogate measure of various forms of risk – primarily market risk. It has become one of the established building blocks for handling investment risk. VaR serves as a good building block for expanding our knowledge of risk management, especially when it comes to developing mathematical tools and techniques.

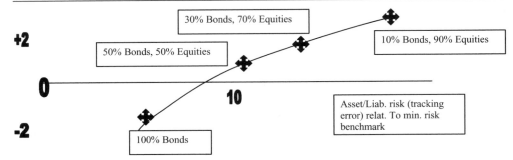

Figure 3.4   Risk v. return trade-off
Source: *British Actuarial Journal*, vol.7, Part III, Institute of Actuaries, August 2001, p. 331.

We need to determine at the outset which risk elements are in operation, then to estimate the overall risk in the bank trading book or portfolio. We can then postulate that you are likely to lose a maximum amount X (i.e. VaR) in the market on any given day, up to 99 % or 99.9 % certainty. This is the maximum exposure, or loss X, you can take with a given level of confidence – any more loss becomes a catastrophe.

VaR simplistically reduces risk to one figure in a financial report. Because of this simple presentation, there is a loss of data granularity and detail. There is also a hidden danger that the real distribution of events can hide a skewed distribution with a "fat tail". The normal distribution figures for variance and probability theory can cope with a skewed distribution, but we have to use alternative flavours of VaR to handle fat tails. This would raise the probable chances of loss above the standard VaR figures computed. See Figure 3.5.

The breakdown of this one figure for VaR is derived from the portfolio of assets which each contribute risk towards the synthetic VaR. The constituent assets in the portfolio will be

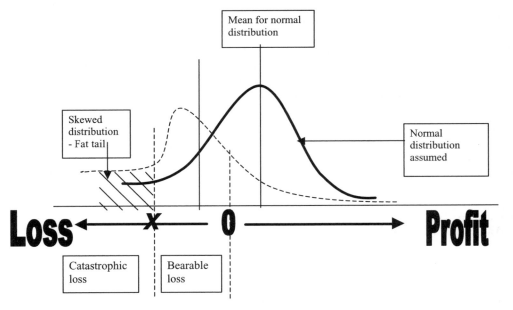

Figure 3.5   Basic VaR diagram

Value at risk (euro (m))

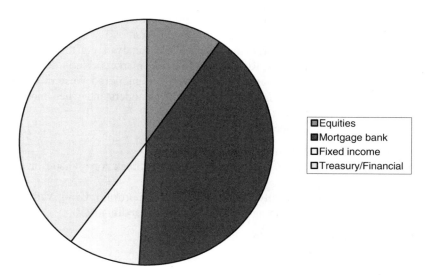

Equities
Mortgage bank
Fixed income
Treasury/Financial

Figure 3.6   VaR of market risk by trading unit
Source: Commerzbank Annual Report 2000, 2001.

decomposed (see Figure 3.6). Risk management practices and studies can then be developed to hedge or counter this potential loss.

Our confidence in the forecast should diminish when we reach the wings of the probability spectrum. A common in-depth analysis of VaR often estimates that your portfolio is safe at the 99.9 % likelihood cut-off line. This is a once in a life-time, or once in a 1000 years event. If this unexpected loss event happens, then the company will go bust when it has not got the resources to cover the losses on the market.

The 99.9 % confidence limit has been called "science fiction" by some risk professionals.[6] This is because the extreme events of the stock-market crash in 1987 and September 11, 2001 intuitively tell us that catastrophes are not once in life-time events. Furthermore, there is nothing in VaR that tells us of the magnitude, or impact, of the event when it occurs. There is the danger that our investment behaviour can be adversely biased by such a low theoretical probability.

The weakness of VaR depends upon opinions, but most agree that:

- The loss amount that exceeds VaR is important. VaR does not tell us by how much.
- There is no utility function associated with this excess measure given by VaR.
- VaR assumes that assets can be sold at their market price with consideration for liquidity.
- It is simple to understand and very widely accepted. People may even come to take it as gospel truth.

VaR reaches its limits of confidence and accuracy at the ends of the distribution, so new approaches can be more appropriate. EVT (Extreme Value Theory) is one way in which we can offer deeper analysis into these rarer events.[7]

---

[6] *Sceptical Thoughts on the Way to Basel*, Riccardo Rebonato, Global Association of Risk Professionals, London, May 2003.
[7] *Operational Risk*, chapter 11, Jack King, Wiley, 2001.

Our "best" financial models need more development to iron out the defects. Yet, Western financial pricing models are being applied all over the world. They should be exported to emerging market economies only with substantial modification to suit local conditions. The history and business cultures there are so significantly different.

This has been the experience of many dealers and technical analysts, e.g. those at the Moscow MICEx or Shanghai Stock Exchange. Russia and the newer markets clearly demonstrate that these can be the graveyard of many an optimistic view on untailored Western financial risk management techniques. We need an inquisitive mind to understand when modelling can successfully be applied, and where its limits lie in real life.

VaR provides effective assurance when:

- Market assumptions hold where theory meets practice.
- Other models or data can be used to back-test VaR to check for realistic or alternative situations.
- Following both predicates, you truly have a risk-managed portfolio. Using VaR alone gives you the semblance that you are doing everything right in handling risk.

A complementary technique is the Monte Carlo simulation.

Monte Carlo simulation

Running a simulation, or a stochastic model, could employ "actors" to play out testing in a mock retail scenario. This is a much more unpredictable method, but you gain in realism. Each time you run the simulation, you will get slightly different results just like gambling at a casino.

Some comedians have alleged that banking is nothing more than playing at the casino. Certainly, a "one-size fits all" risk management solution does not work, so some banks and funds moved away from VaR and other flavours of VaR to concentrate on VaR plus other methods for valuation and testing. Monte Carlo can add some sense of realism, or corroborate earlier VaR results.

Monte Carlo is a means of stochastic testing, where models and visions should meet. It gives a less deterministic view of risk, but runs computer simulations many times to get various results. VaR and more "deterministic" models return a standard numerical answer. In this limited view of risk modelling, Monte Carlo gives us a more imaginative answer.

However, this risk evaluation does not offer a standard view across all tests. It depends which Monte Carlo model you choose, and how many times you run the simulations. CitiCorp, for example was reported to compare alternative investments in one case using the Monte Carlo method, and running it one million times to forecast the default rate.[8]

If you ran Monte Carlo simulation tests many times, and either obtained a majority of favourable results, or chose to ignore many of the adverse results when interest rates rose, then the model is skewed. This would prove nothing more than what you really wanted to show in the first place. Monte Carlo has a potential element of subjectivity or bias, i.e. run it as many times until you derive the result that you wanted to prove in the first place.

But, you can use Monte Carlo of thousands of alternative scenarios to form a test dataset. You can input interest rates, money supply, unemployment or whatever underlying assumptions

---

[8] "Simulations for credit risk measurement", www.PRMIA.org. 19 September 2002.

Table 3.1   Bank portfolio Monte Carlo dataset

	Scenario 1	Scenario 2	Scenario 3	Scenario 4
Interest rate	4 %	5 %	6 %	7 %
Portfolio value	9800	9500	9200	8750
NPV portfolio	9250	9500	9580	9790
Net profit (loss)	+550	0	−380	−1040

you consider as valid input. See an extract in Table 3.1. When you obtain this final dataset, there are no assumptions of normal distribution – this makes the Monte Carlo possibly more realistic and robust in some ways. See Figure 3.7.

Another, and possibly more serious, critique of the techniques outlined is that they adopt a static view of portfolios. Investment choice and values change under market conditions all the time, and there is the danger that you are taking a snapshot of your portfolio that gives you a confident feeling, despite the data being out of date or unrealistic.

These methodologies and toolkits move us away from our comfortable collection of well-understood figures and the mathematical models, seeing as they are only part of the whole risk management exercise. VaR, Monte Carlo and other techniques are only tools to shed light in a very fuzzy investment environment. Otherwise, we can miss the wood for the trees, and switch off all judgement and warning mechanisms in our investment vehicle.

Collective use of mathematical tools

A herd effect is to be observed in the investment world where too many people use the same models, with the same assumptions, stretches and limitations. VaR is already accepted in the industry as standard, so that people trust it. This creates a systemic risk, reinforced by the

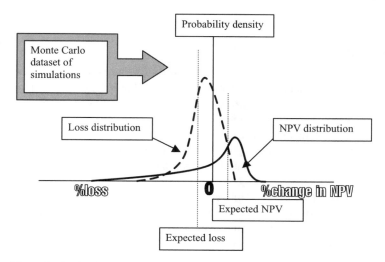

Figure 3.7   Monte Carlo simulation

Table 3.2 Mark-to-market (MTM) example

Financial instrument	Current price	Price change (%)	Current shares held (milllion)	Current value ($ million)	Change in value
ABB	A	+1.2	10.3	i	Q %
BP	B	+3.3	3.45	j	r %
GSK	C	+0.4	1.12	k	s %
HP	D	0.0	2.1	l	t %
IBM	E	−2.0	0.65	m	U %
ICI	F	+0.3	1.1	n	V %
Kodak	G	−4.1	2.5	o	w %
Toyota	H	+2.3	0.2	p	x %
Total value				238.53	
Change in book value				+1.2	
Change in book value (%)				0.5 %	

conformity of regulators and the desire of standardisation of software. Given the tremendous benefits of using standard software and methodologies, this risk may be a risk that is acceptable to most in the finance industry. When everyone accepts the same tea-leaves and risk models, then we are in danger of a systemic risk.[9]

A lot of reputable financial companies are relying on the same standard mathematical models for risk management firepower. This is ironic because every bank and fund hails the benefits of diversification – we should be using different techniques and technologies to reduce overall sector risk.

One of the problems of valuing a portfolio with complex financial instruments or derivatives is that the normal way of stating their value on a trading sheet or in the accounts rests in one line, or one figure. The valuation process to obtain this figure can extend to reams of paper. So, by reporting the short one-liner, the whole financial sector could lose the granularity or detail in the risk analysis.

Position keeping

Position keeping can be seen as a more detailed form of trading control. It does not rely on single figures per se, but on the wider management control task. Thus, positions are monitored to see if they are open or closed, date of closure if open, in profit or loss. Exposure to certain instruments, geographic regions, counterparties, concentration ratios give a broader picture of trading. It is a fundamental form of corporate stock keeping on a dynamic basis, with the search for this investment holy grail being a valuation in real time. It operates in the same way as our high-street store that checks the daily inventory, or the market position or portfolio.[10]

The mark-to-market (MTM) principle exists in the mainstream to value the portfolio based upon the latest trading prices available. This is a control mechanism that forces the portfolio to be periodically valued against the whole market and variances reported. The basic principles are summarised in Table 3.2.

---

[9] Professor Avinash Persaud, Gresham College and Managing director, State Street Bank, London, 3 October 2002.
[10] *Managing Project Risk*, p. 62, Y.Y. Chong, Financial Times Management, 2000.

MTM works well when viewing financial instruments assumed to be traded under certain market conditions, such as:

- A liquid market where the price is very transparent, or similarly, it is quoted in an illiquid market where the asset is hardly traded at all.
- Enough market-makers (who are not colluding) in corporate shares or bonds are quoting prices to create a competitive market.
- The last-traded or current price used to value accounts is representative of true worth. The last-traded price may reflect very out-of-date data. Some glaring examples, such as Leeson or Rusnak, show that even MTM at the current price can be manipulated, so that the trading book may be a sham.
- The price for your quantity bought or sold – this is unrealistic where the block sale is so large that it depresses or inflates the market price.

One of the criticisms of MTM is that it focuses solely on historical data, with less relevance to the future. The crashes in the Russian stock market in 1998, or Argentina in 2001, showed the limitations of using historic data. We implicitly expect the future to look, in some way, like the past. While this is happening, the hordes are making their rapid exit from the market meltdown.[11]

MTM position keeping is faced with greater obstacles where there is a wider extent of control that the trader or fund manager exercises. Nick Leeson at Barings, Peter Young at DMG or John Rusnak at AIB were in the powerful position of being able to create their own (fictitious) accounts and valuing their own portfolio.[12] Most banks and funds define a role for the treasury – partly to police the "rogue trader" danger. This comes under the category of operational risk. Controlling operational risk is a managerial function, and it cannot be easily processed solely by computer analysis.

INVESTMENT MANAGERIAL CONTROL

A successful financial dealing environment requires unification of the various species of investors.

1. Managers require a high level of people interaction skills, of which risk management is only one.
2. Successful trading needs an instant eye for distinguishing a good buy from a dud.
3. Recent entrants of the risk managers, including the quants and geeks, who are familiar with the relative probabilities of the financial risk. CAPM, Monte Carlo or VaR are just a few portfolio dishes on their menu.

So, the market is requires at least three types of investor types – few companies have the desired balance of these types.

The treasurer's role

Traditionally, the role of the treasurer and of the middle office was the in-house policeofficer. The role of position keeping fitted in this domain. The treasurer may reduce losses according to how effective these risk management structures prove.

---

[11] *Sceptical Thoughts on the Way to Basel*, Riccardo Rebonato, Global Association of Risk Professionals, May 2003.
[12] "Night of the regulators," *Global Custodian*, Spring 1997.

Thus, the treasurer acts as the paymaster and policeman of the modern corporation. This is a job function that is extended outside the traditional realm of accountancy. Where front office and back office controls have been exposed as being weak – the treasurer or the chief risk officer (CRO) must beef up risk management. The treasurer and the CRO are two different people, working in autonomous departments. The treasurer and the middle office are given their risk management role on these lines:

1. Risk analysis to evaluate risk scope and business objectives, determining potential sources of danger or risk.
2. Design the risk template, outlining the event, likelihood of the event occurring and the damage from the event. This forms a risk-event matrix or risk register.
3. Define the risk involved, the people and departments assigned to it, and how to solve likely problems.

Trading and risk management

The problem is that all bank personnel do not always work in tandem. The trading arm craves for independence to use its creative powers in order to accumulate more wealth. The risk management department wishes for a more controlled structure. Dealers would like to make profits without unnecessary impediments of excess regulation or risk management – their directors may be prone to agree.

Middle office can intervene at various stages and ask relevant questions. See Figure 3.8. Where the balance of power gets shifted too much towards the risk management function, the chance remains that the bank becomes too cautious. It becomes overtaken by rivals and eventually goes out of business.

The most common type of distribution of powers is easy to guess. We have, in a typical management structure, one person from different departments heading up their respective business areas. See Figure 3.9.

Risk management is represented by its director on the board who has the power to get the bank adequately protected. But, the real machinations and power struggles within the company cannot be seen from Figure 3.9. The risk management department fits poorly in many banks as a poor cousin of internal audit, and with the same low voice.

Back office is the unglamorous repository for the detritus of the dealing splendours. Whereas, most banks and funds place most risk management focus and resources in the front office, the back office often gets overlooked.

> ....years of under-investment are causing a consistent leakage of profitability. Poor status within the organisation and a rapid turnover of staff also combine to ensure that this is a continual, but largely unnoticed and unaddressed, drain on a financial institution's bottom line.[13]

This institutional blindness, as exemplified by the Barings or AIB rogue-trading episodes, must be kept under control by risk controllers and auditors. One of the ways to rein in the rogue staff was to erect "Chinese walls" over which the errant officers could not jump. Another solution was to install sophisticated computer-based surveillance and reporting functions within the

---

[13] *Operational Risk*, Middle Office, p. 27, spring 1999.

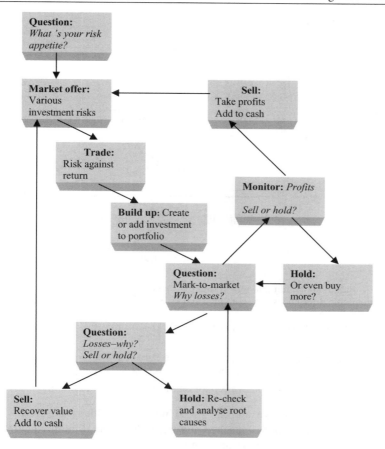

Figure 3.8 A trading strategy

company. These would give up-to-the-minute online pictures of prices and market positions. Trading or lending limits would prevent us from being over-exposed in risky market conditions. We are not out of the trading risk woods yet.

There are too many investor parties with different risk appetites at play. We need to discourage "unsafe" investing, so internal controls are set up. These usually include the various forms of trading limits, and these can be set automatically by the dealing system used. A database of trading limits will exist for deals. These include:

Bank board of directors				
Risk management	Accounting and IT services	Asset management	Retail banking	Investment banking and trading

Figure 3.9 A management banking structure with risk management
Source: Commerzbank Annual Report, 2001.

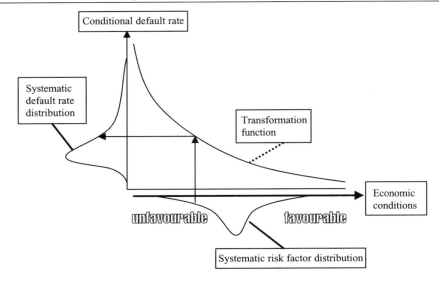

Figure 3.10   Conditional default rate transformation function
Source: "Reconcilable differences", A. Hickman and H. Koyluoglu, *Risk*, vol. 11, no.10, 1998.

- individual dealer limits (Dealer X has $10 000 000 – no margins, close positions at end of day);
- product limits (corporate euro bonds, not outside euroland);
- counter-party limits (e.g. only Deutsche Bank, Bank of New York);
- geographic limits (Latin American FX, not any African or Asian country).

All these limits will be additive, and calculated in real time. Otherwise, there will be a time-lag before these limits have been breached and when the internal trading controllers realise that they have been exceeded. These are simple mathematical handcuffs on traders' hands, but these constraints are not always binding. Trading limits are insufficient managerial control techniques when used on their own.

In fact, banks and funds may be guilty of setting limits too loosely as a strategic risk and not as error in the front-office line management. For example, many financial institutions were guilty of assuming a continuing bull run in the stock markets just before the downturn in 2000. Their past experience had been something of a dozen years of economic growth. This caused them to overlook the extreme left-hand pessimistic area of systematic defaults (see Figure 3.10).

Trading limits take no account of credit risk exposures, correlation between trades and expected returns. The only thing that can be done with a trading limit, if a potential trade has an expected loss, is to set the limits lower. Usually, they cannot perform a reverse trade instantaneously, so the price may have moved adversely in the meantime. Thus, traders cannot be tamed by mere trading limits.

In two high-profile operational risk cases, the trading rebels took over – Nick Leeson at Barings and John Rusnak at AIB. The trading limits were overridden, allowing trades to be unreported, and the whole limits system failed. We have to reinspect automated limits trading systems that profess to being "trader proof". A limit system cannot be applied mechanically to run itself.[14]

---

[14] *Measuring and Managing Operational Risks in Financial Institutions*, p. 137–8, C. Marshall, Wiley, 2001.

Table 3.3 Factors affecting buy-side risk initiatives

Sector	Drivers	Time horizon	Primary difficulties
Institutional investors	Client and fee retention, adherence to mandate	Medium term (1–3 years)	Integrating performance and risk attribution
Retail fund managers	Asset base/fee retention, peer comparison	Short to medium term (0.5–3 years)	Integrating risk analysis, portfolio construction, short-term liquidity risk
Insurance companies	Liquidity; remaining a going concern	Long term (3–5 years)	Breadth and obscurity of asset classes, modelling liabilities along with assets
Hedge fund assets	Attracting institutions	Short term (3–6 months)	Liability analysis, modelling exotic asset classes and complex trading strategies

Meridien Research in *GARP Risk Review*, March/April 2002.

We need to have a good idea about past distributions and the related covariances between the companies – unlikely, given all the possible combinations. Where the shares are not actively traded, we will be using price data that are out of date. The last mark-to-market price is meaningless, especially if you want suddenly to buy or sell a block of 100 million shares. We have incompleteness and inaccuracy of data and that is not conducive for efficient portfolio building.

Even if we could build up such a huge numerical database, investor rationality cannot be safely assumed. The average investor will not bother to consult this database before each buy/sell decision. It is more a case of keeping ahead of the Joneses. Thus, it is more realistic to say that portfolio managers are pack animals that hunt together.

> You had everyone out there owning the same stocks and no one caring about growth rates, because they had to keep up.[15]

The buy/sell decision is often made upon a hunch, and that visceral feeling may be given in a share tip. Boom and bust cycles are built upon such word of mouth. Investor behaviour is driven by various players according to different risk appetites and risk horizons.

Efficient portfolio theory has often ignored the greatest assets in front of us, and these are the human assets. Innate intelligence, investment skill, trust and communication are valuable commodities that often short-circuited by the train of investment thought. "I bought the stock because my friend/colleague tipped it."

There is a risk that people have plunged herd-like into a certain buying or selling craze because others are making the same assumptions of the market – see Figure 3.10. Those with true investment skills can see the market with a clearer head and exercise better judgement. Unfortunately, the fact remains that the existence of some investment skill is rare gift, much rarer than thought. (See Passive vs. Active managers.)

Some of the funds employ "active" managers who set out to beat the stock index, or other suitable benchmark, comprehensively. These tigers typify the "star" system of employing the best fund manager for the highest salary plus bonuses. There is a risk-return trade-off and it

---

[15] *Fortune*, 29 October 2001.

Table 3.4 Passive investment manager (the tortoise)

	Result
Definition	Managers that manage assets without taking active investment decisions in order to track closely the performance of a specified index
Efficiency	Stability and consistency of relative returns; reduces active risk at overall level; could improve active return and lower net costs through stock lending
Costs	Low ongoing costs; contributes to lower future transition costs
SleepWell	Results of passive management are predictable, which provides comfort
Monitoring	Low management decision time; process easily explained
Additional risks	Index benchmark may be inappropriately designed

The Concept of Investment Efficiency and its application to Investment Management Structures, T.M. Hodgson *et al.*, Table 6.2, Institute of Actuaries, 28 February 2000, p. 45.

attracts different investor risk players. Based on this, we see that one portfolio size and shape does not fit all. We can match all personal risk-return objectives with the desired portfolio.

Thus, people will have different investment motives; they may want to take on more risk than the client-risk mandate merits. We mix the risk-bearing and the risk-selling players haphazardly. Let us look at the cautious tortoise and the adventurous tiger professional fund manager. We can look at the passive manager as the cautious investor animal (Table 3.4), while the active fund manager is the tiger willing to take on risk (Table 3.5).

Index tracker funds, such as those that put money into investments in ratios to duplicate the NYSE or S&P or FTSE indices do not charge a large management fee because their composition is already dictated from the outset – there are no excessive switches or "churning" between other investments.

Some investors had been paying for professional advice that was losing them money instead of using tracker funds. One US investment manager claims that investors could have gained even more by throwing darts at a specific industrial sector instead of hiring financial "experts".[16] This view has gained currency among the public during the stockmarket slump in 2000–2.

Table 3.5 Active investment manager (the tiger)

	Result
Definition	Managers that take active investment positions with the objective of outperforming over the long term
Efficiency	Variable – dependent on the level of active return and level of active risk
Costs	Moderate to high
SleepWell	Variable – dependent on the familiarity of the approach and the strength of the brand
Monitoring	Average to high
Additional risks	Realistic setting of expectations; avoid focus on short-term performance leading to costly turnover; diversification between managers in the layer is required

The Concept of Investment Efficiency and its Application to Investment Management Structures, T.M. Hodgson *et al.*, Table 6.3, Institute of Actuaries, 28 February 2000, p. 46.

---

[16] *Silent Investor, Silent Loser*, Martin Sosnoff, Richardson & Steirman, 1986, p. 246.

Unfortunately, there are certain minuses at play that decrease active return on a fund:

1. Management fees.
2. Excessive turnover and broker commissions (churning).
3. Slippage from inadequate corporate governance.
4. Performance slippage from benchmark.

Performance must be checked regularly to avoid the meltdowns in portfolio value. This implies a direct design criterion for a portfolio to be built upon steady growth and not transient "shoot the moon" profits. In essence, the portfolio has to be reliable or resilient, rather than illusory.

It is risk ignorance to believe in the board or the fund manager every single time. Take control of your own money and value it well. There are corporate governance activists (e.g. Warren Buffett) who will gun for these dubious corporate leaders. Some are losing their patience; Bob Monks, a US lawyer founded Institutional Shareholder Services aimed at advising shareholders how to vote. He vowed:

> We have tried to persuade corporate America to change through traditional shareholder actions. But are we getting anywhere with this? The answer is, we're not. So now we're going to try, not as shareholders, but as plaintiffs.[17]

The boards, and their subordinate trading and lending operations, have been very good at conveying news of profits, but they still continue to obstruct disclosure at some stage. Some boards are considerably less adept at identifying the up-to-date extent of losses. So, why do management put obstacles in the way?

Predicting and controlling human behaviour has never been a complete science. Banking and fund management may prefer a more tailored approach, with a high element of IT systems. We examine this in the section on technology in Chapter 7. For instance, one web-based example is RiskOps by NetRisk to manage operational risk.[18]

Fair value is one minor problem within the scope of operational risk management. There are an increasing number of new risk management methodologies and systems devoted to handling operational risk – the type of risk that encompasses human conduct and its effects. It has only been in recent years that market and credit risk have been correctly seen as components of risk in the light of operational risk. The contribution of operational risk to an institution's losses (financial and non-financial) is not easy to assess. But, it is more realistic to postulate that operational risk accounts for something like a large percentage of a bank's losses.[19]

Furthermore, managers may wish to create a portfolio that is less volatile and more predictable. The predictability makes it easier to install risk management measures, plus it eases planning for the future.

If we studied a trend that BP-Amoco went down while the price of Royal-Sun Alliance (RSA) insurance rose, then we have a case to buy RSA as a hedge to protect our BP-Amoco stake. To do so, we can reduce the overall variance and covariance of the stocks and bonds in the portfolio whilst seeking to maximise the mean or average return. Thus, we have the makings of a "mean-variance efficient" portfolio that we can market to public clients.[20]

[17] *Financial Times Fund Management*, 4 November 2002.
[18] www.Netrisk.com.
[19] *"Measuring and Managing Operational Risks in Financial Institutions"*, chapter 6, C. Marshall, Wiley, 2001.
[20] *"Mean-Variance Analysis in Portfolio Choice and Capital markets"*, Harry Markowitz, Wiley, 2001.

Table 3.6   Percentage of companies hiring outsiders

Reason	Percentage who quoted reason
Specialist knowledge	78 %
Extensive past experience	70 %
More readily defined accountability	39 %
Most cost-effective option	37 %

But, there are some problems when we try this portfolio-building approach. We are using historic data that may not be representative for the future trends. The UK official warning that: "The price of shares can go up as well as down. Past performance is no guarantee of future performance etc. . . . " Thus, the fundamental assumption of overall long-term stable variances and covariances can fall apart rapidly, and that means that the portfolio performance becomes very unpredictable and more risky. It can become too complex a modelling exercise to be conducted in-house.

Investment risk experts

Risk management is still an art as well as a science. We have seen the use of sophisticated models based upon correlation between different risks and assets. Many of the parameters are numerical and objective. These provide real benefits when applied properly. We also have to realise that these tools only handle certain types of risks adequately, mainly market and credit risk. When new products are introduced and increasing complex financial modelling overawes us, we deem it fit to call in the investment risk experts.

If computers and automatic limit systems worked all the time, then no one would have to go outside for specialist help, except for the occasional risk management and dealing system supplier. Mechanical-type systems only account for a small part of the entire risk management business process. Many companies do not possess all these skills in-house and there are reasons why they must hire outsiders. See Table 3.6.

This means that in major change projects, some element of accountability and control are reduced because of taking in outside help. Also, cost-effectiveness is not the top criterion in these projects at all. In essence, it is ironic that we hardly place checks and controls over those who are hired to control our errant staff.[21]

More products and mathematical modelling techniques are brought on the market every year. This creates a buoyant market in certain dealing areas. The prospects for derivatives and futures contracts are bright in many ways, but what do they offer fund managers in the way of real value? Many are confused as to the exact answer, so they bring in outside derivatives experts to help them. Some of the problems lie in the complexity of these financial instruments, the extreme leverage they can possess and the manner in which people have been mis-selling them.

The deep mathematical foundations underpinning derivatives and financial futures instruments mean that more scientific knowledge is needed to understand them. Thus, a breed of mathematicians and intellectuals sometimes known as "rocket scientists" or "quants" appeared in various brokerages, banks and funds. Investment risk is not a question of solving solely by

---

[21] 'The 2002 Challenge of Change Survey', Institute of Management Consultancy and Executives Online, www.changemanagementonline.co.uk.

mathematical or scientific means. Nevertheless, the use of mathematics in investment theory seems to be addictive for many.

So, we have to identify the risk style of the professional investment manager. Then, we have to pick the type of fund that our risk appetite allows. It seems that many investment meals do not match the risk appetite appropriately. Another critical look at the menu can rebalance the investment fare.

CASE STUDY: A LARGE UK PLC DEFINED BENEFITS PENSION FUND

This fund wished to improve the annual return on the portfolio performance which was poor. Together with a stated aim of trustees to increase control and reduce risk, it led to a restructuring of the fund. A wider range of control was needed as the management structure was expanded to cope with the greater monitoring role. The new structure included:

- 40 % passive
- 45 % active
- 15 % satellite fund manager types.

A 50 % increase in portfolio efficiency was stated.[22]

It seems obvious that aiming for such a high active return ahead of the investment herd is to accept a level of active risk above and beyond the call of fiduciary duty. Setting realistic, and yet challenging, limits for the active fund manager is a task that will continue to tax the abilities of many in corporate governance. The expectations of shareholders should not be raised too high in the meantime.

An eye for differentiation of, and diversification between, investment managers in the market is required – in reality, few have the required skills desired. We look into this in more depth in Chapter 6: Instinct versus ability.

Who controls whom

Thus, fund managers exist to provide a real service at reasonable and competitive costs. More people now understand that they have the power to shop around. This became particularly so with the increasing exit of the state in providing guaranteed pensions for everyone, and the increase in number of financial regulations. Many of these are more detailed corollaries of the Statement of Investment Principles (SIPs) for investment professionals. These include:

1. Mission and goals
2. Professional appointments and delegation
3. Investment strategy
4. Target investment return
5. Risk management
6. Funding requirements
7. Regulatory compliance.

So far, investment managers can keep within their job as long as they can be seen to conform to SIPs and to exercise skills that others do not. On the investment road, irrespective of the

---

[22] *Structured Alpha: A practical application for institutional funds*, Watson Wyatt, December 1999.

hype surrounding over-regulation, investment barriers are few and far between in relation to the countless new products and the high number of new entrants on the market. Under the changing market dynamics, we have to question the factors that affect the life of our investments from the responsible stakeholders.

1. Which investor parties have the greatest power?
2. Which parties exhibit investment risk management?
3. Are these investment risk management tools effective?
4. Have these risk management processes been practised or used?

Part of the reason why these questions are not asked is that we use a proxy measure for risk management, that of reputation. This reputation commands prestige and respect, but it may be ill-deserved. The investment system traditionally relies on a mutual control and respect between stakeholders. These linkages deserve deeper re-examination.

The risk management monitoring function partly comprises performance measurement. This has become a euphemism for "reality-check" in investment management under recent slumps. During boom times, hiring a "winning" stock-picker is a bit of a cake-walk. Investment funds are looking for the best manager, and that means delivering maximum return, especially during a stock-market drop.

Clients now expect to impose more control over investment funds to manage their money for best return. The technocratic financial system has instigated countless analyses and compliance reports. Unfortunately, these reports are of little effectiveness when the powers at the top are hell-bent on driving the company to ruin. The Enron and Worldcom examples serve to illustrate this point. Investment risk management is not just about analyses and reports, it is about doing. Organic risk management is about investigating people and attacking with risk countermeasures.

4

Investing under Attack

We look at the investor unhappiness with the way markets run and are governed. The stake-holders in the financial markets are outlined. The behavioural traits of CEOs and company executives are analysed. The structure of corporate governance exerts great influence over how they behave, and what they can get away with. We look at the various risk classes of investment vehicles, and treat the investor as embarking on an investment project.

INVESTOR DISENCHANTMENT

The stock-market collapse has emphasised the topsy-turvy world of investor euphoria and dismay. The shareholder public has suffered a crisis in confidence in those charged with the management of their investment, chiefly the corporate directors or CEOs.

> There has been a significant impact from corporate accounting scandals as two-thirds (62 %) of UK private investors are now less trusting of all company reports and accounts.[1]

What is true seems to be a disconnection between real risk and a perceived "good investment" and the investor votes with his wallet.

Certainly, the investor has turned to regulatory safeguards in desperation, but the protection may turn out to be rather cosmetic at times. More realistically, there is a limit to help and compensation that can be provided post facto. Or that the public naively placed too much faith in the FSA, SEC or FDIC in getting back all (or most) of their losses. This market is full of unrealistic expectation.

RISK-BEARERS AND RISK-TAKERS

This struggle between investor creditor and company debtor is part of a mismatch of their risk-return appetites. Yet, there are various types of investor in the risk universe. See Figure 4.1. Some are risk-bearing, some are risk-offering players.

Professional investor/shareholder

This category includes the class of professional investor – those who work in banks, fund managers and financial institutions. There are many sophisticated investors who are busy creating their own pension or playing with more than $100 000 to $1 million. They invest to accumulate wealth, sometimes losing on the way. But, this is a burgeoning section of the population.

These individuals operate in addition to the full-time professional bank/fund managers who are investing far larger sums. Table 4.1 shows factors affecting the buy-side risk drivers for launching risk management actions.

---

[1] "Private share ownership in Britain 2002", ProShare, 23 September 2002, MORI, www.Proshare.org.uk.

Table 4.1 Factors affecting buy-side risk initiatives[2]

Sector	Driver	Time	Primary difficulties
Institutional investors	Client and fee retention, adherence to mandate	Medium term	Integrating performance and risk attribution
Pension plan sponsors	Fiduciary responsibility	Very long term	Breadth and obscurity of asset classes, modelling liabilities along with assets
Retail fund managers	Asset base/fee retention, peer comparison	Short to medium term	Integrating risk analysis, portfolio construction, short-term liquidity risk
Insurance companies	Liquidity, remaining a going concern	Long term	Integrating asset risk attribution with actuarial risk
Hedge funds	Attracting institutional funds	Short term	Liquidity analysis, modelling exotic asset classes and complex trading strategies

The different types of investor classes take various time horizons, trading strategies and asset classes.

A conservative or risk-averse investor would like to preserve the value of the original investment, hence to limit the downside risk, and to make a "reasonable" return.

A risk-seeking investor or speculator, on the other hand, can be eager to engage in "double or quits" wagers on the stock market – such as Internet day-traders. In fact, it is often worse than a zero-sum game; after spreads, commissions, fees and taxes, at least 70 % of these short-term traders lose money. It is an uneven playing field just like a casino's rules: the house always wins.

Yet, there are those in the majority of investors who take a longer term view and believe in the "prospects" of a company. These are the "rational" investors, both big and small, who occasionally get "suckered" into buying a bad stock. The stock-market crashes of 1929, 1987 or September 11th 2001, and the continuing bear run in 2003 offer testimony to the fickleness of share prices. Disaster is good for risk management business but bad for the traditional "buy-and-hold" investor philosophy (see Figure 4.1).

Investment companies/Fund managers

The market is potentially teaming with sharks ,which is why we hire seasoned managers who protect us and nurture our wealth. The directors of investment companies are meant to be professionals who are hired for their ability to create and preserve shareholder value. But, when they fail, the business world either rails against investor injustice, or quietly suffers in silence, which offers no solution. Fortunately, there has been some good research done to search for effective corporate governance solutions. We visit the sections **Fiduciary Risk** and **Corporate Misgovernance** later in this chapter.

---

[2] Meridien Research, in *GARP, Risk Review*, Mar/April 2002.

% fall in GDP

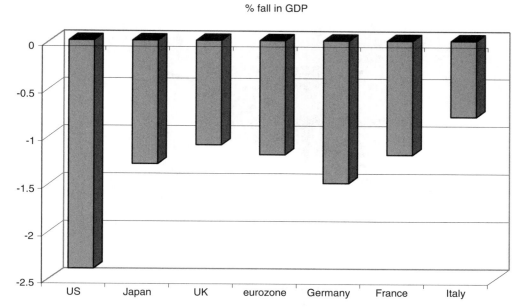

Figure 4.1   Fall in GDP following 2001 stockmarket crash

Investment banks

These are the professionals who often rest at the centre of the market action. There are corporate bankers, brokers, company analysts who have been deemed skilled and ethical to handle the vast and valuable amounts of data in the market. Banks are paid to analyse target companies' prospects, and also to finance and sell these companies to the investor. The chef is cooking, tasting and recommending the same dishes to customers. These roles have conflicts of interest that have led to successful law suits against some Wall Street banks. Some investment banks have split their stockbroker and analytical arms from their investment banking arms into different companies. It will not be a complete solution to the conflict of interest that led to the division along 'Chinese Walls'.

Auditors

Company auditors are external experts hired to provide a "fair and accurate view" of a company's financial health. Yet, the payment from the company, rather than from a third-party source, represents another conflict of interests. Therefore, it is often in the auditors' economic welfare to report favourable accounts if they want to get the company's repeat business.

This is more like the Andersen–Enron case, and it is a phenomenon that has not disappeared, even after Sarbanes–Oxley. These are real threats to the investor, and we should embark on an active form of risk management if we are to load the chances of effective protection in our favour. This is the 'Kalashknikov' part of the dealing with investment risk threats – i.e. how to hit back at threats.

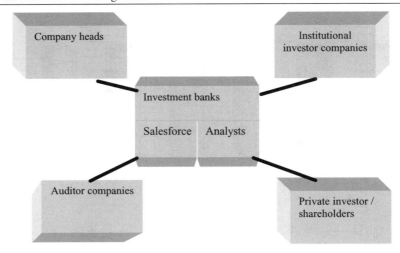

Figure 4.2   Investment players in the market

The first stage within the risk management methodology is to embark on an effective risk analysis and identification of interests. One task would be to look in the risk mirror to determine your risk appetite. Based on the potential perils that face the prospective investor, it would be well to see whether you are:

- Risk-bearing OR
- Risk-seeking OR
- Risk-averse OR
- Risk-ignorant.

A LOOK IN THE RISK MIRROR

Business models do not work where humans function in a non-linear mode. There is no fully developed art or science that fully describes or predicts investor behaviour. They also differ from country to country. Some countries (e.g. USA) have tied their national wealth so much to the stock market. Thus, in a market downturn, they suffer from risk exposure to a fall in national GDP wealth. It depends on the cultural risk appetite. See Figure 4.3.

Let's use a simple categorisation for our risk mirror.

Risk-averse

A plodding style takes conservative choices in the markets. Houses purchased through long-term mortgages and blue-chip large market-cap firms are the classic parking space for their money. Thus, you find this player covering the majority of the market, whether they are 60 year olds with personal savings, or a 20 year old in a company pension fund. A vehicle like a "tracker funds" keeps them within the main herd of investors. See **Active funds v. Passive Funds** in Chapter 3.

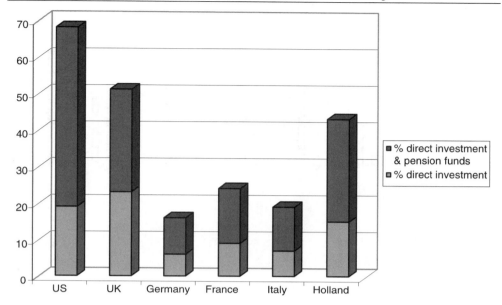

Figure 4.3   Share ownership by country

Risk-neutral

You can spot this nimbler investor taking large, bold strides into markets. They top up their portfolio shopping cart with an occasional dip into more funky things. Mutual funds or unit trusts in developing countries or bio-tech might be worth keeping. Otherwise, following the herd into blue-chips and property is the order.

Risk-takers

We have the courageous minority that are bent on riches, but with different ways of getting there ahead of the herd. Thus, investing in the large "safe" mutual funds are off their radar screen – surely too mainstream. Some illiquid share or IPO would definitely be worth putting a large chunk on the table.

From just every risk-perspective, you could have profited from the upswing if your timing or your term horizon were right. Figure 4.4 shows US equity returns in the past 30 years. Timing is everything.

Some of the street-wise veterans park a little of their profits in a contingency fund, or "get out of jail". So, if they end up on the wrong end of an investment crash, they still retain a small sum for emergency.

The recent market crashes have hurt investment players especially when they have kept little reserve, or even borrowed to invest. They are prepared to bet more than the farm and lose more than the whole shot. Such a leveraged player can behave like some rather well-known hedge funds. See Case Study **LTCM**.

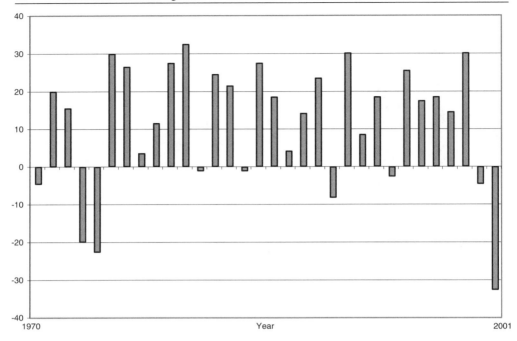

Figure 4.4   % US equity returns 1970–2001

INVESTOR ANALYSIS

Certainly, the financial regulators would like to know which sort of investor player they are controlling. The banking reforms under Basel II would like to get the balance right between an eager pursuit of profits and a sound capital base from long-term investors. See Basel II in Chapter 9. But knowing how to keep a market properly regulated, yet liquid and still attractive for investors, is a harder problem to solve. It depends upon investors' risk appetites and perceptions.

One of the Basel II main challenges is to guard against a disturbing tendency towards banks and funds flocking together in "group-think". This leads to simultaneous organic behaviour that leads to cycles of boom and bust. Basel labels this "pro-cyclicality" where financial institutions plunge into the same investment, or run for the exit at the same time.

> ... we need to know about banks that they exhibit herd behaviour. This is not because they are silly, though they may be silly as well. Herding is a rational response to uncertainty.

Essentially, these investor trackers, work, eat, drink and socialise in a pack. They do not really venture far from the investment fold for fear of getting shot by more rapacious hunters.[3]

In a runaway group-think scenario, the board of directors can develop into a "closed shop" that ignores the wishes of the shareholders. There is a marked tendency for remunerative packages to go far and beyond their contribution towards the running of the company. The *UK Cadbury Report* on directors' pay scales and the Combined Code on corporate structure and risk have been combined to focus on modern company governance.

---

[3] Professor Avinash Persaud, lecturer at Gresham College and managing director at State Street Bank, London, 3 October 2002.

Table 4.2   Types of CEO

CEO bird	Low risk appetite	Medium risk appetite	High risk appetite	Low risk awareness	High risk awareness	Ethics
Ostrich	X			X		Neutral
Dodo		X		X		Neutral
Magpie			X		X	Low
Eagle			X		X	Neutral
Owl		X			X	High

Different business roles need appropriate types of risk players. Some businesses fail because they have the wrong type of key risk player in charge. Need for a risk-reward goal matrix for the private investor. Put these goal definitions into practice and check that they work for you. This is the way to balance the risk-reward ratio with the reserves you have at your disposal. Take another simplified look at the CEOs – it's for the birds.

TYPES OF CEO – BIRDS OF A FEATHER

The components of this corporate style categorisation revolve around risk-averse and risk-conscious. Comfort in assigning your money to a reliable designate controlling your large corporate investment is defined as a "SleepWell" factor for an active type fund manager.[4] For simplicity's sake, we can define five types of company CEO that exist in the marketplace – see Table 4.2.

Each of these CEO birds has a different risk appetite and ethical attitude that directly influences their entrepreneurial behaviour when leading corporations that are charged with the task of creating the nation's wealth.

The eagles have still managed to triumph, but they appear to be fewer in number. Their insightful investment selection and risk management have been their winning strengths. Slower birds that hold and pick investments have not managed to stay ahead of the rest of the flock during the downturn. They struggle or drown rather than ditch the dead weight. We put the distribution of these corporate birds over our skies in Figure 4.5.

The fear and weakness of losing business in a downturn will force the bolder fund managers to follow the pack rather blindly. Just mirror the S&P or FTSE indices and invest with little imagination in the "safest" companies. It will be cheaper for investors to get the same performance by purchasing the index-tracking funds. This is the (hypothetical) danger, and one that may be closer in reality. We investigate passive versus active funds.

The CEO eagle – The M&A addict

This stunning bird of prey is a fine sight as it soars to high attitude. They survey the surrounding companies for opportunities to stake their claim in mergers and acquisitions. They suddenly swoop down upon unsuspecting victims and grab them in their clutches. There is no long-term investment buy-and-hold strategy. Some succeed spectacularly. However, the troubled AOL-Time Warner is one of these species that almost flew (straight into a cliff).

---

[4] "The concept of investment efficiency and its application to investment management structures", T.M. Hodgson *et al.*, Institute of Actuaries, 28 February 2000.

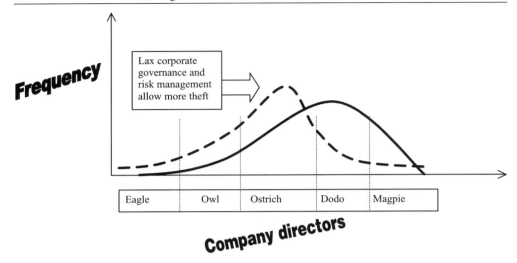

Figure 4.5   Frequency of bird sightings

The CEO dodo – Risk-phobic

You might recognise this plumage that is bright and rather haughty in attitude. They claim to be "with it" in being aware of the risks, but their real attitude can be effectively risk-seeking. Some have called this species the dinosaur, but it seems to keep coming back. Others said : "Let the trend be your friend."

Many investors took Arnold Weinstock of GEC as this sorry dodo. Then, reborn as Marconi, the company flew into a wall. How it wished for the days of the dodo. See Marconi case study.

The CEO ostrich – Risk-ignorant

This bird is so shy that it keeps its head in the sand to block out the real events that are happening all around. The market will force this type of company leader into the grave.

The board of directors at Barings during the Leeson disaster, or the management at Sumitomo lulled by their "Mr Copper", are both market examples. Our point is that we can spot this bird before we lose our money on it.

The CEO owl – Risk-acceptable

If you catch this bird, it flies high above and generally picks out the best corporate decisions. Some decisions may be controversial or painful, but the long-term effects are that the company is nurtured for growth. The problem in the market is where to find such a rare bird as a replacement when it flies away or it retires. It is said by many that Warren Buffett sit in this nest.

The CEO magpie – Risk-seeking

This bird is one to avoid at all costs. That is, they exacerbate the business risks from the reasonable to the totally unacceptable. Like Rossini's opera *La Gazza Ladra* (*The Thieving Magpie*), this creature lines its own nest. A large degree of brazenness, smooth-talk and hard-selling often proves effective camouflage in the corporate forests. These birds behave like the Enron or Worldcom bosses.

Financial newspapers are quick to portray this bird preening itself. Dennis Kozlowski at Tyco was more egregious in his desire to evade tax and to get interest-free loans from Tyco to help furnish his lavish New York apartment. Tyco has lost some $100 billion from its peak of $120 billion. News of his behaviour as Tyco leader affected the shares, which fell precipitously more than 30 % in a day.[5]

There are ways in which we can avoid these dangerous CEO species. Get the AEW (Andersen–Enron–Worldcom) disaster alert radar fitted into your risk navigation aids. It will need a long-term process to force the boards out of their cosseted and closeted "group-think".

COMPANY STRUCTURE AND RISKS

The return of fundamental analysis is to find real value in a company and that is one that finds a concrete upside, and then manages its downside risk. Investment risk management is a form of zoo-keeping whereby we have to cage the financial corporate animals at the appropriate time, and let them out to exercise at other times. A lax corporate governance structure, ineffective auditing and poor risk management allow more CEO magpies to fly over the corporate landscape and lets them steal more. See Figure 4.4. The public knee-jerk reaction to CEOs' malfeasance is "Jail'em!". Yet, this is an inadequate solution. We have mentioned the AEW (Andersen–Enron–Worldcom) danger-alert system to assist us in the investment jungle – see **Risk Warning Signs** in Chapter 6. Can we place more OpRisk controls or tactics within the corporate "zoo" to filter out or counteract the crooks in the market?

Such a filter can make it worthwhile considering a great asset of companies – the value and effectiveness of their risk management structure. This is what the Basel II banking regulations recognises – the need to assess how developed a business is at risk management. Currently, many banks and funds in the Western markets focus on the compliance department and audit group as the sum total of the risk management exercise. This is a narrow corporate view and misinterprets the concept of risk management. Risk management is a corporate asset waiting to be valued and deployed.

We place an explicit check for the establishment of a sound risk management department as a separate and empowered function in the company. Basel II recognises the need for OpRisk to be identified and managed by a specific risk management framework. Not devoting more resources, and specially trained staff at that, is to ignore the OpRisk problem and hope that it will disappear.[6]

CASE STUDY: THE EXECUTIVE BACKGROUND CHECK

Top execs of at least three US companies were disciplined for fabricating their university degrees on their CVs. The disclosure by Peter Turecek, who heads the consulting services group at corporate investigating firm Kroll Inc. said:

Resumé fraud is not new. Companies wanting to check it, or having the political will to check it, is something that has to change.

---

[5] "Tyco's Kozlowski sets sail", www.Forbes.com, 3 June 2002.
[6] "Sound practices for the management and supervision of operational risk", Basel Capital Banking Supervisory Committee, www.BIS.org, July 2002.

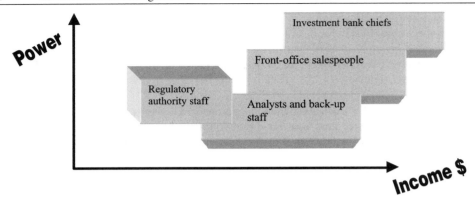

Figure 4.6 Relative power and income

He added that nearly 25 % of the exec background checks he had done revealed false information. Companies are complacent, they assume that if the job candidate has been in an industry for 20 years, some previous company must have checked – but no.

A thorough background check costs about US$25 000, therefore CEOs often skimp to save money and time. Compared with millions of dollars lost in securities fraud and money laundering – padding the resumé seems small corporate potatoes. Yet, Veritas Software Corp fired CFO Kenneth Lonchar after discovering he did not have an MBA from Stanford Business School as claimed. Veritas shares fell 19 % on the day of the announcement. Ultimately, Turecek said, the client companies are responsible. They should do pre-employment screening or background checking, but they do not always do so.[7]

Moreover, the recruitment pool of potential directors for the board is currently so limited that it becomes apparent that it is more of a nepotistic case of "jobs for the boys". Thus, the *Higgs Report* recommends a stronger role for non-executive directors on the boards.[8] Furthermore, the remuneration committees draw up complex salary and bonus structures that may seem to have little or no relation to the actual performance of the company.[9]

Yet, by current salaries, it seems that income and power are distributed to encourage errant corporate behaviour. See Figure 4.6.

Essentially, a basic re-cap of the process would show a conflict of interest; the analysts are meant to be given the task of professional study of the industry and form of companies worthy of devoting valuable money, especially in an IPO (initial public offering). But, the front office or sales department is devoted to maximising revenue and promoting a successful IPO, not minimising downside investor risk. Who has more power?

Furthermore, the regulators have only a moderate level of influence and power. Their power is compromised by the fact that regulatory staff earn much less than those in the top investment banks. From experience, we know that middle-level regulators are paid, say, $50 000 – $75 000, quite a bit less than the banks. Furthermore, many of the regulators are aware of this income disparity, so they would eventually like to find jobs in the banks they inspect.[10] We have to see who has the power and who gets the money (see Figure 4.6).

[7] Associated Press, 3 October 2002.

[8] *Higgs Report*, Department of Trade and Industry, www.DTI.gov.uk, 20 January 2003.

[9] *Turnbull Guidance Report*, September 1999.

[10] Professor Avinash Persaud, lecturer at Gresham College and managing director, State Street Bank, London, 3 October 2002.

Underwriting IPOs of shares was as simple as shooting fish in a barrel. It was the most profitable line in investment banking, without much of the downside risk of proprietary trading. In this scenario, the risk is borne by the company who sees its IPO launched at a low price so success is almost guaranteed for the bank. A feast time was Q1 2000 – a great period for world-wide IPOs, raising some $144 billion of equity capital. Business revenue advising on mergers and acquisitions was knocking on $4 trillion worth.[11]

The open hearings of top US investment bankers held before Congress was a threat that few companies really wanted to bear.

> There is no question that the investing public has diminished faith in Wall Street. . . . my office has announced the results of an investigation that showed the degree to which the investing public has been misled by one of the largest institutions on Wall Street. Unfortunately, several ongoing investigations have revealed similar problems elsewhere.
>
> These deceptions – Enron, Global Crossing and others – have led many small investors to withdraw from the markets. It is absolutely essential that we take steps to restore investor confidence in the marketplace.[12]

There is some evidence to say that the regulators' teeth are only now starting to sink deep enough into the corporate animal to deter the directors.[13]

More major changes are still necessary. For example, the SEC has encouraged investment banks to split from their analysis arms. Thus, investment banking arms have been split from stockbroker market analytical research divisions. This is a tacit admission that the Chinese Walls alleged in the investment banks never really existed. Deeper reform is needed if investors are to return in numbers.

RISK VANITIES

A robber or fraudster normally takes time to plan their crime. Thus, proper risk management is not a sit-back-and-watch process. Risk monitoring is a component of operational risk management and is a continuous hands-on process. Handling operational risk properly is not a completely reactive process, investors must have a proactive risk attitude and devote their resources accordingly.[14]

This is the first element of risk analysis. Stand on a steady business foundation, and then prepare to leap forward. More investors stood on quicksand, suckered by investment marketing hype – very groovy, but potentially fatal. This is the realisation – a dull, grey, concrete base lets you conduct a more balanced business evaluation. It involves evaluating risk scope and business objectives, then determining potential sources of danger or risk.

The slow and reliable tortoise always gets to the finishing line. Warren Buffett was chastised for investing in bricks and mortar or boring insurance; although it does sound boring, many of his businesses still survive and grow. Maybe "boring" is that corporate steadiness and foundation that the business community would rather shun in favour of the more groovy investments.

---

[11] *The Economist*, www.economist.com, 25 October 2001.
[12] "US Senate: Hearing on corporate governance", testimony of Eliot Spitzer, New York State Attorney General Eliot Spitzer, Washington DC, 26 June 2002.
[13] MSNBC News, 26 September 2002.
[14] *Managing Project Risk*, Y.Y. Chong, Financial Times Management, 2000.

A problem that recurs in investment history is that investors tend to have short memories. The fascination with junk bonds, derivative contracts, IPOs and dot-coms came and went just like the Tulip craze in early Holland or the South Sea Bubble in England. This blind buying mania, although rooted in the 17th century Dutch tulip craze, will continue to recur within the tragedies of poor investment decisions. These problems will revisit us in the 21st century.

Every one or two years there is a market fad. Whether it is bell-bottom jeans, wide lapels or pet rocks is anyone's guess. Every now and then there will be a new technology, such as biotech or dot-coms to dazzle the eye, or some obscure country that demands investors' money. Salespeople, investment advisers *et al.* are paid a fee or commission by banks and funds to sell their products to clients.

> (analysts') research was largely and openly used as a sales hook for investment banking clients. Research could also be used to punish companies. In one instance a company was downgraded by Merrill Lynch when it did not get the company's investment banking business, and in another example, a stock was downgraded to please a competitor.[15]

Many of these investment ventures have not got a slightest hope of winning. People are still oversold on junk.

PENSIONS MIS-SELLING

How much sales commission is reasonable? This was a fundamental question during the pensions mis-selling scandal. Worse: *are the best and most suitable investment products being sold?*

There has been a really damaging fall-out from the case in the UK of mis-selling pensions. About 1.1 million people were wrongly advised to transfer out of their company pension schemes. The compensation given to the victims is estimated at £12 billion so far, but this may only be a portion of the damage done. Many individuals and groups have been sold unsuitable pension products that should not have been promoted to them in the first place. There is a real need to protect the investor against the failures of a completely free market.[16]

Who is there to protect the investor? Even the most sophisticated investor requires the assistance of experts. Financial operations need specialist support staff who assist them. Who are these specialists?

- Lawyers – due diligence.
- Accountants/auditors – examine the balance sheet and account statements.
- Bankers provide the finance.

These are part of the old way, those who carry out investment risk management by the orthodox school of risk management.

But does it really fit the 21st century? Even with the "best" experts from the investment banks, lawyers and accountants behind you, you can still snatch failure from the jaws of success.

---

[15] "US Senate: Hearing on corporate governance", testimony of Eliot Spitzer, New York State Attorney General Eliot Spitzer, Washington DC, 26 June 2002.
[16] *Financial Times*, p. 1, 16 August 2002.

CASE STUDY: BOO.COM

Let us cast our minds back a few years to the maelstrom of the dot-com fever. It seemed that just about every Internet IPO idea was worth floating and getting backers to pump millions into schemes for projected huge gains. Share prices did indeed rocket on many a tech stock flotation.

The meteoric rise (and crash) of Boo.com under the controls of Ernst Malmius and Kajsa Leander shows some of the professional qualifications needed for a leading-edge business model. Grooviness certainly sells.

But, just as a rocket, many of them dived spectacularly downwards as reality sank into the market. Well-known backers such as JP Morgan bank were happy to put large sums of money into the venture that was the focus of much publicity. It has been indicated that some $300 million was lost forever in this ill-conceived enterprise. Original investors lost just about everything.[17]

Given the IPOs and dot-com scandals, the lumbering tiger of corporate governance is only just starting to growl and get its claws out. It can only be a good sign in the long run for the innocent investor.

CORPORATE MISGOVERNANCE

So, if the risk-averse investor continues to park good money with bad company directors, what can be done to protect the innocent? The investor has to be both reasonable and proactive.

We have seen the pitfalls from the side of the financial experts who have lost investors' money, partly from a lack of proper communication. This fault can come from both sides, either the salesperson "ramping" a financial instrument that is more risky (or much valuable) than is likely within the bounds of reality, or the investor having a risk appetite that is completely unsuitable. Furthermore, there is a problem with the regulatory moves to make self-disclosure best practice for the industry when the salespeople do not want to, or cannot, reveal the true extent of risk.

Regular people, not Wall Street professionals, have lost a collective fortune by relying on the tainted advice of the biggest and most trusted names in the world of finance.

As one Merrill Lynch analyst wrote:

We are losing people money and I don't like it. John and Mary Smith are losing their retirement (money) because we don't want...an investment banking client – the CFO of Goto.com to be mad at us.[18]

We have to admit that a corporate gagging order, under many slogans ("Don't rock the boat", "Don't tell the customer more than you have to" etc.), is likely to continue despite all legal moves for full disclosure. Faced with this scenario, it is incumbent upon the John and Mary Smiths of this world to take on the role of investigative investor and to evaluate the extant risk and fair valuation themselves. They should forget reputation and actively ask themselves whether the business opportunity offered really merits an appropriate investment.

---

[17] "Delivering on your e-promise: managing e-business projects", p. 105–6, Y.Y. Chong, *Financial Times Management*, 2001.
[18] "US Senate: Hearing on corporate governance", testimony of Eliot Spitzer, New York State Attorney General Eliot Spitzer, Washington DC, 26 June 2002.

What is more appropriate is that investors do not pass the investment mandate so readily to the "experts", but consider the suitability risk. The suitability risk has been defined as: "The risk that the institution sells the client the 'wrong' product, which the client later claims to be inappropriate for its needs or level of experience.[19]

Aristotle was asked what reason was. He gave examples of what reason was, and what a reasonable man would do under certain circumstances. This question still unsettles modern legal thinking two millennia after the Greek classics. The US Supreme Court employs the "reasonable man" hypothesis, to determine what a reasonable person would do under specific circumstances. Degrees of reasonable risk and reasonable return still trouble us today.

Determining a reasonable risk-return performance is a more dedicated and complex task than many banks have thought, even now. One view takes this task as a combination of three horizontal processes cutting across all business lines throughout the corporation:[20]

1. Setting up risk-return guidelines and benchmarks.
2. Risk-return decision making ("ex ante perspective").
3. Risk-return monitoring ("ex post perspective").

It is time for the John and Mary Smiths of the investment world to extend their snouts and sniff out the risk themselves.

What has emerged over recent months is a renewed effort to force "corporate transparency" and disclosure. There are numerous moves to improve corporate governance and we track a handful of them. Will these moves drive the thieving or incompetent directors into the open?

Faced with such corporate uncertainty, we need a risk management strategy to handle the potential danger. We compare this project initiation or remit according to the best practice in RAMP (risk analysis and management of projects). RAMP offers us the risk management actions to choose:

- Avoiding risk
- Reducing risk
- Reducing uncertainty
- Transferring risk
- Insuring risk
- Sharing risk

Nobody loves a loser, and there are few dealing operations in banking and fund management that would wish to appear anything less than a winner.

ACCURACY OF CORPORATE LOSSES

Risk management is a hugely information-hungry process. Keeping an up-to-date record of banking or fund winners and losers is a data-intensive exercise. Completeness and the accuracy of the data are the bedrock for corporate scrutiny. Banks can be strange animals when it comes to releasing data; they may not even be fully aware of their own profitability. The new Basel II regulations will try to enforce mandatory reporting of profits and losses in detail. This is where the Basel II regulations come in to encourage more banking transparency.

---

[19] *Measuring and Managing Operational Risk*, Appendix A, C. Marshall, Wiley, 2002.
[20] *Risk Management in Banking*, p. 54, J. Bessis, Wiley, 2002.

Table 4.3   Risk analysis I

Business line	Loss factor % of value	Expected annual loss	Actual loss this year	Action
Corporate finance	2.8	$11 000 000	$14 200 000	ALERT! Send in forensic investigator from Bank HQ

Table 4.4   Risk analysis II

Bank's business line	Gamma risk weight %	Expected annual loss	Actual loss this year	Action
Bond trading	40	$10 000 000	$12 213 710	ALERT! Send in chief risk officer

Losses are bad news, and sometimes nothing is worse than the embarrassment of a public loss or reputational damage.

> A failure or degradation in these operations tends to make existing customers and counter-parties defect, resulting in an economic loss to the firm. Reputational effects are particularly important for larger more well-known retail banks in competitive markets whose customers can easily transact elsewhere.[21]

Knowing how much you have lost, and why, is a sign that you are making progress in retailing. Knowing how to stop or reduce your losses is an indication of business success. These are known as "risk triggers", while in auditing they are called "red flags". See Table 4.3.

Adapting this sort of analysis would be useful in banking and fund management. Furthermore, on the larger corporate scale, banks under the stiffer Basel II operational risk measures will rarely wish to confess to the central banking authorities that they are "banks at risk". Certainly, banks rated as more risky will be forced to pay higher operational costs in terms of a capital adequacy ratio of reserves held in the central bank under new Basel II rules.

We can adapt one feature, the recording of losses, from the Basel II banking regulations and adapt it for the retail industry. This forms the first one-line building-block approach of our Basel II Loss Database for dealing with operational risk in the finance industry.[22] See Table 4.4.

This is a simple prototype approach towards identifying areas for monitoring, i.e. being risk proactive against solely reactive. It can identify business areas for improvement, certainly when you data-mine by business lines and deeper detail. This is a potentially rich area for business intelligence development.

CLASSES OF INSTRUMENTS AND THEIR RISK COMPONENTS

What is harder to conceive is that many major investment players are unaware of their true risk appetite. Some are even ignorant of the risks involved when investing in the various assets.

---

[21] *Measuring and Managing Operational Risks in Financial Institutions*, p. 246, C. Marshall, Wiley 2001.
[22] MB Risk Management press release, 16 December 2002, www.mbrm.com.

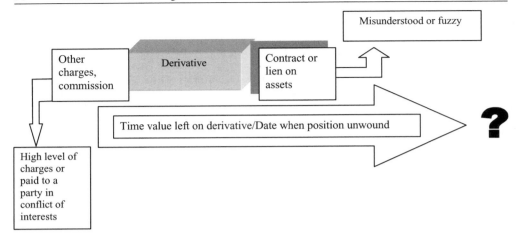

Figure 4.7   Derivatives – value and ties

Financial instruments come in numerous shapes and forms, and new instruments appear every month. However, beyond the marketing creativity of investment banks, there are constants that can be found in all instruments.

Classes of basic instruments, for risk management purposes, can be roughly divided into:

- fixed income
- commodities
- equities.

Investments can be viewed as resources placed in faith into the above asset classes on behalf of sponsors, managers and clients. The risks of these different classes have been defined in brief earlier. This is now complicated by the emergence of another composite class below.

Derivatives

Thus, investors could successfully take protection against adverse movements in currency or interest rates by buying countervailing derivatives or futures contracts. Derivatives have value in risk management for those who fully understand them. The realised value is not fully clear when there are complex relationships with the financial vehicle they are related to – the "underlying" asset. See Figure 4.7.

Lately, there have been further derivative products introduced on the market. Some have diverged from the plain "vanilla" product towards the newer range of "exotics". They can provide real value in hedging the value of assets, or as an investment commodity in their own right.[23]

There are further risks pertaining to one's limited knowledge, sometimes regarding the legal standing of the assets. The ownership liens, contract amendments and linked assets attached to derivatives, especially OTC ones, add considerable risk for understanding the true value of the financial instrument.

---

[23] *Derivatives: The Wild Beast of Finance*, A. Steinherr, Wiley, 1998.

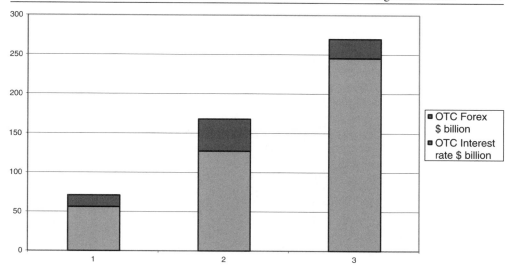

Figure 4.8 OTC derivatives market in the UK 1995–2001
Source: *Financial Stability Review*, Bank of England, June 2002.

Derivative financial instruments have seen an astounding large volume in trading. Most are interest rate OTC derivatives, the minority are OTC Forex derivatives, yet the daily currency volume dwarfs the UK need for trade foreign currency by a factor of at least 50. See Figure 4.8.

Briefly, derivatives can be used for risk managing our investments when managed adequately:

• Used properly, derivatives have uses that can be both imaginative and helpful. Wheat and oil commodity derivatives are clear examples, while weather derivatives are a new phenomenon.

In spite of this, the effect of derivatives is supposed to decrease the total risk. A side effect of a hedge through a derivative is that it generally adds a host of small risks, by adding complications, lack of trackability, etc. One of the more useful aspects of Basel II, and the latest accounting standards, is that it is supposed to promote better asset valuation and disclosure of risk exposure – sometimes at odds with the very complexity of derivatives.

Bonds

These are considered as the lower form of risk as they represent debt and not equity. Debtors are first in line to be paid, especially when the company hits a bad market patch and runs low of reserves.

Bond-holders have traditionally felt a bit more secure, although it is disconcerting to see owners of Enron or Worldcom bonds not considerably optimistic over seeing any significant return on their investments. But, take a more mundane case – let us run along an arbitrary panorama of bonds and their perceived risk associated. Bond holders are near the top when it comes to the safety pyramid. See Figure 4.9.

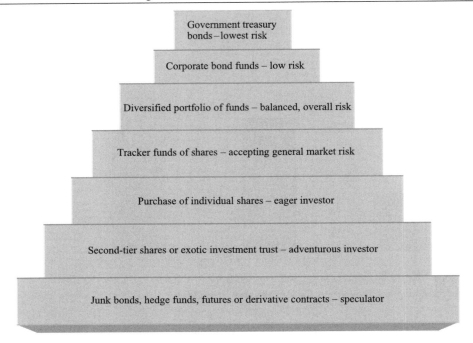

Figure 4.9   The investment safety pyramid

Low risk

US Treasury
The commonly accepted no-risk investment. Backed by USA Inc. Used as a benchmark for all other securities that are deemed to carry a risk premium.

Investment-grade bonds
Bonds for the conservative investor, issued by a reputable company. The timely payment of principal and interest are more or less guaranteed, the risk of default is remote.

Housing bonds
Revenue bonds (e.g. FNMA, GNMA) issued by state or local housing agencies – safe as houses?

Bearer bonds
These bonds pay coupon interest and principal when due to the bearer. These bonds require physical presentation to the bondholder and their ownership is not registered. This makes them

Table 4.5   Performance of dot-com funds

Fund manager performance	Fund value increase p.a. (%)			Downside risk potential results
	Year 1	Year 2	Year 3	
Top 10 % last year	110 %	130 %	−85 %	Demolition of fund
Top 25 % last year	70 %	80 %	−75 %	Carry on job
Median percentile last year	25 %	30 %	−25 %	No promotion
Bottom 10 % last year	5 %	8 %	−15 %	Lose job

easily traded as a very liquid asset next to currency, but it also means that if you lose them there is no fall-back.

Zero coupon
Commonplace bonds that are sold at a discount from face value and easily traded. They do not pay periodic interest payments, so there is no income or dividend, so are not recommended for less adventurous investors. They were sometimes favoured in the investment fund splits. Because all interest is paid at maturity, then these are unlikely to be recommended for pensioners who have a more limited time horizon.

High risk

Low-grade bonds
Usually called "junk bonds", these are unable to obtain a favourable investment-grade listing and are therefore reserved for the adventurous investor or speculator.

But if US Treasury bonds are seen as a no-risk investment because of their solid backing by the US government, how come they pay a higher comparative yield than Japan? The yields do appear very low. Does it mean that Japan Inc. is viewed as a lower risk than the USA?

No, it shows that risk and return is more complex than we had hoped. There are a lot more factors, e.g. currency risk and risk perceptions at work here.

Let's take a hypothetical, but not unrealistic, case, e.g. funds performing during and after the dot-com boom (year 1 and 2) and bust (year 3). These roughly correspond from the boom years of 1998 to 1999, then 2000 downward movements. See Table 4.5.

Trackability for a fund manager's performance can be split into two sources: Systematic and Non-systematic. Thus, the tracking error (in basis points/month) can be reduced to near zero, where the fund manager just about reflects the market's performance when a portfolio of 60 bonds are picked. One way of reading this is that a benchmarked performance 100 % the same as the market is almost guaranteed when a large basket of bonds is picked. Then, we become embroiled in the argument as to why one should employ professionals when we can construct passive tracker funds instead. Many would argue that we should only hire professionals to pick a successful selection of the higher-risk investments, e.g. tech stocks and bonds (see Figure 4.10).

The world technology share prices have fallen by some 70 % from the peak in March 2000. Even the German Neuer Markt was badly hit to such an extent, suffering the effects

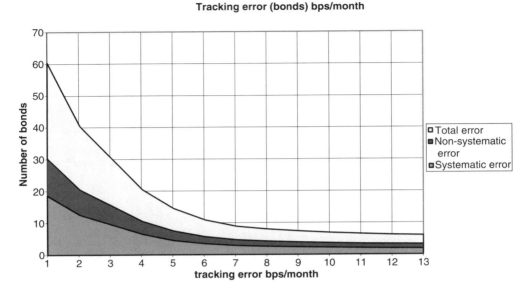

Figure 4.10   Tracking Error

of reputational risk too, that it no longer exists. Bond prices have generally done well by comparison, as have certain commodities such as gold or crude oil, which have performed better than the stagnant stock market.

The good news among the gloom is that not all industrial sectors have collapsed. Many investors have switched from shares to profit elsewhere. Boots pension fund reported a £175 million gain on its £2.3 billion scheme by switching out of equities completely and moving into bonds.[24] But, one pertinent question could be for John and Mary Smith, plus interested fund managers, as to how long a good market for bonds will run before equities become more profitable again?

Equities

These were the mainstay of the investment community, typified by pension funds and the banking world. There was no close rival for their popularity in the dozen years of the bull market from the late 1980s. There are some foundations for determining a company's stock, but these seem to shift like sand. There are many analytical ratios and numerical data that stock-pickers use in their arsenal; some are:

- P:E ratio
- EPS
- cash: earnings ratio
- ROCE
- assets: debt ratio
- equity: debt ratio

---

[24] *Pensions Week*, 12 November 2001.

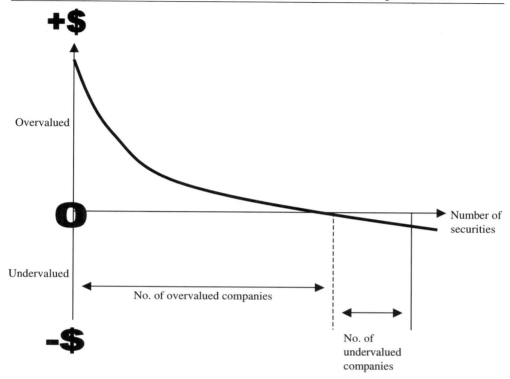

Figure 4.11   Overvalued vs. undervalued companies

- quick (or acid-test) ratio $q = (\text{cash} + \text{short-term securities} + \text{receivables}) / \text{current liabilities}$
- % growth (sales, market share)
- Market capitalisation

and so on.

Grinding numbers out of a computer leads one to a conclusion, but the final decision on a purchase still embodies hope that the stock will increase in value, rather than fall as an overhyped and overvalued company. The overvaluation is "hope value", and it is because of CEO malfeasance over company accounting statements and pictures of the firm's value. This is the "pecking-order" theory, where the party at the top of the corporate pyramid has the best information and investors have the worst.[25]

Alternatively, this could be a ramp up of the company by the company's investor relations department, investment bank or broker. Or, a misjudgement by the buyer or just momentary naivete bordering on madness by the buyer.

A study of seasoned equity offerings show that there is a consistent pattern for overvaluation. It shows that the offering reaches a share price peak when examining against P/E, CAPM or EPS. This is true for share price in the period two years before and two years after the offering.[26]

---

[25] "Corporate financing and investment decisions when firms have information that investors do not have", S.C. Myers and N.S. Majluf, *Journal of Financial Economics*, vol. 13, 1984.
[26] "Seasoned equity offerings, overvaluation and timing", J. Jindra, *Cornerstone Research*, November 2000.

The pecking-order theory has a certain validity because it shows us that CEOs have an inclination to issue more shares and ramp up the market capitalisation. The period of share recovery and the subsequent fall is perfect for the short-term tenure of the CEO – milk as much out of the company quickly, then leave.

Because of a combination of CEO greed and investor gullibility and the asymmetry of information favouring the directors, investors are faced with the stark reality that key company staff can orchestrate an overvaluation of the share price. More work has to be done to determine the extent of this malpractice. The study of US firms came up with sample of 1882, comprising 346 (18 %) undervalued and 1536 (82 %) overvalued companies.[27]

We illustrate this in Figure 4.11. The sample used contained many more overvalued than undervalued companies. If this is fully representative of the stock market, then, the news looks bad.

INVESTMENT AS A PROJECT

However, the danger is that individuals and corporations might not understand the value or operation of the investments being sold. It sounds like another Millennium Dome. This makes for a bad investment project. Under RAMP methodology, there are minimum criteria for a successful and desired result:

- Clearly stated and understood objectives.
- Defined scope of the project investment.
- Clear responsibilities and project ownership of these parties.
- Estimated budget for the project.
- Defined end-state for the project.
- Milestone date of project end.

Under extremely unclear financial engineering or complex business lines where none of the above conditions exist, then a successful outcome is very unlikely. Thus, clients may be occasionally oversold derivative products and inappropriate investment strategies. It is not just the banks and investment funds who have lost. The main losers are the humble private investors.

---

[27] "Seasoned equity offerings, overvaluation and timing", ibid.

5

Investing under Investigation

Calling the best investment in the market has always been a nerve-wracking job. We look at determining the "fair value" of an asset, and the risk involved with it. Investment value discounted for risk under RAROC is examined. There is concern that the financial "experts" have not been more proficient than the common layperson in the selection and management of investments. This makes the due diligence procedure doubly important. We look at the cult of investment reputation. A business plan and an investment methodology along RAMP lines is proposed. We end this chapter with an overview of hedge funds.

INSTINCT VERSUS ABILITY

The finance industry's basic instinct focuses on hiring the best performing stars, and that may include closing eyes to certain work or character defects. One error is that the "star" bank trader or fund manager is really a shooting-star, one that burns up and disappears from sight. Empirical results show that there is only a tiny core of fund managers who are truly stars. These stars are surrounded by the ephemeral satellites who will slip down the market performance stakes. Hiring these satellites at their peak is to risk underperformance, and even fund losses.

Reputational risk is once again means sticking your neck on the block. Banks that realise this stand a better chance of succeeding because their risk perception is correct. Investment banks that held on to a large staff with high salaries and higher bonuses in a down-turn put their balance sheets on the line. Those that shed staff and cut payroll fast put their reputation at danger, being seen as a "bank with a problem", but their financial strength remains.

Mortgage banks that lend money out at low interest rates and high leverage are in this market risk scenario on a different playing field. The fact that the loan is secured on collateral (the property) may be irrelevant – the real estate value can have dived disastrously. "No problem, we can always redo the property."

The American early 1980s S&L banking failures underlined the danger of such lax risk perception. We have to adopt realistic risk attitudes about the finance game.

The use of RAROC to test individual lines comes across as a good start to justify the investment. RAROC enables a company to ask if it is really making an acceptable return for the risk from each particular business line. It is a fundamental question that is worth asking whether to:

- remove (reduce capital)
- reinforce (more capital)
- stay in the business line
- or get out of the business.

The financial regulatory authorities hope that Basel II will eventually force banks and financial companies to report real trading losses. RAROC and similar tools are designed to develop richer profit and loss accounts, not cosmetic trading figures to appease the regulators and shareholders.

One of the problems that bedevil banks and funds is the uneven standards of institutional practices. The media have tended to focus so far on fraud and rogue trading, even when this is in the minority of losses. The FSA and London Stock Exchange warns that "previous performance is not a guarantee of future . . . "

Yet, we are constantly faced with inspecting the value of the track record; poor traders or managers continue where they are protected by the mantra of their previous performance.

These professionals have prided themselves upon their skill in recruitment and due diligence, their greater ability to sift out between good and unacceptable customers or staff. Unfortunately, banks' hiring and due diligence errors have subjected them and their shareholders to significant operational and reputational losses that have financial costs. The Basel Committee reported deficiencies in international banking due diligence know-your-customer (KYC) policies.

> KYC policies in some countries have significant gaps and in others they are non-existent. Even among countries with well-developed financial markets, the extent of KYC robustness varies.[1]

Thus, the Western economies with a long history of developed banking sectors also have large room or exposure for due diligence errors. This risk needs to be rectified.

CHECKING CORPORATE FUNDAMENTALS

We can revisit the traditional series of steps of the investment processes that extend from the John and Mary Smiths, to the bankers and fund managers, i.e. every reasonable investor. The diagram of investment project parties involved is used as a building block for demonstrating how the stakeholders interact in a basic model (see Figure 4.1). In the orthodox models, the steps of managing business investment decisions are sequential. We can insert reality checks that focus upon risk to keep our risk-return view balanced, put back in question at every phase, leading if necessary to a complete revision of investment projects. Let us see these phases in turn:

1. Formulate a business plan.
2. Match the risk appetite to the risk offer.
3. Due diligence, not least to manage reputation risk.
4. Risk support and methodology.

Formulate a business plan

The orthodox theory tends to propound the stable nature of the free market, where information is freely available, and leaders can build sound business cases backed with revenue and cost projections. The business case primarily rests upon the return or profit to be reaped in the future. The investors are, thus, able to make rational business decisions based upon this analysis, discounting the future profits by time decay and risk factors. To start with, there are various schools of investment analysis; but we only look at two (RAROC and NPV) for brevity's sake.

Essentially, the fundamentals of book-keeping/stock control theory are:

$$\text{Profits} = \text{Output} - \text{Input}$$

[1] *Customer Due Diligence for Banks*, Basel Committee on Banking Supervision, BIS, October 2001.

or

$$\text{Deliveries} - \text{Stock level} = \text{Sales}$$

Net present value

Discounting future revenue to take into account interest rates is one way we can risk-manage the value of future cash against present cash.

The basic way to do so was to estimate a prevailing interest rate r for the next few years t. So, we can derive present value (PV)

$$NPV \equiv \frac{\sum d_t F_t}{(1 + r)^t}$$

Imagine a bond that pays $12 per year over 2 years when interest is at 10 %.

$$\text{First year } PV \text{ interest} = \$12/(1.1) = \$1.09$$

$$\text{Second year } PV \text{ interest} = \$12/(1.1)^2 = \$12/(1.21) = \$0.99$$

The more advanced application of this simple investment technique is to run it over the portfolio. This "what-if" analysis reduces the value of the portfolio to one benchmark figure – net present value (NPV).

Take an example bank portfolio using its customers' bank deposits of $10 000 000 at 5 %. It reinvests this money into bonds that yield 10 %. Using simplified numbers to demonstrate, we can run a NPV analysis. We take the PV of all assets over time held, subtract the PV of liabilities over the same period to gain the NPV profit.

But, if you took a large position, and the interest rates rose, then you made a net loss. Financial instruments are often valued in terms of the cash flows they are likely to bring in the future, hence the fundamental tool, NPV. One minor problem for NPV users, everything works according to theory because the interest rates are known and constant throughout – it is a static model.

The trouble with the NPV school is that the numbers look very simple and the model rather naive in assuming fixed interest over the years. What we needed was something more functional and funkier. With more insight, we might be able to discount future cash inflows for the risk premium. Even more advanced pupils of this school talk of practising "what-if" analysis.

RAROC theory

Risk-adjusted return on capital (RAROC) uses a discount to treat profits as properly adjusted downwards to taking the risk. So, use the net return and subtract a risk premium

$$\text{Risk-adjusted profits} = \text{Net return} - \text{Risk premium (e.g. in an insurance company)}$$

$$\text{RAROC} = \frac{\text{Risk-adjusted return}}{\text{Risk-adjusted capital}}$$

$$= \frac{\text{Revenue} (- \text{Expenses} - \text{Expected Loss}) + \text{Return on economic capital}}{\text{Capital for covering worst-case loss scenario to desired } \% \text{ confidence level}}$$

% confidence level can be 95% or 99% depending upon your scenario evaluated.

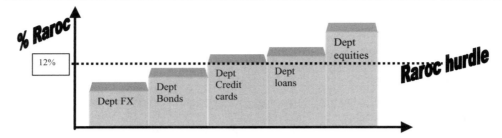

Figure 5.1   RAROC

The critical acclaim the RAROC model received initially was well deserved. When applied, it analyses performance within business units, and focuses attention on departments which are excelling. Thus, those making high profits, or above threshold levels, are compared against those that were under the set limit of profits.

You can benchmark different companies, or different operating divisions within the same corporation. Those business lines, or even departments, having low RAROC levels could be overcapitalised. By cutting their capital allocated, assuming that you still cover the loss events adequately, you raise the RAROC and release capital that could be more profitably invested somewhere else. See Figure 5.1.

Yet, examination of the business-line cases using a simple and ruthless RAROC can be a little spurious. A snapshot picture of RAROC across business lines does not take into account the time periods for which profit levels are volatile. Thus, wiping out the bonds department would have been fine during the dot-com IPO boom, but it would have killed a golden goose that made very good profits in any bonds bull run after 2000.

Another important factor is that some departments cannot be backed with revenue and profits projections. These departments provide the company with essential services and backup products. If RAROC were the sole driver behind whether to keep a department or axe it, risk management would be first for the chop; accounts and settlements would be second in the firing line. Both have considerable costs and are likely to be seen as cost centres. They might be sent instantly to the scrap-heap in favour of a cheaper "outsourced" solution in a recession.

RAROC is a very useful analytical tool, and is amenable to the use of computers, but this may be a strength and a weakness. People are often not very good at numbers and statistical analysis, thus humans are somewhat number-agnostic. Computers are very good at crunching numbers but are people-agnostic. Therefore, computers are unable to make rational and accurate decisions as to whether a company CEO or a counter-party is good for your business.

People and company leaders are responsible for much of the making or breaking the value of assets. Based upon this RAROC analysis alone, we embark upon a very narrow univariate school of investment analysis. Nevertheless, RAROC has proved useful in providing benchmark levels and enabling analysis between a corporation's business lines. Because the theory is understood and widely available, it will continue to hold promise in companies willing to manage risk.[2]

However, these professional views on risk tend to ignore several caveats in force. "Let the buyer beware" surrounds the questions over the models used to value assets on the market

---

[2] Erisk, www.Erisk.com, October 2002.

and time of commercial entry or exit. The real options view practises asset management flexibility. A further complication is the extent of any potential portfolio underperformance or extra operating cost processed. A customer could end up feeling badly used or misled. The conventional investment world-view cannot always work when faced with such a mine-field.

RAROC and VaR are fine analytical tools, but they are the first casualties when investors or top management have decided to pile into the next asset fad. The head-first rush into the telecoms companies during the dot-com era was one of the latest in the never-ending saga of hype initially triumphant over substance. There is a systematic bias for bank analysts to be overoptimistic about companies where the bank has taken an interest – even those with little fundamental prospect of wealth creation. The holistic, or organic, view and understanding of the stakeholders above would tend to make such a study irrelevant. The business plan is flawed if our business view is blinkered from the outset.

"Take JPMorgan Chase, or Citibank or Credit Suisse, banks with very sophisticated approached to risk management . . . Despite their sophistication, perhaps because of their misplaced sophisti-cation, they have been full and present victims of all of the last cycles. They have lost considerable amounts of shareholders' capital on the dot-com bubble, on Enron, on Worldcom, on Global Crossing and potentially on their syndication of collateralised debt obligations. Yet, they have not failed, perhaps because the market believes they are too big to do so, thereby limiting panic."[3]

Spot the business stakeholders first and their real motives.

DUE DILIGENCE

There are ways of delving deeper to dig up the truth. Sometime, it is like peeling an onion because the truth makes you cry. Or, you could laugh when you find out that the emperor wears no clothes. See Figure 5.2.

➢ A wide community feeling of confidence in a company affords little value of true investment protection. Prestige can be "fig leaf" risk management– see: Reputational Risk. It offers little real effective protection, and when the figleaf is removed, then everyone laughs about it.
➢   Size is of no protection – TBTF "Too big to fail" is just a mantra. The harder they come, the harder they fall.
➢   The "comfort factor" that the accounts have been audited by a top-class "Big Five" auditor and has been advised by a respected management consultancy can be exposed as worthless.
➢   An industrial tendency for restatement of booked revenue and profits engenders scepticism in GAAP and IAS accounting standards, together with the corporate auditors.
➢   The manner in which investment banks and brokers hold interests in companies and promote their shares must be called into question. Various conflicts of interest are at stake; formerly brushed away dancing under the totem-pole of "Chinese walls".
➢ Corporate forecasting methods and mathematical projections of revenue, profits and the usual company "gods" are not always worth worshipping; a lesson to be learnt hopefully before the company goes bust.

Figure 5.2   Stripping the clothes away from a risky business

---

[3] Professor Avinash Persaud, Gresham College and Managing Director, State Street Bank, London, 3 October 2002.

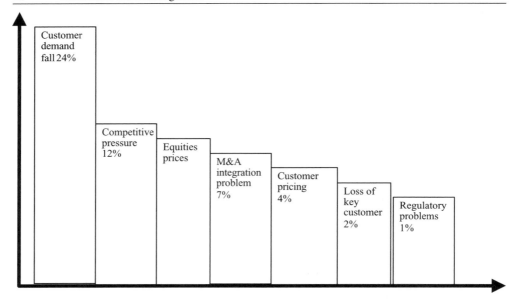

Figure 5.3   Primary cause of stock drop (number of Fortune 1000 companies)
Source: *"How Safe is Safe Enough?"* A. Darlington *et al.*, Insitute of Actuaries, 12 June 2001.

Traditional corporate analysis and orthodox investment risk management should be viewed with a jaundiced eye once the mistakes keep recurring. You cannot rely on the institutions and regulatory agencies alone to offer protection. They may be unaware of the illegal acts undertaken, the litigation may take a very long time, any compensation may be dwarfed by the loss incurred.

It is likely that once the first stage has been passed, the process of matching the risk appetite and the risk offer is a merely cursory exercise. There becomes little to derail the investment train. We have seen that a large proportion of strategic business decisions resulted in a significant stock price fall in Fortune 1000 companies. See Figure 5.4.

Many reasons may exist to explain the corporate marriage rationale, e.g. synergy between businesses, stronger teams, better sales and revenue figures from the M&A, but more often, the real results delivered from M&A disappoint. Let us, however, note that this rate of success, estimated at 25 %, is in line with other projects, such as financial IT system projects. Your dice are loaded at least 3:1 against your M&A succeeding.[4]

There is so much momentum and ego raging within the investment groups, that it is considered cowardly to back out of the original investment decision. Thus, under such a closed mindset, a due diligence or oversight check is merely a rubber-stamp of the decision to proceed. The risk-analysis and risk-monitoring processes are considered weak, irrelevant or suspect.

RISK SUPPORT AND METHODOLOGY

The key to proper risk management is to have an empowered risk-analysis and risk-handling process. One part of the risk-management puzzle can be offered by RAMP – the methodology

---

[4] *Decision-Making Perspectives on Due Diligence Failure*, Benjamin Powell and Phanish Puranam, London Business School, London 2002.

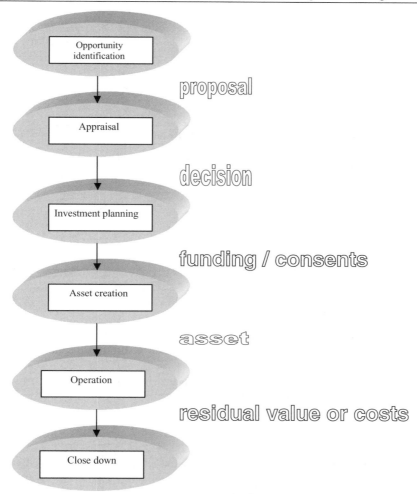

Figure 5.4   RAMP: the investment life-cycle

created by the Institution of Civil Engineers (ICE) and the Insitute of Actuaries (IoA). Because of the long foundations of ICE in engineering projects, coupled with the expertise of IoA in financial analysis, we have the potential of hard-core mathematical analysis wedded to project management control. RAMP holds great promise in handling investment projects, and should be further investigated for those in the financial sector wishing to promote greater risk management.[5] See Figures 5.4 and 5.5.

INVESTOR CYNICISM

What we have seen in the past 20 years within the business community is a cycle of boom and bust, of euphoric optimism followed by a real sense of investor cynicism. The 'Big Bang' UK financial community changes in 1986 heralded a spirit of greater competitiveness, and a

---

[5] *Managing Project Risk*, Y.Y. Chong, Financial Times Management, 2000.

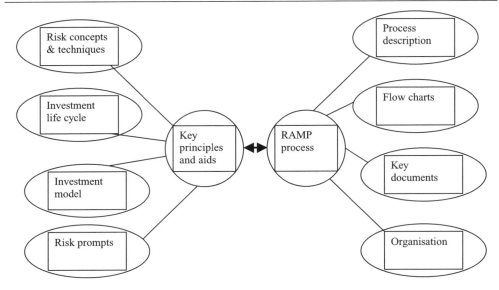

Figure 5.5   Components of the RAMP approach
Source: www.Actuaries.org.uk, Institute of Actuaries, 2000.

greater openness – a fairer deal for the investor. So we were told. The supposed impartiality of investment advisers has now been widely questioned after the mortgage endowments scandal and pensions mis-selling in the UK.

RAMP explicitly advocates the need for a balanced view and the astute use of common sense within risk and project management.

CASE STUDY: LTCM[6]

Both Mr Merton and Mr Scholes of LTCM adhered to the efficient-market hypothesis that the market competently prices all financial assets and available information. They believed that derivatives dissipate economic risk. Merton even argued that improved hedging techniques rendered equity capital unnecessary as a cushion against risk. The prototype was LTCM.

With hindsight, it is extraordinary that Messrs Merton and Scholes failed to realise that LTCM concentrated risk acutely. Part of the hedge fund's strategy involved purchasing risky assets from other investment banks. However, LTCM was also financed with loans from those very same banks. This sounds a bit like the Lloyds' Names scandal. Thus, the risks were not really being transferred.

LTCM was born with good breeding. John Meriwether provided the capital in LTCM, while Myron Scholes (one of the Nobel prize-winners for the Black–Scholes model) bolstered it with his unimpeachable academic credentials.

People flocked to the hedge fund with the top brains in the business. It initially made good profits for its customers. Then the once-in-a-thousand-year extreme event, or "perfect

---

[6] "When Genius Failed: The Rise and Fall of Long-Term Capital Management", Roger Lowenstein, Random House, 2001.

storm" happened. The Russian sovereign debt default in 1998 "spooked" markets. The hedge funds were extremely exposed and liquidity ran dry. Asset prices fell, and even a hedge fund that could sell short or take bets on a downturn fell down.

When LTCM failed in September 1998 it had capital of only $800 million, against its total market positions estimated in billions of dollars. The Federal Reserve felt it had to bail it out with a $3.6 billion loan because it believed there was a real danger that the world's financial system might be harmed. With the top brains at LTCM snatching failure from the jaws of profits, the Fed managed to save LTCM in order to avoid the risk of market melt-down.

LTCM pleases nearly everyone in the risk reasons: TBTF, top reputation, glitzy mathematical models, systemic risk etc. And then failure. It is also many regulators' nightmare. Picking through the lessons helps us to track tell-tale signs of future players who offer a mini-LTCM but clothed in different apparel. RAMP gets us out of the closed mindset of the emperor who wore no clothes. It brings us into closer detail of the project and business process description and the risk concepts and details. Otherwise, we can have our eyes too firmly locked on the prize.

Regulations require these HLI institutions to set up reporting and accounting systems. Nevertheless, they will continue to operate in some form. Losses will occur, where and when they do, from complete mismatches in risk appetite and risk offer.

However, these procedures are wholly developed, in light of the high leverage and risks that they take. We should monitor the surviving HLIs to prevent a new LTCM episode from recurring. Regulatory bodies can keep a rein upon the HLIs only when they operate within their jurisdiction. But, the BCCI episode shows us the lack of international cooperation between different regulators. The problem is compounded when HLIs operate offshore without any adequate control. Part of risk management protection is realising the limits of power.

Nevertheless, hedge funds based offshore mean that we are unlikely to eradicate them, and we will revisit HLI corporate failure again at some time sooner than later. HLIs work on high-risk principles of being extremely highly leveraged, or betting with borrowed money. Their great advantage is that they can make profits in downtrends in the market. Most players buying bonds or shares outright in a falling market means:

Table 5.1   Hedge fund features

Feature	Comment
Investment efficiency	High variance. Investors expect high alpha return but the actual results may differ significantly from anticipated. Large tracking variance and errors.
Costs	High management fees; usually increased even more when returns are high.
Comfort factor	Not comfortable for the easily worried. Unfamiliar modelling and analysis. Bad PR in media.
Control	Intense monitoring required because of volatility and high leverage. Managers need scrutiny because of opaque remuneration structure.
Risks	Market risk – volatility needs more scrutiny. High leverage requires more ALM risk control. Mandate risk because of less corporate transparency and high management fee structure.

Source: *Hedge Funds*, John, Caslin Institute of Actuaries, 22 January 2002.

1. Hold and keep (expect the market to rise).
2. Sell at a loss (write off in the trading book).

Hedge funds do not have this limited choice. See Table 5.1.
  Used well, including hedge funds within a portfolio can create benefits for the fund manager.

• Raise the number of days in year with positive returns.
• Reduce the spread of returns.
• Change skewness of returns from negative to positive.
• Increase the average monthly return in the portfolio.
• Reduce the variance of the returns.

  Hedge funds can also increase the returns of portfolios. But, care should be used to ensure that their inclusion does not unduly raise the whole portfolio risk. Their complexity requires more care in portfolio design and greater monitoring. Traditionally, hedge funds have been reluctant to disclose how they operate, report how much they are profiting/losing. Where institutional investors decide to use hedge funds as a suitable investment vehicle, then they could choose:

• Tailor-made fund of hedge funds.
• An existing basket of investments (fund of funds).
• Directly investing into hedge funds.

All approaches still require degrees of caution and monitoring.[7]
  A large LTCM disaster will happen again, in one form or another. Yet, there were the initial successes of other hedge funds that made incredible returns on their capital. This sort of performance will continue to entice thousands of customers.
  Why worry? Some of the most "respected" banks operate just like hedge funds.

  Banks are more like hedge funds than we care to think. They lend several times their capital, they borrow short-term to lend long-term . . . . The bigger the bank, the bigger the tumble."[8]

  Given the leeway under which a hedge fund now operates, there is an argument that HLIs should be forced to disclose what their strategies are and what their current market exposures are. That is, to fall under the same measures for corporate governance as the other banks and funds. This obviously compromises their corporate confidentiality and their room for silent manoeuvrability; HLIs would definitely oppose such regulation. What we have is a trade-off between transparency and confidentiality for operational flexibility.
  Investors should consider the deeper issues of designing hedging mechanisms, especially the opaque or "non-transparent" ones.[9] Then they need to review corporate governance and risk-return principles within our organic risk management methodology. Organic risk management may not prevent all LTCM recurrences, but they are the basic investigative building blocks for selecting appropriate investments.
  You need a full business solution, and that means follow-up and enforcement.

---

[7] *Hedge Funds*, John Caslin, Institute of Actuaries, 22 January 2002.
[8] Professor Avinash Persaud, Gresham College and Managing Director, State Street Bank, London, 3 October 2002.
[9] *Risk Management in Banking*, Chapter 16, Joel Bessis, Wiley, 2002.

6
Risk Warning Signs

We look at the behaviour of top management in modern corporations. We examine their great love of M&A despite the unfavourable track record. Given the trend for many CEOs to be inept or greedy, investors have to adopt a warning system to detect a company's destruction earlier. This we call an AEW alert system. We look at accounting and credit ratings to serve as some form of alarm signal. The risk management offered by the legal and insurance sectors is examined. Given their shortcomings, we look to alternatives in risk management.

PREVAILING RISK ATTITUDES

An efficient mental risk-return calculus is a critical component for business success under uncertainty.

> ... the overall risk perception held by the public is often worse than reality. Risk management can assist you in making more profits in areas where over-conservative investors stay out. The upside is that, if risk is really low, your rivals will be over-valuing the risk. The downside is that, if risk is really higher than you think, you will stand to pay the price of the risk hazard or damage.[1]

The efficient portfolio theory and mainstream mathematical models only set a basic foundation for analysis; they do not represent the risk management goal itself. Thus, they can become inclined to set a level of return that is not proportionate to an acceptable level of risk. We have seen that investors and managers often inadvertently end up being risk-seeking.

Sophisticated financial modelling can lead companies into a false sense of security where theory has not been adequately back-tested to check if it conforms to reality. Thus:

- they have lower assessment of the risk probability and impact;
- the impact of worst-case scenario is less dramatic than imagined;
- the maximum return is potentially higher than thought;
- such phenomena of risk misperceptions are often observed in practice, but not always admitted.

Weak banks and companies that are more prone to failure have inherent shortcomings such as a CEO and board that are likely to embark on unsuitable strategic missions. Reputation and prestige of the guilty party, as we have seen in the Credit Lyonnais case, may be enough to stop adequate risk management exercises taking off in the first place.

Furthermore, the internal checks and balances offered by the oversight board may have been overridden, so defects in the company's structure are prevalent.

At the lower organisational level, there will be risk management weaknesses that allow major errors to occur. The Leeson or Rusnak cases are examples of a failure to incorporate suitable control elements. Financial modelling errors are examples of less glaring unintentional mistakes in risk management.

---

[1] "Bringing risk management up to date in an e-commerce world", Y.Y. Chong, *Balance Sheet*, vol.8, no.5, 2000.

Setting up a departmental risk management function will monitor a risk hazard, and train staff. Under the trend of short-termisim in career and instant gratification, there are limits to how much passive personnel watching can achieve.

It is traditionally incumbent upon the industry watchers and regulators to monitor the operations and losses on a "watch list", then to sound alarm bells. Yet, this corporate warning is too late for many shareholders. The auditors are meant to perform a regular financial health-check, as is done before a merger or acquisition.

REPUTATIONAL RISK

What due diligence is meant to do is to protect you before you buy. *Caveat emptor!*

Unfortunately, the banks and funds have concentrated on white-collar executives cramming themselves into a large boardroom for a long discussion, possibly punctuated by lunch and drinks. Bankers, financiers, accountants, lawyers, technical specialists and backup staff all enter into the fray. This makes the due diligence a top-heavy, unwieldy and often ineffective process. This is because there are people of the like mindset who are often intent on take-over or merger.

CASE STUDY: ENRON

There can be few companies that suffered a reputation risk as disastrous as Enron. It continues to loom large in investors' mental risk radar whenever anyone mentions something akin to "restatement of earnings". Enron's golden assets proved irresistible to many. A more ambitious firm always comes along, bigger and brasher, richer and slicker than the previous fraud. The investor lemmings who rushed headlong into Enron's golden wonder shares lost out. The SEC is sometimes held to blame, but no exchange or regulator can discover and halt all frauds. This case continues to unwind with few professions coming out covered in glory.[2]

Sadly, empirical tests bear us out, that the normal corporate due diligence is done poorly in general. Dynegy CEO Chuck Watson confirmed that the planned $9.5 billion takeover of rival Enron would go ahead. It had "nothing but upside", he said.[3]

We can try to explain why M&A often proceed even when the due diligence points to a potential failure. Dynegy was within a whisker of taking over Enron despite banking analysts questioning whether Dynegy could have inspected the company in adequate detail within such a hurried due diligence.[4]

Ambiguous evidence and management stubbornness can override the due diligence findings, even in the face of corporate failure. Risk appetite overrides the limit for bearing risk – eventually they give up after the event failure. During 1999–2000, 11 556 US M&A cases of >51 % equity were announced. Only a tiny proportion, 383, did not complete as the project momentum carried most through.[5]

Most M&A failed to meet their targets. Management stubbornness or self-interests against shareholder benefit (a k a "agency theory") are attributable. One major perk could be a larger salary or bonus upon M&A; bigger workforce and more sales and revenue. Based on fulfilling

---

[2] "Enron and corporate law: all guilty", *Economist*, 30 January 2003; "Enron's trail of deception", BBC News, 13 February 2003.
[3] "Dynegy set to buy Enron for $9.5 bn" *CNN Money*, 9 November 2001.
[4] "Dynegy set to buy Enron for $9.5 bn" *CNN Money*, 9 November 2001.
[5] Thomson Financial Data, 2001.

Table 6.1   The five principal causes of failure in M&A activity

Reason for M&A failure	%
Incompatible cultures	57
Synergies non-existent or overestimated	54
Inability to implement change in new organisation	49
Clash of management styles/egos	42
Inability to manage target organisation	24

Source: *M&A Survey*, Towers-Perrin, August–September 2002.

sales and growth performance targets, the CEO's stock options start to kick in. Such remunerative packages are deceptive and only lead to executive greed, further putting the company at risk.[6]

The innate greed pattern, coupled with the short-term tenure of the CEO, lead executives to extract as much out of the company rapidly before a forced exit. CEOs have a temptation to get a percentage of an ever bigger pie – that pie becomes commensurately larger under M&A. A leader's overambition creates an overvalued company within M&A, whose chances of success are loaded against it. This subsequently leads to a boom–bust cycle in the share price. See Table 6.1.

The case around the directors' table may for be clear for M&A, but the damage and failure afterwards are visible for all.[7]

How can we improve on the due diligence process? Due diligence can work, but not for every firm. We can instigate a more flexible "slimmed down" due diligence. Due diligence can be cheap and quick, a rapid detective investigation, not an expensive boardroom affair.[8]

It can progress from simple elements such as:[9]

- Internet search on name e.g. local community website or Google.com.
- Check for name in library or newspapers.
- Check criminal record or court appearance in public office and legal documents.
- Asset liens and tax judgements.
- Real-estate holdings in property register.
- Trawl companies documents for record of directorship and holdings in other companies.
- Call in a private investigator.

Gathering together the findings, with the accounting experts' input, we can track the company's health or movements in a *risk map*.

Post-Andersen and Sarbanes–Oxley, there is some doubt that they will reveal the true corporate health in a timely and accurate fashion for interested investors. Both the US Sarbanes–Oxley Act and European legislative directives are designed to make CEOs and accountants more accountable when signing financial statements. These legal moves stand or fall on the crux of whether these key staff signed a financial statement knowing of any irregularities.

The auditing industry is still very concentrated in the Big Four, even after corporate audit and management consultancy are split. Apart from the lack of choice, there is also the spectre

---

[6] "Stock option accounting can be materially misleading", D. Crumbley and N. Apostolou, *Journal of Forensic Accounting*, vol.3, 2002.

[7] *Decision-making Perspectives on Due Diligence Failure*, Benjamin Powell, Culverhouse College and Phanish Puranam, London Business School, London 2002.

[8] *GARP Risk Review* (Global Association of Risk Professionals), Issue 08 September/October 2002.

[9] "Black tech forensics – collection and control of electronic evidence", G. Stevenson Smith, *Journal of Forensic Accounting*, vol.1, 2000.

of these four companies having the same type of operational procedure, more or less, from each other. Buying one company's auditing services instead of another does not necessarily represent a qualitative improvement, nor a substantial quantitative discount in the daily rate charged.

The current legal and accounting system militates against swift justice and compensation for those who have suffered loss.

> In 1998 there were nearly 2 million pending civil tort cases. The cost of the U.S. tort system for 1999 was over $200 billion.... The RAND Institute for Civil Justice studied transaction costs and determined that about 43 cents on the dollar goes to the plaintiff. The other 57 cents goes to transaction costs, which include attorney fees paid by the plaintiff.[10]

All professions are policed by their own institutions to some extent. This does not mean that billed rates are reduced. There are associations of bankers, insurers, lawyers, accountants etc. There is some recourse for complaint and reporting breach of contract or trust. The lawyers, for example, have the Law Society, while accountants have the Joint Disciplinary Tribunal. A client's complaint is not always satisfactorily resolved by any means, but it is usually an inexpensive way to whistle-blow on the professional. It is a cost-effective manner, but often not the end process, to start getting compensation. It would be better not to get ensnared in the first place, so you need an alert system.

AIRBORNE EARLY WARNING (AEW)

An advanced airborne early warning (AEW) system is the air force AWACS or E-3A Sentry aircraft.

Such a sentry in the finance industry would be an AEW warning, i.e. Andersen–Enron–Worldcom, a sensor to awaken us to potential danger. This AEW sentry could check for tell-tale warnings in the wake of a possible problem company, such as problem accounting statements. See Figure 6.1.

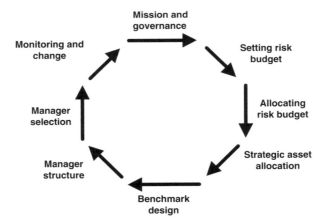

Figure 6.1   AEW Corporate Governance model
Source: *Risk Budgeting*, R.C. Urwin *et al.*, Institute of Actuaries, February 2001.

---

[10] *A Paradigm Shift to True Litigation Management*, Michael R. Boutot, International Risk Management Institute, www.IRMI.com, August 2002.

The Comptroller of the Currency already has an AEW or 'Canary' that carries a series of banking benchmarks that act as an alarm when target banks are deemed to be operating in too risky conditions. This warning provides some ability to prevent disaster, rather than to react too late.[11]

INTERNATIONAL ACCOUNTING STANDARDS (IAS)

International accounting standards (IAS) or the latest US GAAP (generally accepted accounting principles) accounting guidelines will reform the auditing world in the post-AEW investment climate. The revised accounting drafts are of major relevance to banks, funds, insurers and all types of corporation.

In particular, the latest IAS 39 and FAS 133 spell major revisions for reporting and valuation that enforce a stricter manner of stating corporate accounts.[12] These have particular significance for the statement of derivative valuations in the corporate accounts. This has a direct implication in the daily mark-to-market exercise where the company is exposed to fluctuating values of derivatives.[13]

Similarly, FRS17, the new accounting measure for funds requires them to state an actuarial valuation of funds' assets and liabilities that are regarded as a stricter and harsher view. All parties, investors, accountants and audited companies are arguing over the animal that is called "fair value". Like the blind man touching different parts of a camel, it is a difficult creature to pin down.

In fact, a previous financial disaster, the US Savings and Loans collapse, led to new CAMEL regulations to bolster the banking sector. Bank regulators examine subjects and judge them on a scale of 1 (best) to 5 (worst/likely to fail).[14] The criteria are:

- capital adequacy
- asset quality
- management quality
- earnings performance
- liquidity.

In all, the companies audited may well complain that the new accounting standards are too strict and draconian, while being costly to implement. Thus, for example, the IAS cousin in the USA, as defined by the FASB, has shown more leeway for the corporate heads than might have been allowed in Europe. US company stock options held by key staff are not normally treated as expenses and deducted from corporate profits account. The usual practice is excused by the reasoning that the valuation of the options is either too complicated or inaccurate, so firms tend to leave this entry as a footnote in the corporate accounting statements. The FASB has stated that it will review this practice. Meanwhile, the IASB has decided that the options should be treated as corporate expenses – a standard for EU auditors starting 2005.[15]

IAS standards serve to give us better foresight of corporate illness before it hits us. Some companies will invariably slip through the net, but we should (hopefully) stand a better chance of catching a cold rather than a debilitating sickness in the pre-AEW era. The new IAS are hoped

---

[11] Comptroller of the Currency, "Early Warning Analysis & Stress Testing: Tools to identify weak banks", May 2002.
[12] International Accounting Standards Board, www.IASB.org.uk; Financial and Accounting Standards Board, www.FASB.org.
[13] International Accounting Standards Board, www.IASB.org.
[14] *Modern Banking in Theory and Practice*, p. 233, Shelagh Heffernan, Wiley, 1996.
[15] "FASB to review accounting rules for stock options", *Financial Times*, 13 March 2003.

to be part of a stronger corporate AEW radar to detect errant performing or corrupt companies before they implode and cause further public damage. IAS and new FAS procedures can only be part of a risk management toolkit, not the whole answer. A wider corporate picture is needed.

CREDIT RATINGS

Credit ratings are just one of the benchmarks of banking and fund management industrial standards. They are a good attempt to protect against potentially wayward performance in the financial markets, but they represent only one technique. They provide a short single figure or code e.g. AA, B−. The research figures distilled into one succinct summary may be fine for a university, but it can be dangerous when looking deeply into market investments.

Risk management systems embody the knowledge or assumptions of industrial best-practice norms that have been built up over the years. Thus, the up-to-date credit rating of counter-party firms are essentially a reactive move to risk-monitor companies, quite possibly using data that might be up to 12 months old. Also, bank decision makers may take the individual ratings and amalgamate them, thus losing data accuracy or granularity. This introduces risk of its own. See Table 6.2.

There are real dangers about using credit ratings as a proxy for full-scale risk management, of which due diligence is just one tool. When the ratings are up to date and accurate, they work well in defining an extent of risk attached to a company or investment. If not, they can fail you.

Credit-rating agencies used in the risk management exercise can be late or irrelevant where the search is done post facto, i.e. the decision has essentially been made and all that is needed is a rubber stamp. The process of estimating the risk from past data reflects the subjectivity of credit ratings published. Where balance sheets and similar audit data are used, we are imposing two layers of subjectivity. This error is increased where the published information is out of date. Thus, you have distilled a mass of complex (and sometimes dubious data) into one single figure or grade. This sifting process can have inherent faults at play to provide a misleading result.

Table 6.2 Credit ratings and decision making

Bank scale	Probability of default (%) (PD)	Rating	Bank grading	
1	0.015	Aaa		Good – buy
2	....	Aa1		
3		Aa2	Investment grade	
4		Aa3		
5		A1		
6		A2		
7	0.085	A3		
8	....	Baa1	Borderline	Cross-check before buying
9		Baa2		
10		Baa3		
11	0.8	Ba1	Speculative grade	Avoid
12	1.2	Ba2		

Source: Standard and Poors, 2001.

The ratings procedure

The credit raters are not to blame as such; they only review the data and aspects of a company presented. It is a consensual process, in that the agencies do not barge in uninvited, nor do they pay surprise visits. The company visited pays for the inspection, or it may have been requested and funded by a party intending on buying a large stake or take-over.

If the firm wishes to hide or misrepresent the truth, then it is difficult for the rating agency to find out the accurate picture. The rating agency may be given a short time of a day or less to make an inspection of the company. More complex inspections can take a bit more time on site.

Follow visits may be done in one or two hours some time or years later. Such visits can be rather superficial inspections, depending upon the conditions, but time is tight and the extent of cover-up would be difficult to spot in many cases. So, deep information is unlikely to be revealed where intent of deception remains.

Nevertheless, many unbiased analyses are made by the credit raters where a "favourable assessment cannot be bought". Rating agencies disagree more often on banks and insurance companies. The strength of a balance sheet in a financial company can be difficult to assess, even after several on-site visits.

Where the subject field is broader, there is likely to be even more room for controversy and disagreement. Sovereign, market, interest rate or currency risk carry a lot of attention. The room for surprise is quite large. The rouble's dramatic devaluation in 1998 or the Argentinean peso in 2001 reflect how experts can get it wrong.

Yet, banks and financial institutions cannot blame the credit-ratings agencies. This former get-out clause is further closed where the banks themselves choose to gauge their own risk rating under the Basel II AMA (Advanced Measurement Approach) or IRB (Internal Ratings Base) system proposals. Yet, the blame for a bad investment decision cannot reasonably be laid at the door of the raters. *Caveat emptor* clearly states that caution had to be exercised by the buyer, and no ratings agency forced investors into Argentina or WorldCom.

Frankly, it is not the job of the rating agencies (Moodys, S&P, Fitch) to be the world corporate police officers. All they do is survey past data and monitor news releases or pay a short visit to the companies themselves. The ultimate decision on investing money after the assessment of fundamental enterprise risk rests with the owner of the capital of the person who is mandated to make the choices. The passing the buck:

"I only made the decision because the credit-raters told me it was a good company", is an insufficient excuse. To say anything less would be cowardice, and chicken capitalism thrives.[16]

Business investment decisions must be made by the investor, resting upon a straightforward train of processes:

1. Formulate business plan.
2. Marry risk appetite to risk offer.
3. Manage reputational risk/due diligence.
4. Risk support/risk monitoring.

Not only is risk appetite directly linked to risk offer, but risk appetite is also covered by regulatory capital. Risk support means that the danger of capital becoming inadequate to cover expected losses automatically signals an alert to the bank. What we have created is a web-based system for warning of banking danger areas.[17]

---

[16] *Cowardly Capitalism*, Bel-Ami, Wiley, 2002.
[17] MB Risk Management, www.MBRM.com, December 2002.

Table 6.3   Basel II standard-certified risk-taking bank

Business line level 1	Business line level 2	Beta risk factor	Regulatory capital subtotal	Expected annual loss	Actual loss this year	Action
Corporate finance	Muni./Gov. finance	18 %	$17 600 000	$16 000 000	$12 213 710	
Investment banking	Asset management	12 %	$15 400 000	$14 000 000	$12 213 710	
Trading & sales	Market making	18 %	$13 200 000	$12 000 000	$12 213 710	ALERT!

Table 6.4   Basel II advanced-certified risk-taking bank

Business line level 1	Business line level 2	Gamma risk factor	Regulatory capital subtotal	Expected annual loss	Actual loss this year	Action
Corporate finance	Muni./Gov. finance	Gamma 1	$9 250 000	$11 000 000	$8 256 000	
Investment banking	Advisory services	Gamma 2	$8 750 000	$10 000 000	$7 750 090	
Trading and sales	Market making	Gamma 3	$8 500 000	$9 000 000	$8 806 012	CAUTION!

The spectre for shouldering risk increases under the latest Basel II standards where "higher rated" banking and financial institutions choose to rate their own risk under AMA (Advanced Measurement Approach) or IRB (Internal Ratings Base). This essentially means that the banks will develop their own ratings systems (geared towards showing that they are lower risk banks) and justify their models to the regulators. Naturally, it would be in the banks' best interests to portray themselves as lower risk to the regulators and the credit-ratings agencies. It is going to be very interesting what sort of assumptions and theories underpin their models.

Example, the Basel II system could end up looking a bit like Tables 6.3 and 6.4 for a bank.

Business lines

A bank or fund is usually the sum total of several business lines. Each of these business lines has an associated risk to its assets that Basel II wishes to label Beta or Gamma. The total risk exposure can be summed as the total of the risk-weighted assets. Thus, best practice in one department does not mean it translates into a bank's best practice.

We have defined the risk appetite to risk offer relationship in another line of our Loss Database that evolves into a Basel II compliant system. A standard-certified risk-taking bank will have higher regulatory capital assigned because its risk management processes and system are adequate, but not extremely sophisticated. An advanced-certified risk-taking bank will have lower regulatory capital allocated because its risk management is highly developed and is evaluated as a lower overall risk. The risk of losses increases, and this should be reflected in the Beta or Gamma risk weight.

The long-term investors can almost be in danger of extinction under the rush of the incoming speculators. More traditional wealth-creation business lines involving "hard" assets and less turnover or "churn" attract lower comparative costs and risk.

Moreover, under the advances of the Internet and online dealing, we have the increased presence of naive traders in the jungle. For such a public, there are a score of animals that can seek to prey upon such victims; smart operators, banks and brokers can play the role of scavengers. These people may be naive gamblers, even more tempted by margin trading and buying highly leveraged derivatives contracts, even with borrowed money. Thus, there is little in the way of risk management to protect us – a fool and his money are easily parted.

There are other methods in risk management for the investors from the traditional ones offered, they are:

- risk avoidance
- risk retention
- risk reduction (e.g. diversification)
- risk hedging
- transfer of risk.

Maybe fund managers and bank professionals have too much information at times. It is a mess and too much to process efficiently. Everyone is perennially too busy. They do not have enough useful data to make the best investment decisions. Risk management is partly the presentation of useful and readable information, then the translation into action and concrete risk countermeasures. So, in the absence of a clear solution, they take Occam's Razor for a business decision. Stated very simply, if there are two or more choices, then the simpler and better option is likely to be one that offers the least line of resistance. Thus, when confused, call in the experts and dump the problem (or risk) on them.

LAW AND RISK MANAGEMENT

The risk manifests usually itself when the (creditor) party tries to reclaim what he feels is rightfully his due. This includes documentation risk and the formation of incomplete or unenforceable contracts.

Lawyers are one of the first row of experts to manage risk. Companies demand and expect a 'water-tight' contract to cover eventualities, usually of non-payment or underperformance. Legal management of risk was considered an isolated fiefdom of the solicitors, barristers and judges. Similarly, accountancy was a completely separate profession. Investment banking was the same. This is an unrealistic risk management system, which needs to be holistic if we are to have an effective protective system. Otherwise there are loopholes and gaps in contracts.

CASE STUDY: THE UK FOOTBALL LEAGUE

A more recent example was the 2002 inability of creditors (the UK Football League) to win compensation for ITV Digital going bust when it had already bought the football television rights from the League. Essentially, for simplicity's sake, the loop-hole was that when ITV Digital went into liquidation, the companies that owned the majority of it were not liable for damages.

> This is a bone that sticks in the craw of many shareholders or victims of corporate damage or underperformance. A limited-liability company can wind itself up and the directors walk away. Shareholders and other plaintiffs (e.g. victims of railway accidents) can end up with nothing. This situation has to change (see: Corporate Misgovernance). The ITV Digital contract with the UK Football League cost the League £180 million. Many experts believe the British football is seriously threatened by the perilous state of its finances.[18]
>
> The League had a contract, but could not enforce it. This will often be the case if a contractual party (a limited liability company) goes bust. Thus, incomplete or unenforceable contracts mean risk and vulnerability to loss.
>
> In other words, joined-up-thinking that marries the needs of businesses to the operating logic of the legal profession would help our quest for rapid and cost-effective legal cover.

What the law covers

There are a few fundamental goals to consider when dealing with legal risk (sometimes called basis risk) management:

- cost
- time
- probability of winning lawsuit
- effectiveness
- completeness of contract
- enforceability
- redress, e.g. ability of party to pay damages.

Completeness of contract

This is a potential problem because of the complexity of the legal system – even more so when we deal with separate state jurisdictions within the USA, or with national and EU levels of laws.

Redress: we can question the ability of the guilty party to pay damages once a favourable decision has been granted.

The question must be asked regarding "enforceability". We live in a global economy, so can effective legal measures can be brought against parties that operate offshore? Our view of the jurisdiction, especially over offshore cases and the wide usage of the Internet, leads us to offer more questions initially, rather than answers.

What about those who conduct fraud in the USA and Europe on the Internet while based in China or Russia? Our experience in Russia, China and southeast Asia leads us to believe that the laws on paper look very good, but the real effectiveness of enforceability is lacking. Nothing can be done to punish these people who cannot be extradited.

We include the recovery rate within the Loss Database because it will be the basis for projecting the probability of getting compensation or insurance. This means that we have further transactional data when we are faced with making a similar investment again in the future. Recovery rates are sector-specific, lower for telecoms. Thus, the dot-coms had many

---

[18] BBC Sport Online investigation, www.bbc.co.uk, 22 October 2002.

"99 %" members, i.e. those whose equity value listed on the exchanges fell by 99 % from their peak. What is the recovery rate for your investment that you envisage?

The regulatory risks, risks of change in company law and the risk of lawsuits from clients, employees and every other stakeholder are further hazards. The list of financially unclassifiable risks, means that any perceived "legal risk management" is generally assigned to the legal department. These are the "residual" risks that companies consider fit to be handled by their legal department. This need not be the best way to organise legal risk management, but it is a return to the separate silos concept of viewing risk.

The "not my problem" syndrome does not work because the judge can rule that "whistle-blowing" is the duty of a responsible director or company manager.[19]

It is no longer just the duty of the police to investigate. When lawyers, actuaries and accountants become aware of major trangression during their duties, it is sufficiently arguable that they are in breach of civic and company law if they do not inform the proper authorities. Thus, losses suffered, e.g. as result of incorrect accounts or money-laundering, must be reported.

Similarly, the silo risk view is potentially erroneous because it tries to pass the buck. Thus, professional indemnity insurance cannot always be relied upon to save your bacon. Grounds of negligence can override the quest for damages, so all you are left with is nothing.[20]

However, plaintiffs can sue and still win considerable damages. Risk assessment over likely award and chances of loss now become a priority before a case is initiated. This will be more commonplace in the area of executive underperformance. Stakeholders can hit back, and win, through the legal system.

CASE STUDY: MERRILL LYNCH VERSUS UNILEVER PENSION FUND

Britain's sleepy pension fund trustees woke up to the scenario that they could sue their fund manager – and win. Tradition-bound fund trustees were more inclined to fire the fund manager and leave it at that. Furthermore, they could allege grounds of underperformance against a chosen benchmark, instead of being fobbed off by the typical market risk reasons. Thus, the fund manager claimed that it was running the fund on an adequate risk-managed basis, using the Barra model.[21] This is what the pension-fund trustees of Unilever found when it sued its fund managers, Mercury Asset Management (now owned by Merrill Lynch). They won damages of about £80 million for negligence.[22]

One of the interesting points of this open-fund trustee versus fund manager conflict is the choice of battlefield. The fund trustees could have picked professional negligence based on a reckless investment stance, one that was not properly risk managed. In fact, they chose the comparison of underperformance against an agreed benchmark. Mercury had undershot the UK equities benchmark by a concrete 10 %, and that was not in dispute. A guideline for fund trustees and holders of the investment mandate is to set out fixed benchmarks for agreement. A potential legal wrangle over whether a fund manager was, or was not, risk managed would probably not prove a fruitful ground to wage war.

---

[19] *RBG Resources Plc* v. *Rastogi & ORS*, Westlaw.Co.UK, 9 January 2002.
[20] *Alexander Forbes Europe Ltd* v. *SBJ Ltd*, Westlaw.co.uk, 9 January 2002.
[21] "In the dock", *The Economist*, 20 October 2001.
[22] "So sue 'em", *The Economist*, 5 October 2000, and "Merrill settlement: a boost for index funds", www.Forbes.com. 12 June 2001.

The final Combined Code is in the listing rules of the London Stock Exchange and is mandatory for all listed companies in the UK. It requires the boards to maintain a sound system of internal control to safeguard shareholders' investment and the company's assets. Directors should check the effectiveness of the company's internal control and review all controls, including financial, operational and compliance controls and risk management.

Further developments with regard to Combined Code for corporate governance in the UK reinforced processes for identifying, evaluating and managing key business risks. They aim to protect the corporate wealth through sound leadership.

One alternative to speed up the legal process and cut counsel costs is to choose arbitration. This body can be stipulated in the initial contract. Sometimes it can work out to be swifter and cost-effective.[23] Yet even arbitration can cost more to instigate than conventional litigation routes, given the lack of choice stated over arbitration bodies.[24]

Given the dissatisfaction over level of service and professional costs, there is a growing trend for people to manage risk themselves. Once again, in an organic business world, we are in danger over losing the corporate command-control battle.

Sarbanes–Oxley Act for audit control

The ideas that back up the Sarbanes–Oxley Act in auditing can be transferred into the banks and investment houses, especially when it comes to launching "hot" IPOs and bond issues. The legal framework for auditing work has now changed in the US post-Enron. "Simply stated, the current status quo for corporate governance is unacceptable and must change."[25]

The Sarbanes–Oxley Act was passed into law in August 2002. It laid out firm rules:

- CEO and CFO to certify company financial statements. It became a criminal offence to make such a certification falsely knowing (and "knowing" is the key word) that the report was intentionally misleading within the definition of the Act.
- Enforced rotation of audit partners where the audit partners (the specific persons) have performed full audit services in each of the five previous fiscal years of service.
- Prohibition of non-audit services where the accounting firm already performs audit of the client.
- Document destruction or alteration now attracts new criminal penalties where the intention is to impede any US government investigation.

Already auditors are being faced with a mandatory change every five years so that they do not get too cosy with the customer as in Enron. The effectiveness of any legislation is governed by roughly the same factors as a successful project. It needs:

1. Scope.
2. Risk monitoring.
3. Enforcement.
4. Performance (i.e. punishment or financial redress).

Sarbanes–Oxley can prove itself particularly potent particularly in the last two factors. An investor can look to Sarbanes–Oxley for some sympathy and support, but will have to search elsewhere for anything close to complete investment protection.

---

[23] *Risk Management in Russia and the Baltic states*, Y.Y. Chong, Financial Times Publications, 1998.

[24] "Cost of arbitration: executive summary", *Public Citizen*, Washington, DC 1 May 2002.

[25] "Strengthening compliance through effective corporate governance", S.S. Bies, Annual Regulatory Compliance Conference, Washington DC, 11 June 2003.

Insurance

Insurance is looking at the other side, assuming that there is a significant chance that external risk events will strike or that the corporate leadership will be anything but sound. There are residual risks that are difficult to calculate, or know about for sure if they never happened to you. These are particularly true in operational risk. Part of this ignorance or uncertainty is because companies have not created, or cannot gain access to, the relevant knowledge base (see: Basel II and Loss Database).

The investment risk of fixed capital assets can be insured on the institutional market, such as houses or industrial plant equipment. There are risks of specific catastrophic events to insure against, e.g. fire, flood or storms.

Marsh McClellan insurance company sees systemic risk as that which affects the whole enterprise. It takes the definition:

> Enterprise risk management: the process of systematically and comprehensively identifying critical risks, quantifying their impacts, and implementing integrated risk management strategies to maximize enterprise value.

This is investment risk management in the banking sense.

Insurance has a choice of risk strategies (sometimes more than banking):

- Accept it, finance the risk burden.
- Transfer it, e.g. insurance.
- Mitigation, damage-limitation exercises.
- Leave business completely (bankruptcy).

Insurers and bankers come from different parts of the risk spectrum. Different types of risk expertise are found on both sides of the insurance–banking border. Banks handled risk pooling, for credit risk, as well as risk financing. Banks' access to capital markets gave them better access to capital than insurers. Banks took credit risk in lending operations as their normal bread-and-butter, and worked under market risk as an intermediary, e.g. a broker.

Insurers worked in direct acceptance and management of risk. They engaged in risk pooling – taking unrelated risks so that the average losses are regular. Otherwise, they could choose risk absorption where they could afford to take the risks because of stronger financial backing, or risk financing to maintain liquidity to pay for the risk events. Insurers have the structural tools to provide risk management support:[26]

- captives
- risk funding
- risk transfer
- risk financing.

Insurance business was traditionally about transferring risk. It created value in pooling risk, therefore lowering upper-band risk limits to any single party. It could also pool different types of risks under diversification to obtain heterogeneity of the risk portfolio, thus lowering risk impact of any one single risk. It would transfer risks to the people who have deeper knowledge about these specific risks and/or who could afford to insure them. The captives act as specialist intermediaries between banks that are worried by operational risk and want insurance cover for it, and the international reinsurance and retrocession market.

---

[26] *Insurance in the Management of Financial Institutions*, T. Leddy, Swiss Re, London, 12 June 2003.

Insurers can advise about management of certain risks, and financial markets being used to transfer risks. The justification for insurance is, thus, the right specialist information with adequate financial backing. Note the Lloyds' Names scandal, which dealt in specialised risk and reinsured it within the same group of companies. The wrong information and skills, with localisation of risk burden, cropped up again in the Investment Fund "Splits" fiasco.

Specialist knowledge over what the insurance policy does not cover, how much it costs, alternative forms of protection are basic business starting points. Sometimes, this start line is ignored for businesses that think they are covered. At the most basic level, the evaluated expectation of risk should be more than the insurance premium paid, i.e.

$$\text{Risk expectation} = \text{Sum of all (risk event} \times \text{damage)}$$
$$\text{Risk damage expectation} > \text{insurance premium paid}$$

This test will generally give a negative result, where the premiums plus the costs of transfer are greater than the damage. Therefore, the insurance company profits. Such a calculation would give a satisfactory result only if the client had an asymmetry of information and knew better than the insurance company his *a priori* probability of suffering damage. The 1980s' Lloyds' errors in home appliance insurance came about because the insurance companies miscalculated that there was a lower risk of electric gadgets going wrong. The resultant malfunctions and claims cost Lloyds' insurers more than average losses.

With the increasing use of derivatives and the impending deadlines of Basel II, we should see more variety in the types of insurance policies to cover foreseeable loss events. Insurance provides a safety net for sustaining losses where the costs in a single period would be too punitive. If the risk is deemed too large to handle singly by the company and collectively by shareholders, the risk must be transferred out and dispersed among a wider pool.

Insurance is the latest but one line of defence against risk, after capital reserves and before benefiting from bankruptcy law. It does not protect against risk but just smoothens the risk over time, transforming risks into costs. Pooling by transferring to institutions with more capital; or transferring to those who know the risk better.

Insurance results in a transfer of insurable risk into a tail credit risk and a host of legal risks. For these reasons of legal friction and contractual costs, insurance ends up a very incomplete market. A lot of risks are not covered at any price other than at excessive levels because of the paucity of up-to-date market information and the risk-aversion of many companies. If financial markets were as incomplete as insurance, a considerable number of arbitrages between market segments would not be possible, and trading would be minimal.

The effects of large impact disasters, certainly after the emergence of terrorist waves post 9/11, and the collapse of stock-market prices are causes for concern. The major worries for the insurance industry are that they:

- will not be able to pay the insurance liabilities of clients' claims
- will reduce their cover by expanding exclusion clauses, so that clients will find self-insurance protection more attractive
- will cut costs so that operational efficiency in the insurance companies diminishes, so that client satisfaction falls and business leaves.

This means that there will be more regulations from Basel II as the insurance business overlaps with that of pure banking. The insurance industry needs to be innovative.

When we are unsure of a specific type of risk, e.g. with complex damage or liability risk, a convenient get-out is to pass it to the insurer. You can protect yourself better against investment or corporate failure – for a premium. Thus, a popular policy was the D&O insurance – the Director and Officer cover. A company could cover the performance of its key staff, as well as protect against shareholder lawsuits through purchasing this policy. Unfortunately, with the rise in company scandals and accounts restatements post-AEW, this D&O cover has become more expensive. So, General Electric found its D&O policy quadrupling within one year.[27]

Market players should familiarise themselves with the idea that buying insurance not solve all their risk problems. Furthermore, investors and company chiefs should acquaint themselves with the basic techniques of risk maps and loss databases to provide advance warning of potential corporate damage. Funnily enough, the insurers are the ones who are most likely to have understood the benefits of a loss database and created one, years before the banks and managed funds.

Do the groundwork – you need to be:

- Assessing areas of risk weakness or corporate vulnerability.
- Assessing cost-benefits of buying in risk management expertise or cover.
- Assessing areas of non-coverage for corporate cover.

Read the small-print beforehand in great detail, there are obvious advantages to be gained.

Corporations and individuals have become used to retaining risk that would have been insured. Insurers trap the cost of losses over time, charging their expenses for the risk burden. Insurance provides a safety-net for sustaining losses where the costs in a single period would be too punitive. The normal view was that a corporation takes a diversified portfolio of investments plus their associated risks. The increasingly common perspective will be to view enterprise risk management (ERM) status of the client.[28]

This means that clients will be assessed upon the value and quality of their portfolio, plus to what degree they have the tools, techniques and business processes to manage risk. This is analogous to the Basel II view of operational risk. The insurer would work progressively with the client to develop strategies, implement them tactically and monitor business performance. A hands-off "just post us the premium cheque" will be less commonplace. More detailed inspection will take place before policies are signed.

If the risk is deemed too large to handle singly, the risk is farmed out or dispersed. The directors and shareholders will tend to shun investments where the insurance premiums eat too much of the associated profits. The idea of ceasing to buy insurance is not new, the investor can take on the total potential loss.

Risk retention: self-insurance

This is an alternative where a large corporation such as IBM, Exxon, BMW can retain a large risk because of the size and strength of its balance sheets. Another choice would allow companies to forget insurance and incorporate other hedging instruments themselves. The rationale is that the total savings on insurance premiums for the company are more than the

---

[27] "GE hit by huge rise in D&O cover", *Financial Times*, 12 March 2003.
[28] "Enterprise risk management in the financial services industry: from concept to management process", www.IRMI.com, November 2000.

substitute hedging costs of the portfolio. The hedging instruments would match or exceed the total insured losses for an adequate substitution. Banks may adopt self-insurance (SIR) retained part for only a portion or threshold level of the potential operational risk hazard. The rest that they feel unable to handle would be covered by the captives.

Yet, the matter can be different where the big losses surround the downside risk.

CASE STUDY: INSURING BIG OIL PROJECTS

The engineers build and fund the pipelines and refineries, the in-house lawyers draft the contracts and revenue-sharing agreements (PSAs). There are chiefly the sovereign or political risk factors to deal with, and the danger of collaborating with partners who are not entirely trustworthy. This alone takes a wealth of data and investigation to ascertain whether there is a suitable base for profitable PSA operations.[29] There are day-to-day operational risk management physical features to maintain security of operation – guards, perimeter fences, CCTV, smoke detectors, anti-blast rooms etc. There are three obstacles for them:

1. There are unclear areas for residual risks that are difficult to calculate. These can be the chance of lightning striking the plant, to unforeseen human error mixing chemicals. The uncertainty is a big weight on the mind and the wallet. Because oil companies focus on exploring and production, less attention is spent compiling statistics on the areas and operations where they have experienced damage. This is where the insurer's loss database comes into play.
2. Oil firms have less experience implementing risk management contracts and derivative instrument strategies. Their key expertise is production, and financial matters and hedging is not their chosen field.
3. The smaller companies will have limited funds to cover some of the enormous damage that their operations could produce. A blow-out can be lethal and the liability very expensive. Certainly, the smaller companies including the "minors" cannot keep a contingency fund to pay out damages.

For these three reasons alone, oil companies find it more convenient to farm out the risk to insurers.

The view of long-term value theorists is that such sudden losses or short-term volatility offer too much potential for damage to the portfolio. Once the company's long-term earnings are discounted for short-term losses, the calculus still comes out in credit territory. But, such huge drops in stock prices in 2000–2 remain highly worrying to fund managers. The comparison and substitution of increasing insurance premiums after September 11th 2001 against other forms of loss cover will still continue.

The usual insurance practice is pooling, transferring to institutions with more capital, or transferring to those who know the risk better. We have seen that a loss database, plus the associated actuarial skills, puts the insurers way ahead of the banks when it comes to analysing risk. Backed up with easy access to large sums of capital for insuring potentially huge disasters, these loss risk managers could be on to a winning business.

There can be no bigger or more well-known capital or knowledge base for risk transfer than Lloyds, London. The capital for covering losses and claims is derived from a large reserve base built up over a long time, as in the three centuries of the company.

---

[29] E.g. *Managing Project Risk*, Y.Y. Chong, Financial Times Management-Prentice Hall, 2000.

CASE STUDY: THE NAMES AND LLOYDS, LONDON

Corporations and individuals (known as "Names") in the insurance syndicates were happy to take on specific risks in exchange for a premium for the client. As long as the claims for damages paid to the clients remained less than the total premiums, the Names raked in the profits and insurance companies were on a roll.

The fiasco of collaborating with Lloyds as a private investor (or Name) bearing unlimited liability is a prime example of risk seeking. The risks were diversified to other insurers in the same area – a contradiction. This incestuous relationship succeeded in concentrating, not diversifying the risk. The Names disaster is one of the worst to hit Lloyds, both financially and by reputation. The need to mitigate risk is paramount, and to distinguish between reputed risk management and real performance.

A few incidents spilt the cosy apple cart. A few disasters, such as Exxon Valdez and Hurricane Andrew really piled pressure upon the insurance industry. Then the huge claims from victims of asbestos poisoning almost brought the insurance sector to its knees. The ramifications from the US September 11th 2001 attacks continue to exert real pressure upon the insurance market reserves. Lloyds is due to face a $2.7 billion net loss from claims following the attacks.[30]

The ramifications of September 11th for reinsurance are that people will buy and pay more insurance premiums. The insurers will buy more reinsurance, but both insurers and reinsurers will restrict their risk offer and coverage. Supply shrunk, demand rose – insurance prices have already risen substantially.

What is needed is an industrial shift from pure insurance to risk protection services. Outsourcing tail event risks is a good business practice, but a better procedure is to work in partnership with risk experts to manage these risks. Business continuity planning is the typical part of active risk management, rather than simplistic outsourcing. Mitigating risks by pooling within the same insurance group is called "spray and pray".

The risks are that:

1. The insurance companies will not have enough capital reserves to pay the insurance liabilities of their clients' claims. See Figure 6.2.
2. The insurance companies will expand their policy small-print so that their clients find that certain conditions nullify, or reduce, their insurance coverage.
3. Operational weaknesses within the structure of the insurance companies continue so that client satisfaction diminishes.

The insurance industry should learn and expand skills. Instead of designating risks bought or eliminated from policies as being "uninsurable", we should train ourselves to be active risk managers beforehand. The unintended result so far is a host of uncovered risks; risks that could be avoided are pooled. This produces a lack of risk awareness and risk mismanagement. We must move forward.

Sharing, transferring or mitigating risk

Basel II allows insurers to adopt a more active investment style, and to compete with banks, or to assist in financing them through risk hedging enterprises. Basel II allows insurers to take a wider role in finance and operational risk management for banks.

---

[30] www.FT.com, 20 December 2001.

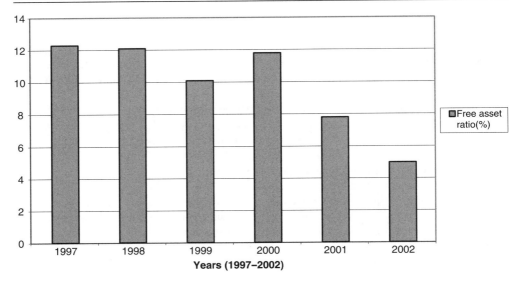

Figure 6.2 Free asset ratio for UK life-insurers

- They can undertake risk funding for banks which gives a finite medium-term (a few years) and monetary cover for resultant losses. This gives loss provisioning for expected and designated unlikely operational risk events.
- Insurers can carry on with risk transfer, a traditional role. When large-impact risk events occur, a bank's P&L has the advantage of loss transfer to the insurer.
- Or, insurers can select a risk-financing strategy with the bank, a new role. The insurer becomes more of a co-investor with the bank rather than an external risk transfer party. If a large-impact risk event results, a bank's P&L has not the protection of loss transfer, although there are benefits for the bank's balance sheet from having an insurer as a partner to share the loss.

Whatever option is selected, there are a number of risk factors or issues that need to be addressed for project success:[31]

- Credit risk of both parties.
- Basis (legal) risk.
- Settlement timing of the compensation pay-outs.
- Moral hazard of the contract parties – especially careless or corrupt behaviour that contributes to bringing on the loss incident.

So what are the options for the insurance companies?

The trend towards lowering or avoiding insurance premiums through risk retention or self-insurance is troubling the insurance industry. Nowadays, insurers experience financial pressure to support a relatively high fixed-cost base in the face of declining premiums.

Insurers' efforts to cope with this loss of business have encouraged the alternative risk market. The trend is for offering the pricing of risk management products that enable insurers

---

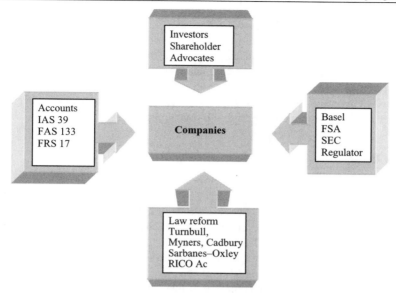

Figure 6.3 Legal and accounting reform pressures upon the companies

to behave more like corporate financiers or banks. This way, they avoid overcompetition among themselves for a declining pool of conventional insurance premiums.

All assets of value can be covered by an insurance policy in theory. Thus, although it is possible and common for assets to be covered and traded, we are now coming to an age where we have to question whether the insurance companies have the funds to cover claims.

Lawyers, insurance and technical specialists will add their risk management expertise to kill or expedite the final deal. There seems to be little significant reworking of the chain of events and parties within investment projects. Sometimes, more risks come when adding parties to investment ventures – this can provide management problems.

One of the factors that we propose is a greater sense of realism within valuation risk, that means a customer casting a wary eye upon billing. The old days of "gold-plating" investment projects or buying in the best brains based on mere reputation may be meeting their end. The Combined Code and Myners Reports within the UK have signalled a drive towards getting real value for money. They are already being implemented.

Another factor is that Basel II banking regulations promote greater market transparency over disclosure of losses, and that means getting past perceived reputations and corporate excuses. We propose a greater sense of realism within reputation and valuation risk. The good news is that moves for enforcing corporate governance and increasing shareholder value are gaining momentum. See Figure 6.3.

As we saw from real life, reputation risk management is not real risk management for the industry – it is totem worship. The use of a "top" auditor, or employing the services of a bank split by Chinese walls from its other operations, becomes fully realised as courting disaster. An AEW risk radar helps us see farther. There is a Russian saying that advises: "When you ignore history, you are blind in one eye. When you ignore the future, you are blind in the other."

After looking at the recent business disasters, we look ahead with both eyes towards a brighter investment future under real risk management.

SEARCH FOR RISK MANAGEMENT

We have seen that orthodox methods of handling risk offer us business advantages. But there are limits to which traditional financial techniques are stymied by the entrenched self-interest of various stakeholder groups. "Organic risk management" explicitly recognises fundamental obstacles presented by self-interests, and identifies potential areas for conflict, underperformance or loss. This more realistic market view or risk map forms the basis of an integrated business methodology for concrete progress in managing risk.[32]

Alternative theories

People are always trying to push out the envelope of financial modelling. What other modelling tools offer us a potentially successful outcome? Some people are tempted by a tentative use of stochastics, where parameters bearing shocks can be modelled. Physics and quantum mechanics have truly lent us a new breed of rocket-scientists and chaos theory deserves a mention.

Research in thermodynamics and entropy have also played some part, where the number-guru "quants" have entered the dealing-room. Yet, further proof is needed to prove that these are suitable and robust tools for financial markets.

A further shock for financial markets is that there may well be something called innate trading gift, or luck, that piles of money and mathematical models cannot define.

Causality and managing investment risk

Making a good level of profits is fine; understanding why you made them is even better. Unlocking this secret, as with Leeson or Rusnak, is something you have to find out even if you get a nasty surprise. Establishing lines of causality is a more rigorous process than attributing success to mere luck. As we have seen from empirical study, few managers really win profits consistently; those in the "best in class" category are eagerly recruited. Most managers are actually birds of the same feather, but with different results. They nest in the satellite "best in class – subject to slippage" category, and are sought after by companies willing to pay large incomes to attract them. Then, they find out later what performance slippage means.[33]

More complex sets of factors enter the risk equation, some of them political and these were identified in our earlier stakeholder analysis. The mechanical processes of investment risk management can be derailed completely under simple linear causality when things go wrong under a complex, political world.

Common strands seem to exist for certain disasters we have examined:

- Continuous risk hazard.
- Lack of effective managerial action.
- Large political dimension to problem.
- Wish to avoid reputation risk.
- Ignored warnings until too late.
- Devastating disaster.
- Atrocious PR after the risk event.

---

[32] *Operational Risk Capital Allocation and Integration of Risks*, E. Medova, Judge Institute, October 2001.
[33] *The Concept of Investment Efficiency*, T.M. Hodgson *et al.*, Institute of Actuaries, 28 February 2001.

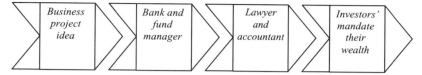

Figure 6.4   Value-added chain

The finance industry had a similar business process where risk management reports were shelved and forecasts ignored. The Leeson, LTCM, Rusnak etc. disasters were (ironically) the best thing to happen to the industry. These were the "Gestalt" shocks that prodded the industry into ever-increasing effort in risk management. The accounting IAS 39, FAS 133 and the Basel II regulations are renewed efforts to ensure that good banking lessons are not forgotten.

The most valuable part of the risk management cycle is a brain-storming session or presentation with the top executive committee. Here the risk managers can present their analysis of business risk and debate options to handle it. It must not be just a paper exercise, it must be the best sales exercise to win whole-hearted support and budget of the directors.

More importantly, we can encourage top executives to get through just talking about managing risk, and get them involved in actually *doing* risk management. Thinking about risk is fine, what is better is taking measures to deal with risks and reporting any residual risks to top management.

This goes beyond the features of operational risk, expanding upon certain facets to bring us closer in line with how an organic corporation really works. Successful risk management is predicated upon the adept chaining of related processes to create value-added.

Value-added chain

As we noted, the word "fiduciary" is derived from Latin meaning "to trust". Given the modern economy's division of labour and the innate "luck" of some people at the investment game, we do have to trust the experts somewhere. Or do we?

Then we have to examine value-chain risk or fiduciary risk. Each link offers potential value by bringing in its special skill or connection. But there is always the weakest link. Furthermore, we should think of asking questions, or monitoring the performance from each business link (see Figure 6.4) in the chain.[34]

- Can we trust them with the control of our money at all?
- What value do they add to our portfolio?
- What is the measure of their added-value for us?
- What we can do to try to ensure that they do not lose some, or all of it?
- What measures of recourse can we employ to obtain redress or compensation?

The emphasis upon the business interaction of people, and their innate skills and capabilities, is germane to our thesis of organic risk. Technology is only the secondary factor in determining a company's wealth management. There is a multitude of dealing and risk management systems

---

[34] *Competitive Advantage*, Michael Porter, Free Press, 1985.

on the market; many are sold, few are truly successful in managing the risks specified (see Chapter 7: Systems to manage risk).

> Neither *money nor technology* will solve fundamental business design flaws. Risk management is an activity that is labour-intensive.[35]

Mathematical modelling or the use of modern computing technology is often a side-show to the central theme of analysing businesses as organisms that are in the process of growing (or dying). People's skills determine whether the business develops or dies. Furthermore, this organic risk becomes integrated with the other conventional aspects of risk that the Basel Committee neatly split into credit risk, market risk and operational risk.

The new Basel II regulations have already proposed some of the foundations for organic risk management elements to deal with operational risk. Basel II does make an attempt to integrate market and credit risk.[36] We can go further and develop other organic risk management techniques, which have a wider industrial application than Basel II.

RISK MANAGEMENT TO PICK UP THE PIECES

There are additional techniques to deal with the risk spectre.

Scenario analysis

Scenario analysis lets us think wider to encapsulate more dramatic risk events. These include the Exxon Valdez and Hurricane Andrew extreme risk events that drove many companies to the brink of bankruptcy. There cannot have been a more damaging and unthinkable recent disaster than September 11th.

CASE STUDY: BUSINESS CONTINUITY, LESSONS FROM SEPTEMBER 11TH

This sad episode was a tragic extreme risk event, and we must use it as an opportunity to learn. The knock-on effects are yet to be definitely measured, let alone reliably observed. The economic downturn effects caused by the attacks are reckoned at 1.8 million jobs lost in the USA, of which about 250 000 were in the travel sector. The full extent of human misery has not been computed. The consequences on risk management have been tremendous.

Business processes under organic risk management must recover their original shape as easily as possible, in the same way a wound gets healed. The lessons learned included that communications are vital in the case of disaster. It is essential to have an up-to-date list of employees together with the means to reach them.

Dependency on key personnel is one of these few operational risks that are better mitigated than prevented. One way is to adopt insurance key-man cover. Another way is to assign top back-up staff, and to maintain an up-to-date staff roster with 24-hour contact details. These are potentially intrusive and expensive procedures and may have been unthinkable before the September 11th calamity.

The natural wish to cut corners, allowing slack procedures and lowering costs, work against disaster recovery. Full disaster-recovery backup is a high-cost exercise which is

---

[35] "Bringing risk management up to date in an e-commerce world", Y.Y. Chong, *Balance Sheet*, vol.8, 2000.
[36] *Operational Risk Capital Allocation and Integration of Risks*, E. Medova, Judge Institute, October 2001.

rarely used by definition. Cost-benefit analysis or RAROC alone would tempt a company to axe disaster-recovery and business continuity measures in order to cut costs.

These safety measures will not be properly maintained as long as the tools and processes for disaster recovery are de-prioritised as non-critical business processes. An example is a recovery site being used as well as extra capacity. The downside risk is that, in case of disaster, the first task is to make ready the recovery site.

The limits of thinking and use of business imagination are widened under scenario analysis, consistent with a set of given possible future events for brainstorming.

Scenario testing has been applied in preference to other modelling techniques in some cases because it is easier to comprehend. For example, the pension funds around the world have used simple what-if scenarios at times to determine the money left to cover the payment of pensions.

Let us say that scenarios of 4 %, 6 %, 8 % and 10 % rates of return were taken up by some banks. These were somewhat conservative given the double-digit real returns on the stock markets in the 1990s. Yet, as we have seen, investor behaviour can be irrational and place too much weight upon recent experiences. This is unrealistic against the evidence of a probability density function (PDF) for percentage returns. A comparison of market values against PDF numbers gives a more objective view than being caught in a buying mania. See Figure 6.5.

A long-term share price growth of 5 % should not be far from the median. We have not embodied the chances of a fall in long-term share prices, but the short-term collapse post-2000 should already have forced the consultant advisors, actuaries and client funds to think in terms of more pessimistic outcomes.

Unfortunately, pension funds should have foreseen the impending difficulties in the value of stock markets, and made provisions accordingly under more pessimistic scenario analysis. A 4–6 % annual return would have kept the pension funds more secure, but many got carried away in the optimism of the stock market and have not kept provisions in reserve for future bad debts.[37] Life insurance companies also guaranteeing 8 % pay-outs to their policy-holders was a disastrous move when stock market returns fell to record low levels.

For pensions and life annuities, things have generally gone from bad to worse.

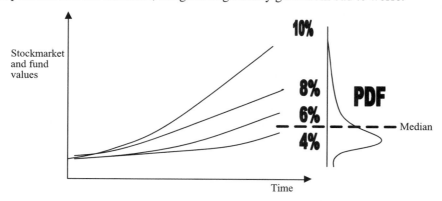

Figure 6.5   Stockmarket and fund values against probability density function (PDF)

---

[37] Chart 156, p. 87, *Financial Stability Review*, Bank of England, June 2002.

CASE STUDY: GUARANTEED ANNUITY PAYMENTS

Another example includes defined outcomes and contingency (insurance) coverage of annuity repayments to policyholders:

- Worst case (2 % return)
- Likely case (6 %)
- Best case (10 %)

The upper and lower limits can be assigned by industry experts who define these values in a brainstorming "Delphi" session. The unravelling outcome that we face is not ideal for either banker or policy-holder, but it paints the naked market truth in a light where it is possible to reconstruct something out of the mess.

The UK pensions mis-selling episode was estimated to have cost around £12 billion to future pensioners. The UK disaster over shortfalls in endowment mortgages has been variously projected to cost many times more than this figure. A benevolent summary of this situation is a business-like patch over what could prove a very messy and expensive mistake. Some would call this compensation exercise a fudge, but it has given a limited redress for victims, and it has put in place damage-limitation procedures.

Scenario analysis does not complicate the risk models, but simplifies their application. Well-designed scenarios can bring to light weaknesses of risk management systems, including modelling vulnerability. Results help to identify critical procedures necessary for reducing risk and conserving capital, returns, market position, core competencies and reputation. Scenario analysis should lead to changes in the way to allocate capital, or planning contingency procedures.

Scenario analysis suffers from being less standardised than the more established VaR, and it makes little use of complex mathematical modelling. There is less in a way of a formal methodology or modelling tool, but it rests upon widely accepted engineering and actuarial techniques. It is often a difficult technique to sell internally within the company.

Stress testing

Stress testing subjects a portfolio or a set of market positions through the strains of various situations to see how they perform under these extreme situations. This can start with the simple "what-if" analysis, by changing a few variables in a model.

Stress testing is designed to diagnose exposures to extreme market volatility that are missed by VaR analysis. VaR is not designed to capture extreme market events. Stress testing must be done with an investigative view.

Once a risky situation has been identified, financial executives can decide to manage an unhealthy exposure through various choices:

- Simply unwinding the position.
- Pricing it differently.
- Buying protective instrument.
- Preparing a liquidity or funding backstop.
- Restructuring the business.

An uncritical view on risk that is not sufficiently calibrated can end up overallocating capital, increasing company operating costs and reducing RAROC. Inadequate stress testing can leave a company undercapitalised until a huge disaster strikes. Thus, it has to devise risk mitigation devices, which include contingency capital as the ultimate line of defence.

Bayesian probability

Maybe the Bayesian school can offer us some insight in operational risk by defining management causality that cannot be measured adequately using VaR, RAROC or EVA (economic value-added). Bayesian networks constitute a branch of Bayesian conditional probability theory, e.g.

$$Prob(A) = Prob(B) \text{ given } Prob(C)$$

Where A, B, C are discrete events.

$$Prob \; (company \; defaulting) = Prob \; (20\% \; share \; price \; fall) \text{ given } Prob \; (bad \; CEO)$$

This has some potential for creating deductive causal links in the loss database.

The use of Bayesian probability has uses in VaR in that we can build conditional VaR modelling.

Artificial intelligence (AI) and expert systems

Bayesian probability underpins some of the principles of artificial intelligence (AI) to discover relationships or patterns. These form part of the trend for knowledge management to dig the wealth that lies at the bottom of the bank's and fund's databases. Some research shows that AI has benefit for the way in which we study stock-market movements.[38] Customer relationship management reflects this drive towards profitable data-mining.

ATM machines use expert systems derived from AI principles to link the transactions with possible stolen bank cards. For example (\$250 withdrawn from Site A) + (\$250 withdrawn from Site B) + (\$300 spent at Store C) using Card X = 75% sure that this card has been stolen.

American Express has been working with such a system based on AI for nearly 20 years. Citibank developed a computer-based credit-scoring system for profiling customer creditworthiness 15 years ago. Now, we have progressed and there are more compliance issues to handle in the 21st century.

CASE STUDY: ANTI-MONEY LAUNDERING

Additional banking regulations have come in post 9/11 to combat money laundering. These measures go further than the US RICO (anti-racketeering and institutionalised crime) legislation. Spotting a few unusual financial movements within millions of daily transactions is not a humanly possible task. An automated anti-money laundering system has been used extensively post 9/11 to track down potential Al-Qa'eda movements of money. It includes elements of AI and human expert system programmed into the computers.

The IBM and Searchspace Compliance Sentinel collaborative project in various banks addressed compliance risk directly as all transactions are passed through the workflow engine for review, analysis, identification and audit. Automation is the only way banks can provide an efficient process for compliance monitoring and meet regulatory demands to combat OpRisk.[39]

---

[38] *Artificial Intelligence and Stockmarket Behaviour*, R.S. Clarkson, SIAS Actuarial Society, 1999.
[39] www.Searchspace.com and www.ibm.com, 22 June 2002.

Table 6.5   Scale of relative probability

Every 5 years or more	Every 2–4 years	About annually	Every 6 months	Each quarter or imminent
1) Very unlikely	2) Unlikely	3) Occasional	4) Frequent	5) Very probable

Table 6.6   Scale of relative impact

−$50m	−$25m	Near nothing	+$25m	+$50m
1) High loss	2) Medium loss	3) Neutral	4) Regular profit	5) Very profitable

Yet the battle between humans and computers is not over. The world chess champion Garry Kasparov lost to a computer "Deep Blue" in one game during 1997. Humans can never admit to being infallible. One comparative study was undertaken between skilled insurance credit underwriters and computerised credit-scoring models in loans businesses. It showed that these options often derived different conclusions about individual credit-worthiness, but they tended to agree over the average credit risk of groups. It concluded that business would do best to integrate computer-based scoring models and human judgement within the credit process. The human role in business is far from over (yet).[40]

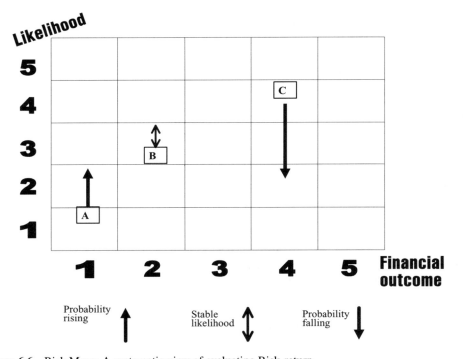

Figure 6.6   Risk Maps: A systematic view of evaluating Risk-return

---

[40] "Commercial credit scoring: robots versus humans?", *Erisk*, January 2002.

RISK MAPS

Based on all our previous theory, we can identify or map out banks that have an initial high risk exposure. There also banks that appear fine now, but have a dynamic risk exposure that will make them vulnerable later. This transience may pose a risk in itself and the change requirements may become too much for their management culture to cope with.

Table 6.5 shows a scale of relative probability.

Building a scale of relative impact, i.e. $ million (loss or profit). Table 6.6 shows a view of probable profit outcomes.

Figure 6.6 shows a risk map for three possible events: A, B, C.[41]

---

[41] *How Safe is Safe Enough?*, A. Darlington *et al.*, Insitute of Actuaries, 12 June 2001.

7
The Promise of Risk
Management Systems

We look at the current state of risk management systems. Installing a risk management system is critical for the continuing business success of a company. Implementation is such a complex process that it requires a project management methodology. We suggest RAMP as one possible alternative for imposing management control. We look at some examples of system failure.

Finally, we outline the definition of the client's needs for the system. These needs are translated into reality by an invitation to tender (ITT) process. A risk management project plan example for implementation of the selected system is presented in the RAMP context at the chapter end.

CURRENT STATE OF SYSTEMS

Financial institutions will chose their risk management paths and associated IT (information technology) systems. A real-time online dealing system performs as the eyes and ears of modern trading. Linked to a risk management nose for trouble, institutions should be able to trade more securely and more profitably.

There is strong competitive advantage to be derived from a powerful union of business and IT. We have to look at the varying results and levels of success within the IT of many banks and funds. There has been a mountain of literature published about the wonders of working in the new information age. The dot-com craze certainly heightened this sentiment. But, the resounding crash of the IT sector showed that there are real limits to marketing hype. There are potential faults on both sides of supplier and client that raise unrealistic business expectations in IT system delivery. Banking and fund management require skilled coordination between IT and risk management that is focused on business success.

The complexity of financial markets has increased because of the development of newer products and services in an increasingly global economy. Derivative instruments also require a higher level of quantitative techniques to cope with them. Back-office clearing and settlements systems do not always keep up with these technological advances, so mismatches will be frequent with the advent of new trading products.

> One of the most prevalent problems is that the antiquity of the major clearing and settlement systems in the back office has meant that they lack the flexibility to be able to handle the welter of new financial products emanating from the front office. Because of this, there is frequent recourse to manual intervention and Excel spreadsheets, with all the attendant potential for error that this entails.[1]

Investor understanding in this respect has declined. Even bank top management has often shed little light upon this extremely unglamorous failure. A huge financial loss arising from

---

[1] *Operational Risk*, p. 27, Middle Office, spring 1999.

a rogue trader is much more understandable than a consistent and innocent seepage from the back office and settlements. Risk management must be focused on accurate goals.

Was the IT project conceived in a manner where initial goals were realistic? These have to be gauged against the bank's resources and the IT supplier's own input. When the business culture of the financial institution proves unsuitable to implementing an appropriate system, this quicksand can sink a project before it is launched. Realistic expectations and a good idea of project risk-return are essential pictures for top management to formulate before calling in technology to solve a business problem.

It is advisable to consult RAMP or PRINCE[2] 2 methodologies before plunging into the deep end of complex risk management systems. Buying solely upon a salesman's pitch or IT director's recommendation can be a sorry choice. Companies need the guidance of a methodology such as RAMP. This is a blueprint that is filled in with data and finalised at the end.

RISK MANAGEMENT METHODOLOGY – RAMP[3]

Activity A: Analysis and project launch

Define risk strategy.
Appoint a risk analyst or problem owner.
Outline the objectives and investment project scope.
Estimate people and skills required, investment complexity, budget and timetable.
Establish an investment project plan with baselines.
Estimate the "most likely" outcome, plus alternative pessimistic scenario.

Activity B: Risk review

Identify project risks, both likely and unlikely.
Analyse risks and their frequency plus probable impact.
Generate mitigation options and discuss them briefly.
Create a risk matrix applicable to this project (cf. Basel II Loss Database).
Consult a Delphi group of experts familiar with similar projects.
Spotlight risks needing deeper scenario analysis and mitigation measures.
Pick cost-effective mitigation for each risk.
Define plan for each mitigation option.
Devise actions for handling residual risks.
Check risk measures with third parties.
Plan financing of the risk management measures.
Get approval for commencing the risk management project with key stakeholders.

Activity C: Risk management

Implement the risk management plan.
Check that risk management plan is compatible with current management processes.
Check that contracts, financing and insurance are compatible.

---

[2] *PRINCE 2*, Central Computer and Telecommunications Agency (CCTA), UK, 1999.
[3] *RAMP (Risk Analysis and Management for Projects)*, Institute of Actuaries, 1999.

Confirm that that the risk management plan is properly staffed, resourced and funded for successful implementation.

Monitor the expected plan results against realised.

Monitor changing market conditions and the extent of risks present.

Revise plan actions where necessary.

Evaluate whether the investment project should continue.

Activity D: Project close down

Summarise the risk events with impact in relation to risks predicted.

Pick out the residual risks and risks unforeseen.

Conclude how successful the project was in financial and risk management terms.

Close down the project with a report for key stakeholders.

Putting this into the RAMP context we can derive a risk management project plan. This is presented as a brief example at the end of the chapter.

FINANCIAL IT SYSTEM SUPPORT

Financial IT development projects took a massive boost in the mid-1980s following "Big Bang". Open systems running on common client-server architecture became the industry standard at the beginning of the 1990s and system choice for banks and fund managers increased. There are now numerous vendors, e.g. Algorithmics, Barra, Erisk, Misys, Reuters, Sungard, who will be happy to entertain you. The hardest job is to select which one (see: **Value for Money**). Finding the right supplier can provide real business value-added service at a competitive price.

Technology has enabled a huge number of private investors to take part in whatever investment at a touch of a button. This has resulted in an unprecedented widening of the clientele within global exchanges. But, technology increased the potential for IT and systems failures, commonly lumped into the catch-all "operational risk". Some banks have met spectacular failures, or have been taken over by more capable and risk-aware banks.

Choose substance and not style in risk management systems. Many system vendors promise to provide you with the "best" systems for every business line. We must choose the "best" IT systems supplier to design and install our specific business environment.

Good use of IT is not about buying fancier computer boxes and designing jazzier websites. All computer-based financial modelling tools and complex IT systems promise to help you. The Loss Database for Basel II is one product that holds a lot of potential. The question is whether it will deliver. The key to success lies in its project implementation.

The Basel II Loss Database project

The new Basel II banking regulations are geared to raising the overall level of risk management in banking and fund management portfolios. Basel II will enable regulators to request advanced operational risk-managed financial institutions to set up and maintain the Loss Database. It has two business drivers, one a mandatory requirement and an optional "nice-to-have".

- First – all financial institutions wishing to have the status of an "Advanced" risk-managed company must comply with the Basel II. One of the requirements is the formation of the Loss Database.

- Second – there is the goal of detecting consistent patterns of loss, and extrapolating from the data to predict the likely level of future business losses.

The ultimate objective is to reduce their level of losses and increase the predictability of the remaining losses. The downside risk of this project is an expensive business and an IT white elephant that does not meet business expectations.

A large global bank can have an expensive loss database, both in terms of number and value of loss items, plus the huge project costs of creating the database. They cannot afford to get it wrong because to do so would be both costly and embarrassing. Backing out a failed loss database project from all global branches would also be a high-profile noticeable loss (compare: Reputational risk).

An operational loss database, driven by the desire for good management or by the regulators, represents a large investment. An empowered band of financial specialists can reap real rewards for the company, supported by IT systems staff to "drill-down" within the loss database. This data-mining involves finding out lines of causality for:

- who
- when
- how much was lost
- how much could have been lost
- why it all happened in the first place.

Loss databases will have to prove themselves against resilience-based approaches. These data will be analysed time and time again under different data-mining angles. The real test will be that of continual testing and review for cost-benefit analysis.

The loss database is a potentially good corporate risk management tool, but, it is likely to fail where it attracts little support within the corporation. Loss data are input for risk management decision making, and it needs a lot of massaging into acceptable reports before it can help to formulate director-level actions. The initiative stands or falls on whether top management supports and funds it.

The benefits are easier to predict than the costs. An advanced-certified operational risk-managed bank will have lower Basel II regulatory capital charges because its risk management processes are highly developed and evaluated as a lower overall risk. From previous regulatory examples within credit risk, a bank could find its regulatory capital reserve falling by some 6%.[4]

How much this will translate into similar savings for OpRisk is to be decided by the regulators interpreting the Basel II guidelines.[5]

Risk appetite becomes more directly linked to risk offer, but risk appetite is also covered by Basel II regulatory capital. Risk support systems alert the danger of capital becoming inadequate to cover expected losses.

The loss database business rationale may be a search for lower risk ratings and knowledge data-mining, forced on them by the regulator. The compliance "Big stick" approach of the regulator may be better at explaining the need for the database, instead of the more complex business cost-benefit analysis.

Losing money has never been in the interests of a bank, nor of its clients. Yet banks and investment funds continue to lose money without knowing where or why. There is some hope

---

[4] *Quantitative Impact Study 3*, Basel Committee for Banking Supervision, May 2003.
[5] *Enterprise Risk Management*, Professional Risk Management Association (PRMIA), London, 13 November 2002.

Table 7.1   Loss data requirements

Date	Loss (£k)	Business line	Result	Cause-effect business lines	Exposure rating	Relief party	Relief amount (£k)	Net loss (£k)
1/3/04	136	Asset Mgmt	Client lawsuit	2–4–5	0.4	AON	36	100
2/4/04	43	FX trading	Late trade	7	0.9	None	0	43

| Gross loss | | Event | | Likely casuality | | Risk transfer | | Final net loss |

that this integrated database, linked to advanced modelling tools, can help make investing less risky. It will most likely be a complex and expensive project to set up, mainly because of the complexity and size of the data collected. See Table 7.1.

The formation of a complex loss database is a knowledge management structure that we are actively constructing. It requires a lot of data and system integration to link the disparate elements in a global bank. Some call this risk management system a "data warehouse" where information is packaged into one compatible format for analysis (see Enterprise application integration – EAI). The benefits are the harnessing of market intelligence to understand: who, when, how and how much money has been lost. Then, we can reinforce risk management procedures to avoid such a loss recurring, or to reduce the loss when the hazard strikes again.

CASE STUDY: ALGORITHMICS SYSTEM IN A BANK[6]

Bayerische Landesbank uses Algorithmics' Algo Collateral to manage its current and future cross-product margining requirements. BayernLB uses Algorithmics to update its trading limit systems with intra-day collateral balances. A banking regulatory data warehouse is then updated with capital requirements and collateral trade costs. Algorithmics Collateral also checks for valuation discrepancies and monitors data changes.

Such systems perform various essential functions, namely:

- valuation modelling
- mark-to-market
- risk alerts
- regulatory compliance.

Getting to the concrete system stage is putting everything from theory into practice. The IT task sequence is relatively simple in theory, but complex in execution.

1) Deal capture data must be collected in a timely manner from the simple trading ticket upwards throughout various application systems.
2) Standardise or pre-process the data into an acceptable and usable format. This can be done using enterprise application integration (EAI).
3) Transfer into another application system – in this case the risk management system.
4) Analyse and distribute output and reports to relevant systems and departments.

---

[6] Algorithmics, www.algorithmics.com, October 2002.

Once the system design is successfully implemented, it has the potential to offer specific competitive advantage to the business. These have functional benefits of risk modelling analysis, risk monitoring, procedural alerts and regulatory compliance. IT systems used by experienced staff can reduce the risk exposure in bank portfolios successfully and cut down losses.

Integration and straight-through processing (STP)

STP would help us reduce losses where the buy and sell orders are either mismatched or lost. STP can reconcile trades and place them in accounts automatically by software packages. It would be admirable to have fast turnaround and cut down mistakes on trades. Trade processing errors can be costly, and they can be cut out using STP. Exceptions are costly; automating exceptions when processing trades can reduce costs by 25 %. Yet only 30 % of 500 financial institutions surveyed have fully automated exception reporting.[7] STP will help us detect errors within our bank or fund, but will STP ever be implemented?

STP is the ideal sold by many systems vendors. But, in the real world where a front office may have a 100 IT systems and subsystems, STP may be part of the Holy Grail. The prospect of no accounting errors or orders mismatches is not borne out by reality. If an accounting error creeps in, how are we to flag it or reconcile it? It would be wishful thinking to wave a magic wand over the risk elements of fraud, mismatched orders and operations mistakes.

The idea of STP (see Figure 7.1) convey seamless processing between all three stages or departments, without any hitches or significant delays. There is no universal IT package that will fulfil all functions in the front, middle and back office.

Reality offers that one system vendor will eventually be called into the bank or fund and be instructed to connect its new system to all the existing legacy systems. This means that we are looking at a reduction of the number of IT systems and subsystems instead of an agglomeration under one "Big Brother" system. A bank may think of buying a "vanilla" IT package, but they really come in many different flavours.

The systems market is diminishing with the cut-backs in financial institution expenditure and more banking M&A. This means further cuts in the choice of systems suppliers. Choose one that survives.

Algorithmics, Barra, Sungard, eRisk, Pareto *et al.* are financial system vendors that offer "risk management" systems in one form or another. A web trawl can reveal a hundred names or more for systems providers. All systems suppliers write one IT system and hope to resell

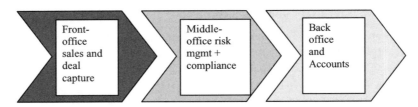

Figure 7.1   Straight-through processing

---

[7] *Exceptional Progress: STP, Exception Management*, Sungard, November 2002.

it many times. Their profits lie in amending previously written systems, not in tailoring each one from scratch for each customer. They are the greatest recyclers of our time.

For example, Reuters, Barra or Sungard should stress that there is no bog-standard "one-size fits all" package. Theirs is an adaptable systems tool-kit backed by a bespoke consultancy service that includes tailoring to the business and portfolio of the specific bank or fund manager. A company may buy a systems package with a fixed price, but have to add 300 % for the amendments, project implementation and support services.[8] Even then, project success is not guaranteed in any way.

IT systems project failure

Numerous cases of cancelled or failed IT projects in the finance industry happen on an alarming scale. Many within the banking world are unreported because of reputation risk, i.e. risk of losing clients or looking foolish in front of rivals.

There are four major reasons for IT systems failure:

- The risk management system was initially unsuitable for the bank or fund and could not be successfully tailored for use.
- The skills base of the business project implementation was not properly understood or resourced.
- Organisational politics or budgetary problems hindered progress.
- Operational errors or poor systems design ruined chances of success.

CASE STUDY: IT OVERLOAD

Intelligent technology is programmed and managed by people, so there is a lot of room for human error. IT systems failure (freeze or black-out) is one of the most well-known disasters under the operational risk category. The London Stock Exchange trading system fell down in 2000 because it could not cope with the load of processing traffic. Its IT system facility was managed by Arthur Andersen. The New York Stock Exchange had to install trading "breaker circuits" to stop the unusually high volume of programmed trades crashing the dealing system.

Spectacular IT collapses in traffic happened because of human-organised hardware or software problems. These can be "directed" or "undirected". The notable hacker or virus attacks are sent to specific destinations such as trading rooms. An electricity supply overload, flooding or short-circuitry in the computer room, or a drill piercing a telecoms cable in the street – all man-made. From personal experience in banking, all have happened to us – they could happen to you.

Disasters and system disruption arise from a variety of hazards:[9]

- 56 % failure in hardware, software, telecoms, power.
- 24 % natural disaster: fire, flood, earthquake.
- 20 % malicious intent, including September 11th.

All of these IT threats can be managed or mitigated, not eliminated.

---

[8] *Delivering on your e-Promise: Managing e-Business Projects*, Y.Y. Chong, Financial Times Management, 2001.
[9] *"White Paper on Sound Practices to Strengthen the US Financial System"*, Sungard, December 2002.

Tying financial system functionality to promise

A company's best move may involve buying in an IT vendor's outsourced risk management services. IT systems and services have been outsourced for many years now. Risk management services in the financial sector have generally involved external outsourced vendor systems and experts. But, value-added services rely upon the deep understanding of the specific business in question. The implementation of key risk management systems bought for the bank and adapted from insurance initially sounds fine; delivery can be something else. Tailoring it for retail banking uses can spell a disaster, it need not be cost-effective in time or money.

Successful risk management initiatives must come from the directors at the strategic planning level. Incremental addition of risk management systems or procedures may prop up the business weaknesses, but they may not cure the structural illness of the organisation. The Barings and AIB disasters showed that the directors either did not understand the target banking business, or were not too bothered to monitor real performance.

A global enterprise dealing in several foreign exchanges requires a central resource for effective internal corporate control. Otherwise, you end up with different divisions in parts of the world with varying standards of business operation and risk. One of these enterprises could have a business failure that could bring down the whole corporation.

A survey of US directors revealed:

- 43 % of company directors cannot identify, plan for, or safeguard against risk.
- 36 % do not understand major risks facing the company.[10]

Companies that identify, plan and manage risk reap large potential business rewards. A basic view of corporate wealth formation, and risk horizons, is that it is created by the:

1. Directors' strategic leadership planning (long term) ➜
2. Traders or fund managers' profit from tactical market moves (short term) ➜
3. Risk management systems in place and effective (short to medium term) ➜
4. Portfolio or assets of company appreciate in value (long term).

RISK PRIORITISATION

The fundamental flaws of system design in the financial company must be addressed before technology. Errors can come about from undertaking a too short review and analysis of the company needs before quoting the price for the contract. The immediate need is to establish a coherent risk management strategy, rather than a hotch-potch buying of fashionable technologies and top names. It requires a plan and a project methodology.

What we find when designing dealing environments for banks and funds is that risk management and IT initiatives can be conducted piece-meal. The may be happy to pay $5 million for a group of star-traders properly kitted out with the latest technology. They are reluctant to shell out $500 000 for a risk management system that backs up best-of-breed redesigned business procedures.[11] Fixing the problem after the risk event occurs can cost hundreds of times more than prevention.

A clear prioritisation with coordinated goal setting is required for mapping and management of the risk areas and technologies. A risk map of designated business operations areas coded

---

[10] *US Directors Survey*, McKinsey, May 2002.
[11] *"Delivering on your e-Promise: Managing e-Business Projects"*, Y.Y. Chong, Financial Times Management, 2001.

red, amber and green can demonstrate the project priorities. These can be input into the user's needs analysis for creating the design specifications in the "user system requirements" (URS).

Giving the go-ahead

Bringing the changes required for the desired risk management processes will be an arduous task in itself. We deal with so different groups of people, crossing departmental boundaries. All these introduce something novel into the company, and change management skills will be needed to bring these new business processes to fruition. Definition of performance criteria, underperformance penalties and budgeting is likely to be contentious. Securing support from the directors will be a prerequisite for getting most large-scale projects off the ground.[12]

Various representatives from the major departments and stakeholders involved are invited to sit in a Delphi group to offer their views on the investment project. Sometimes there are consultants brought in to present an impartial opinion of the corporate project risk map.

BUILDING RISK MANAGEMENT SYSTEMS

After selecting the desired staff, we have to install the technical elements of risk management. It has to be emphasised that IT supports the business and not the other way around. The business department should not go out alone to shop for the "best" risk management system; neither should the IT department.

Financial risk management has to rely on specialised software. There are relatively small firms that usually work with a limited number of clients. An extra customer won can make a difference between boom and bust. Sales overcommitment can take over the aims of delivering the most suitable product for the client at the best price. This sales scramble can lead to excessive promises.

Value-added systems rely upon the supplier's understanding of the business in that situation, the implementation of adequate security procedures and good quality staff. The business functionality inherent within the risk management system may prove unsuitable for the specific bank or fund. You can buy technology and marketing hype instead of system utility. We can take a subjective view of technology for the sake of demonstration. See Table 7.2.

Finding the "best" risk management system

Searching for the "best" risk management system and service delivery constitutes a major project in itself. This is known as the ITT (invitation to tender) process where we follow a rigid methodology to get the best for us. It is likely that a more suitable product and service can be obtained at a better price once we have gone through all ITT steps.

Table 7.2   Traffic-lights/relative technology maturities

	Technology	Time to maturity (months)
Limit usage to minimum (red)	Original CAPM	0
Proceed with caution (amber)	Organic risk management	12
Invest as appropriate (green)	Loss database	36

---

[12] *"Sound Practices for Operational Risk"*, Basel Committee for Banking Supervision, July 2002.

The invitation to tender (ITT) process

If you consider creating critical risk management functions within your company, you have two general choices:

- Build in-house, or
- Buy from an outside party.

Build

This dictates that your company has the adequate internal resources and scale to undertake such a major task. With Basel II, this is further complicated by the small pool of talent able to handle compliance and technical issues for market, credit and operational risk. Given the extreme novelty of the Basel II "Three Pillars", we will probably face a medium-term shortage of able personnel to understand and implement the new regulations.

Specialised risk management has a dearth of skills available. Thus, the company is committed to having the business skills in-house for understanding the risk management issues, and outsourcing the technical skills for implementing the new system. This entails getting the cocktail of talent right, i.e. combining financial skills, risk management, change management, project control, mathematical and IT systems experience.

Buy

It is more probable that you do not have all or enough of all the resources to carry out this large project. "Buying in" is the preferred option when companies do not want to "reinvent the wheel". Some external personnel will handle part of the risk management, some the IT side. This can range from specific technical tasks that require specialist advice, to wholesale design and implementation of the entire system.

There are security issues at stake here because few banks and funds wish an external party to know their finances and risk management status. Confidentiality clauses are written into contracts, and "Chinese walls" emerge to promise non-disclosure of sensitive data to another client. The trust works both ways and it behoves a client to provide accurate data to the system supplier.

It is likely that the project size and risk management complexity will force a combination of build and buy-in, with most companies preferring the buy-in route. Once inviting risk management firms to design and install the business solution, some methodology must be used to select the most suitable suitor. It is crucial to select the best long-term business solution provider, not just for Basel II, but quite possibly for Basel III and all the follow-on work. We have often gone into banks and fund managers and seen the client allied to the wrong business solutions provider. The ITT is a bidding process that is worth conducting carefully.

BUSINESS FUNCTIONALITY REQUIREMENTS

The supporting detail of the grid, used for further analysis and line management purposes, is contained in a risk functional cross-matrix, see for example Table 7.3.

Red warning lights show us the most critical systems to redesign or overhaul. Where departments are already operating well, and currently get the green risk light, then there is no immediate need to replace that subsystem. Nevertheless, systems engineers will often replace that subsystem too and install a completely new one that is guaranteed to be compatible with the rest of the new integrated system.

Table 7.3   Risk functional cross-matrix

Department	Front office	Middle office	Back office and accounts
Function	Mark-to-market positions	Basel-type monthly compliance reports	Reconciling mismatched Forex trades
Performance status (1 – good; 5 – bad)	5	3	1
Risk code	Red	Amber	Green

A lot of the system satisfaction revolves around the functionality, that is, fulfilling the needs of the users. The needs analysis comes out in the defining document that is usually called the "user system requirements" (URS). See Table 7.4. Such a vital document, in summary, is circulated to interested system vendors in a communication flow, initiated by the "request for information" (RFI). This is a preliminary document that defines the summary of needs, and the firm's plans for upgrading systems. It gives enough data to inform systems builders if they can meet the client's needs, or not.

The final URS is analysed in full and sent to short-listed system vendors in a contractual document, usually called the "request for proposal" (RFP). It contains some data such as the user's functional needs.

User's functional priorities

When you are designing a risk management system, you are searching for best:

- price
- functionality
- time taken to implement
- confidentiality/security
- reliability
- after-sales support.

How you prioritise and assign weightings to these criteria is a subjective matter, and it defines your company's exact situation. Even getting the best price–quality ratio and product involves the client in a calculus that offers more room for abstract judgement, rather than costs and figures alone.

You will have to check interfacing and efficiency of sharing data with the new programs. Otherwise, system integration difficulties can bring your risk management system that "speaks" English into a German bank with a French accounts system. The company's central IT department may specify an Esperanto of XML as a mediator language for translating between the bank's myriad systems. XML serves as a universal format for translation that also ports well to the Internet. Shared data can be sent over all the bank's operational centres world-wide in this way. The complex design issues and the need for linking many disparate systems grow ever more insurmountable with a global corporation.[13]

A world-wide financial company is likely to have several risk management systems, including all the "legacy" systems. This indicates a need for sophisticated integration, with the bank's risk management system at the epicentre. The system can sit in the middle, linked by an EAI intermediary layer or module – see Figure 7.2.

---

[13] *"Delivering on your e-promise: Managing e-Business Projects"*, Y.Y. Chong, Financial Times Management, 2001.

Table 7.4 User system requirements

Department	Front office: Forex	Middle office	Back office and accounts
Requirements	*Current system* The new system has to replace our whole Forex front-office dealing system. This trading group has 32 dealers (plus 1 FX group head) using Reuters dealing systems. The treasurer and 5 other users in middle office and Back office and accounts must have access to this system. All these users have Compaq EVOs 512 Mb RAM under Win XP. *Datafeeds* There are also live price feeds coming in from the Bloomberg system, our affiliate bank in New York and our central bank. There are approximately 5000 daily trades made during the day (07:00 to 18:00 London time). We require mark-to-market position reports at midday and at the close of business day. *Availability* We want 99.95 % system availability during the business day.	*Current system* This group includes 15 staff, including chief risk officer. They use Barra and Reuters Kondor + systems. *Reporting* They process market reports for the front office and back office. Other destinations are FSA, BoE and our HQ in Germany. There are an estimated 25 daily reports processed per day. Other reports are produced weekly, monthly, quarterly and yearly. Dealers require daily reports and valuations of their portfolio. These must be generated for their positions within 15 minutes of their request. *Basel II compliance* B-II reports are required for FSA. We will require assistance meeting these standards for AMA (advanced measurement) level. We will want you to help us meet compliance for further EU regulations too.	*Current system* This groups consists of 24 staff including head of accounts. The current system is provided by Midas-Kapiti (MKI). *Capacity* There are about 15 000 daily trades (equities, bonds, FX) made during the day (07:00 to 18:00 London time). Currently, some orders are taking 4 hours to clear the back office. There are requirements to bring this down to 1 hour maximum on average. We are reconciling about 40 mismatched Forex trades per day. This may come from unknown counterparty. The list of clients is run in an Oracle DB that is slow to access. *Reporting* There are 140 types of reports coming from back office. This takes a lot of workload that we are trying to cut down.

The interfacing and data conversion difficulties between the different business programs and suppliers may tend to work against easy linking of an enterprise-wide risk management system.

For this reason, the company may take a strategic policy for IT standards, e.g. something on the lines of:

For all global offices. To standardise our IT systems, we stipulate that:
All mainframes will be supplied by IBM, all servers by Sun Microsystems or Compaq, all PCs from Compaq or Dell, all operating systems either IBM-AIX or the latest Windows. Bloomberg will be our preferred dealing systems supplier and integrator, with MKI for back office and Sungard for risk management. Deviation from these standards will have to be approved by IT department beforehand.

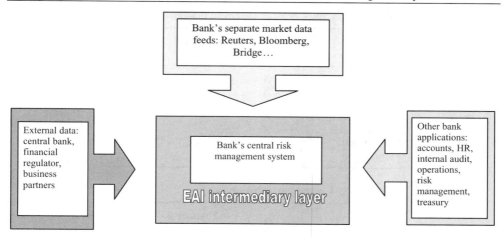

Figure 7.2   Risk management systems and EAI

No supplier ever meets 100 % of your needs perfectly. A compromise solution can be devised to fit your specific business requirements. Various interpretations surround the notion of "best system supplier". Judging rival suppliers is the most complex part of the ITT selection. It comprises designing and selecting the "best" supplier and then integrating its risk management system into your company. You select the "best fit" with your performance demands.

The ITT matrix evaluation needs a lot of company raw data to compare with suppliers' ability to meet these requirements. Use all information to score their likely performance. It is viewed as an audit of their risk management overall skills. The ITT process reduces the probability of picking an unsuitable system or supplier.

Business flirting – the user's system specification

Business functionality plus conclusive "value for money" seems to be the conclusion of the ITT process. Many of the desired business functions can be graded by your team into:

- **Red** – mandatory, this could be a show-stopper.
- **Amber** – medium priority, a function that is nice to have.
- **Green** – low priority, not essential.

Business flirting – the supplier's reply

Then, the risk management supplier can respond to your functional requests:

- Already provided by us.
- Can be provided by us (estimate costs and time for this).
- Cannot be provided by us.

The definition of a suitable business function can be done top-down. The risk management system has to fit your business line, and not the other way around. See Table 7.5.

Then we can define the function by whether they meet the product lines that you are already dealing. See Table 7.6.

We can demand the specific function down to lower detail. See Table 7.7.

Table 7.5 Supplier's risk management functions

Business line	Supplier A complies	Supplier B complies	Supplier C complies
Investment bank	X		X
Retail bank	X	X	X
Savings bank	X	X	X
Insurance company	X		X
Life assurance	X		X
Pension fund		X	X
Mutual fund		X	

Table 7.6 Risk management by product line

Product line	Supplier A complies	Supplier B complies	Supplier C complies
Forex spot	X		X
Forex futures	X		X
Commodities (grain)		X	X
Commodities (oil)		X	X
Energy derivatives		X	X
Bonds (sovereign)	X	X	X
Bonds (US corporate)	X	X	X

Judging the ITT beauty show

The screening process of the suppliers can be long drawn-out, but it has to be methodical and it has to be done well. This mix of weighted-criteria process is sometimes called a beauty contest. It can be done in secrecy with sealed bids to only invited suppliers.[14] Or it can have all interested suppliers bidding. The selection process is certainly more objective with the 'lowest bid wins', but it can leave out the user's needs considerably. Therefore, the argument for user functionality has to be spelt out for all. You can include the system criteria, or priorities, you deem important. See Figure 7.3.

Table 7.7 Risk management functionality

Function	Specific	Supplier A	Supplier B	Supplier C
Mark-to-market (MTM)	Delta	X	X	X
	Gamma	X	X	X
	Vega	X	X	X
	Theta	X	X	X
	Convexity sensitivity analysis	X	X	X
	Discontinuous product (Binary option)		X	
	Discontinuous product (Digital option)		X	
	Real-time charting	X		X
	3-D charting	X		
	Export to Excel	X	X	X

---

[14] E.g. refer "Contractor Qualification", Ron Prichard, www.IRMI.com, August 2000.

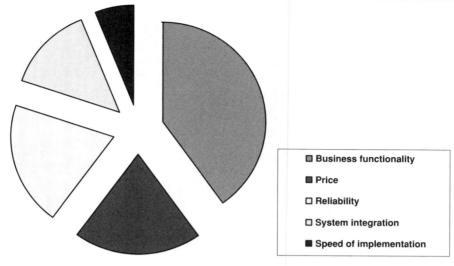

Figure 7.3   System priorities

System priorities

An extract of the selection matrix for your ITT is shown in Table 7.8 with more criteria and three supplier companies: A, B, C.

The winner, supplier C, can be graphed to determine its relative compliance with the user's wishes. Using a radar graph, we see that the winner covers the most area for the major selection criteria (Figure 7.4).

Once you got this far, the ITT does not in itself guarantee the best system available anywhere, but it cuts down the chance of being sold an inappropriate risk management system. It was worth getting this.

Table 7.8   Supplier selection matrix

Criteria	Max. marks	Supplier A	Supplier B	Supplier C
Business functionality	30	21	20	24
Price	10	7	7	5
Speed of implementation	10	6	7	6
System integration	5	3	3	4
Reliability	5	3	3	3
Security	5	4	3	4
Scalability and global support	3	2	1	2
FSA certified risk-compliance	3	1	1	2
Financial strength of supplier	3	1	2	2
Experience in industry	3	1	2	3
Reputation in financial sector	3	1	2	3
Presentation skills	10	7	5	7
Our general confidence in them	10	6	5	8
Total max. possible marks	100			
Overall marks		63	61	73
Our decision		Second	Third	First

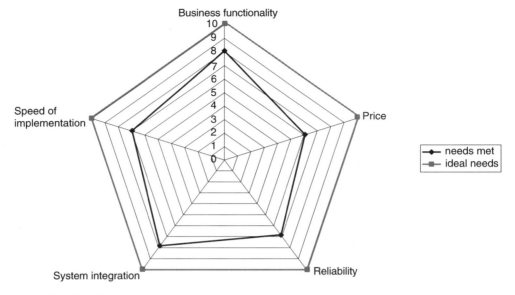

Figure 7.4   Meeting the user's system needs

Project life cycle

On the client's side, the project performance can be anybody's guess until the software func-
tionalities have been tried in operation on go-live day. Some systems and technologies are on
a life cycle, both in terms of maturity as well as industry acceptance. When you are way ahead
of rivals, then you may be on the bleeding edge phase of the life cycle where there are few
teachers available to learn from. See Figure 7.5.

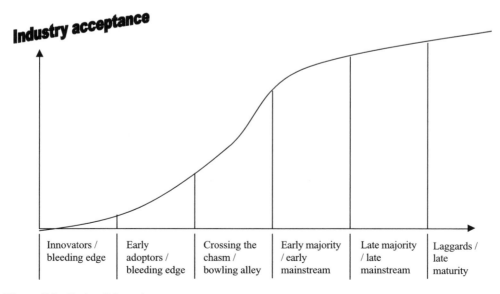

Figure 7.5   Project life-cycle

Financial software houses seek a bigger market share, so underselling is never likely to be a flaw. We still find some banks wondering whether the software suppliers want to be committed to delivering service, or was it really just sales spiel?

We should concentrate on justifying the business case and establishing goals before shopping for systems. Senior executives should then try to meet the defined risk management objectives first. Risk management systems serve to improve overall company performance by meeting business needs, not to serve as a goal in its own right.[15] Building a strategy for implementing risk management is as important as creating the risk management systems. Both need a plan.

RISK MANAGEMENT PROJECT PLAN

We can take the RAMP template for risk management to derive the project plan.

A – Our risk strategy

This is to provide effective and timely support for all the banking staff to cope with market developments over the next 10 years. Meeting challenges for the bank include:

- Evaluating and reporting of strategic long-term risks for the board of directors.
- Handling new products, particularly securitised assets and equity derivatives.
- Online, real-time mark-to-market pricing for front office.
- Basel II compliance reporting up to AMA (advanced measurement approach) operational risk level. We will want to meet compliance for further company disclosure policies, which we believe will tighten with future legislation.

Middle office will continue to be led by our chief risk officer. We intend to recruit an extra 12 staff over the next three years. We plan for all our new risk management systems to be online and operational by 1 January 2005. The capital spend on this system is forecast at €7.5 m spread over three years. Our annual budget is forecast for €15 million, commencing on that date. Online availability will be 99.95 %. Our customer satisfaction among our users will rise by 10 % from current benchmarked levels within three years.

B – Risk review

We have analysed the project risks and tabulated their likely frequency with our company staff and consultants who are familiar with such projects. We have estimated probable impact, highlighting extremely damaging events in a risk register (Table 7.9). Where such project risks are critical, i.e. potential show-stoppers, we have outlined likely alternatives for risk mitigation. The project risk register for this project is outlined for the first six risks only. Residual risks are listed at the end.

C – Risk management

Implementation of the risk management plan ("plan") is congruent with the strategic aims of the company to be a competitive investment bank in western Europe. This plan fits in with current management needs and envisaged development of business processes up to end 2009.

---

[15] Phil Dinsmore, vice president, ERisk, www.Erisk.com, January 2002.

Table 7.9 Project risk register

Risk	Prob.	Impact	Mitigation
Project budget overshoots significantly	*15 %*	*Depends upon overshoot (amber). Contract states where 100 % vendor's fault, then they pay. Our contractual contribution to them is capped at 12 % of total budget for force majeure disasters.*	*We have signed-off project budget of €7.5 m and a contingency fund of €900 000. We have contract terms to force vendor to pay for all their errors.*
Bank wants to cancel project	*10 %*	*This has a major (red) impact. Will leave our risk systems 5 years behind our main rivals.*	*Board has to understand that this project is mission-critical. We have signed approval for up to €12 m and 14 man-years labour.*
System supplier goes bust	*18 %*	*This has a major (red) impact. Modest risk (amber) if supplier taken over. Will probably add 2 months to our systems implementation schedule.*	*Pick a supplier company that is large and robust enough to maintain independence.*
System not up to users' expectations or usability	*22 %*	*Experts believe this has a major (red) impact. Only modest impact (amber) if supplier taken over quickly. Will probably add 2 months max to our risk systems implementation schedule.*	*There are likely to be some user grumbles. Train all staff beforehand. Brief all users long before so expectations are in line with delivery.*
Hardware downtime >1 %	*5 %*	*This is a modest (amber) impact where were are talking minutes. Any more downtime >45 minutes becomes major (red).*	*We have a service level agreement (SLA) with the vendor. Red impacts are compensated by vendor at $1000/minute downtime.*
Hardware lost in natural disaster	*<1 %*	*All power appliances have shielded electricity supply with backup for 2 hours. We estimate chances of full loss at c. 0.002 % based on industry figures (i.e. so slight that we have green risk).*	*IT centre is locked within blast-proof doors with fire and water alarms, manned and guarded 24 hours/day. Hardware insured by Royal Insurance for €10 m replacement cost.*

The contracts for all stakeholders and suppliers are listed in Appendix A. The contractor IT system contract is in Appendix A.2.1. Financing terms and conditions from the bank are listed in Appendix C.1.2. Insurance policies for this project are held in Appendix A.2.1.

The plan is to be staffed by a full-time project manager, resourced with three full-time persons and two part-time from middle office. It is adequately funded for successful completion by the board who gave the plan full support 1/3/2004. The chairman's annual speech reiterated this support.

We will use Primavera Project to monitor the plan progress against realised events.

The project manager is empowered to make revisions in the Plan. Where actions have amber to red impact, there will be a meeting of the project steering committee to agree changes. Low level (green) changes can be agreed where necessary between the project manager, bank line managers and supplier's staff.

Periodic evaluation over the investment cost-benefit and the progress of the project will be conducted monthly.

D – Project close down

We will summarise the risk events with impact in our risk register for risks recorded. The residual risks are to be listed together with ad hoc mitigation measures. We estimate very good chances (82 %) of a successful project.

The project will conclude with a wrap-up meeting, scheduled one month after implementation. There will be a report for key stakeholders detailing variances and errors recorded. Recommendations for project amendments and maintenance will be made then.

The project plan is a risk-managed blueprint for success.

8

Realistic Risk Management

We focus on various forms of business risk, and the manner in which many investors focus on the "wrong" ones. Operational risk is the umbrella category that is the source of many of the troublesome business hazards. Then, we examine the risk of business damage within two groups – intentional and unintentional. A form of intentional loss is the desire to defraud an outsider, as typified by the Nigerian 419 scam. A short look at emerging markets and operational risk is also taken at this stage.

Then, an example of unintentional investment damage is examined in the Split Capital trust fund case within the UK market. Given the important role of human beings in these examples of loss, we example the extent of financial damage caused throughout the corporation – from the top CEO to fund managers and traders. The "star" hiring system in many firms poses many unforeseen risks. The emphasis on the human source of business risk leads us to coin the term *organic risk management* within the operational risk category.

We extend our search to determine what investment and management skills are desired and how we can find them through organic risk management. These skills are rather elusive and sometimes illusory in the job market. These management added-value skills, or Alpha, become more understood and sought after within the financial sector. Furthermore, these skills are subject to the ebb and flow as time goes by. The corporate performance rises and falls within this periodic cycle.

Binding these skills inside an appropriate organisational structure gives us corporate governance with an acceptable risk-return profile. This is the challenging goal of modern corporate leadership as encouraged by investor activist groups today.

INTENTIONAL DAMAGE

We start with the intentional damage to the investor. There are many kinds of business risk, and we have focused earlier on mainstream treatment of market risk and credit risk. Yet, it is the most nebulous one, operational risk, that sticks in the mind foremost. The risk events that come within this category tend to attract most of the news coverage. We can pick out fraud and theft as notorious examples. It is often seen that someone purposely planned to cause massive business damage. Fraud, or theft, is the major phenomenon that usually strikes the headlines first. It is a considerable fear of loss that grips the company management – with some justification.

Fraud, theft and loss

Fraud is estimated to cost £14 billion a year in the UK in direct costs. It is thought that this figure rises to $400 billion fraud loss annually in the USA.[1] This is without counting the cost

---

[1] "Interview as a forensic-type procedure", T. Buckhoff and J. Hansen, *Journal of Forensic Accounting*, Vol.3, 2002.

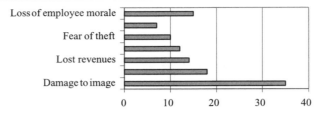

Figure 8.1   Business security drivers (relative importance)

of prevention, the costs of investigation and mitigation of post-fraud damage. Yet, it is not the primary motive for action within the company.[2] Reputation risk is the factor that forces people to act in order to save the business (and sometimes also their career). See Figure 8.1 Ironically, it is the quest to maintain the *bella figura* within the business community that forces top management to control operational risk. Whereas a more rational business approach would more likely have been rewarded with consistent results.

So, the risk management stance is almost entirely predicated upon a desire to keep up appearances in the business world. The commercial leader's risk posture looks rosy, but is not suitable for the hard-nosed reality of business risk management. When a major business loss event is detected, the corporate psyche goes into panic mode, and staff are forced to take prompt reactive steps. The main avenue for redress is to turn to the power of the regulatory authorities and full legal process. Taking legal action post facto is more expensive than any good preventative risk assessment.

As things stand, companies and individuals are more receptive to countering external fraud risks, such as the obvious 419 scam. Yet, there are potential internal threats that are often believed to be less likely or damaging than those from outside.

Fraud perceived as the main criminal threat

We have so much information at hand in the Internet age that we are meant to be able to make an intelligent and informed investment choice at speed. Any web browser and a bank of telephones for local and international calls equip the modern investor with up-to-date news and research tomes of choice. This attitude can be downright dangerous at worst. Any form of self-proclaimed investment invincibility is naive at the very least.

The advent of cheap and widely used telecommunications opens up the investment world as never before. Conversely, e-fraud repackages of old criminal techniques are made easier by the Internet. It appears that about 2 % of credit card transactions online are deceptive or fraudulent.[3] Law enforcement agencies are swamped and follow behind with a time-lag, from the technical challenges and the lack of international cooperation. Internet Fraud Watch reported that, in 2000, 82 % of the solicitation methods were through websites. Once the lure is in place, victims are easy prey. Given the vast number of phoney invitations that come via email spam, this is a numbers game that guarantees that some suckers will fall victim. Online auctions are a great way to scam customers into paying for goods that do not exist, are fake, or that will never be delivered. A better known example involves the infamous Nigerian **419**s.

---

[2] *Security Business Drivers*, IDC, 2002.
[3] "How fraudsters set traps and take the credit", *Financial Times*, 21 May 2003.

419 – not a number, but a way of life

Every year, a significant number of investors have letters, faxes and emails sent to them with an attractive proposition. It certainly looks like a lot of easy money to be made for a small outlay. That is why, for instance, a significant number of investors are caught every year in the Nigerian-based 419s scam. This con trick is also referred to as "Advance Fee Fraud" or "419 Fraud" after the section of the Criminal Code of Nigeria. See Table 8.1.

Table 8.1   The Nigerian 419 – a real-life example

Fraudulent letter	Notes
"URGENT BUSINESS & PROFITABLE TRANSACTION"	1 A typical come-on.
Dear Sir,	2 Big upside lure.
In order to transfer out $112m (one hundred and twelve million US dollars) from our bank.	
I am Mr.X – manager of United Bank in Nigeria. There is a dormant account opened in 1998. I discovered that if I do not remit this money out urgently it will forfeited.	3 Invitation to secret confederation.
The owner of this account is Mr Edward Zzzz, a Director of National Petrol Chemical Service. Sadly, he died in 2001. The account has no other beneficiary.	4 There is no downside risk or danger of detection. Reiterate the big financial gain offered.
I want to transfer this money into a safe foreign account abroad but I don't know any foreigner I can trust. This money can only be sent to any foreign account because the money is US dollars in the name of Mr Edward Zzzz – a foreigner just like you.	5 Your part in the scam.
I assure you it is a genuine business. I only got your contact from our chambers of commerce. You are the only person that I have contacted for this business for now.	6 Calming reassurance. It's just you and me in this sure-fire scheme.
To secure your participation, I need $100,000 in the account listed below to start all official paperwork. So please reply urgently.	7 A smaller, realistic sum to get the sucker into the scam.
Then the transfer is approved and is sent for final clearance and signing of the payment release form. I want us to meet at the overseas paying clearance in our Lagos, Nigeria office face to face to sign the original binding agreement. I can meet you at the airport and offer all help in local contacts.	8 The kicker – come to meet us in our country in person. You can trust us!
I will use my position and influence on staff here to effect legal approvals and transfer of this money to your account. I am sure of your capability to handle this matter in strict confidence and trust.	9 Reassurance again.
I shall destroy all documents concerning this transaction after we received this money, leaving no trace anywhere.	10 Assurance of operational secrecy and confidentiality.
At the conclusion of this business, you will be given 40 % of the total $112million amount, 40 % for me, while 20 % will be for expenses needed for other parties needed during this transaction.	11 Our cut of the profits.
I welcome you to our profitable business.	12 Final assurance and contact details.
Yours truly,	
Xxx	
Manager	
United Bank for Africa in Nigeria.	
Account: 1234567	
SWIFT: UBA NG	

The investor receives an invitation to an offer too good to refuse. There are many variations of this con job, but they display common traits of incredible cupidity and gullibility. The investor is invited by a fax/email/telephone call to enter into an exclusive transaction. There is a large cargo of oil, or a frozen escrow account, that can be milked if you play according to the rules. The naive investors get milked for some time and may even end up in Lagos airport, Nigeria. If lucky, they are happy to get back alive in one piece.

The con artists operate offshore from fake addresses or use a mobile telephone, so they are nearly impossible to trace. They are considerably assisted by their victims – most foolish investors are unwilling to admit to the police that they have been swindled.[4] This is because even the most thick-skinned businessman is reluctant to confess that he has been dishonest, plus very greedy, and worst of all, unbelievably stupid into the bargain. Once again, avoid suffering *damage to image*.

This sort of jungle law has to change if security is to thrive. Fraud creates a loss for the industry as a whole. It enriches the fraudster and pushes up insurance rates. The fraudulent success encourages a whole horde to continue work at thousands of SOHOs (small office, heist ongoing) scams around the world.

Some of the force behind the 419 scam is the ability of the gang to recruit operators from all ranks to get information from inside the company. One key gang member would set up bank accounts and transfers; an IT-literate accomplice would target email users to send out millions of spam emails. Other key allies might be a secretary or cleaner who is able to garner important unshredded papers. This means that letterhead post with key names, telephone numbers, email addresses and bank account details can be collated. The financial damage to the investors can be collossal.

Our experience in Eastern Europe, Latin America and China shows us that there are millions of educated people, eager to enrich themselves on the Internet – by any means available.

There are many forms of such unscrupulous "pump and dump" investment schemes. These may fail spectacularly, although they may not be illegal as such. The dot-com bubble reminds us that some forms of pump-and-dump practice are not deemed fraudulent, and like the 419 scams, no one goes to jail. Thus, this is going to die out as long as there is free access to the Internet. Furthermore, this is one business that has become a lot easier during globalisation. Worse, many companies have insecure networked telecoms and computer technology that allow easy penetration or hacking for fraud.

Losses from the Nigerian-based 419 and associated fraudulent schemes exceed $5 billion.[5] These losses are listed in a "Loss Database", but these include only those victims who have bothered to notify the relevant authorities. Counting financial losses accurately will continue to be a problem to dog banking authorities and regulators for a long time. It cannot be done with any certainty in the emerging markets.

OPERATIONAL RISK IN EMERGING MARKETS

Our risk horizon has to be adjusted other than the orthodox investment theory advises. Banking on conventional reputation, mathematical modelling and an established legal framework all have limited use. We cannot take the quick linear, orthodox view of investment risk in the emerging markets.

---

[4] Police contacts on 419 fraud: US Secret Service at 419.fcd@usss.treas.gov or UK National Criminal Intelligence Service at 419@spring39.demon.co.uk.
[5] The 419 Coalition, Harrisonburg, VA, 22802, USA, http://home.rica.net.

Every now and then, within the flux of world history, there is a potent mix that attracts investors. It was the Asian "Tiger" economies once; then Russia, Latin America or any other emerging market that is flavour of the month. What are the come ons? Some reasons are:

- A big consumer market.
- Cheap labour.
- High foreign direct investment.
- High availability of underpriced natural resources.
- Political stability.
- Educated work force.

Parachuting in the experts

The mainstream train of building investment expertise in the emerging markets rests on the twin tracks of speed and economy. Yet, predicting major market and political movements cannot be built upon *expert local knowledge* after two days at the airport Hilton hotel. The changes just after the army onslaught on civilians in Beijing's Tien An Men Square or the events following Gorbachov's fall from power in 1990, or any Latin American putsch cannot be evaluated by an armchair expert who is in the country on a whistle-stop tour. This cannot be cost-effective in the long run as the local knowledge gained is superficial and the chances of committing market mistakes are commensurately higher.[6]

A real-life view of handling risk means messy problems – and that requires managing operational risk effectively. Many companies are poorly structured to handle operational risk overseas; in fact, they behave more like risk-ignorant investors.

CASE STUDY: CHASE MANHATTAN IN RUSSIA

One HR officer from Chase Manhattan in London was assigned to Moscow, charged with staff recruitment. The screening process is a vital risk management process, yet it was of primary importance for her that: "I don't want anyone who has worked for the KGB!"[7]

This is somewhat risk ignorant as it shows a profound lack of knowledge about Russia. The KGB trained and operated in the USSR in a variety of functions:

- Home security (FBI-like)
- Counter-intelligence (CIA-type)
- Overseas relations (Foreign Service)
- Immigration control (INS)
- Tracking movement of certain proscribed goods (ATF)

Aside from some grisly and undemocratic tasks, KGB training was generally of a high standard and aided the rise of one extremely capable president – Vladimir Putin. In some ways, dismissal of the KGB, or its successor the FSB, is not only risk ignorant, it can be a risk-seeking attitude. Cutting your nose off to spite your face is a sure way to lose good business contacts in an unfamiliar market.

So, investment analysis is made doubly hard in these countries when you have only budgeted for a short stay, and you only make contact with poorly connected local people. Finding out

---

[6] *Risk Management in Russia and the Baltic States*, Y.Y. Chong, Financial Times Publications, 1998.
[7] *Emerging Markets Forum*, London, 1997.

who owns and controls which companies becomes a headache under such limiting conditions. You may wish to scrutinise the cross-sectoral holdings of related companies within the Russian FIGs (financial industrial groups). These were like split capital funds with a similar level of opacity. They are unstable where they concentrate assets in cross-over holdings that create a spider's web of resources that can cave in, like a wobbly Korean Chaebol or Japanese Keiretsu groups. What we saw in Russia is that the FIGs possess a more opaque and unstable structure than you may initially have suspected. There is a lot of hidden wealth, but the chair may decide to keep it under wraps in cross-holdings, or sheltered offshore in Cyprus or the Bahamas.[8]

Therefore, an innocuous company collapse can have wide repercussions and threaten the survival of a large industrial sector. This same ground will be the graveyard of many a foreign fund investing in the emerging markets.

Then, everyone piles into the market, forcing up prices of stocks and bonds. The economy overheats and goes into a recession. We've seen it all before, but it will happen again. Why? To see these things in the historical context is to recount the Dutch tulip mania of the 1630s up to the dot-com craze of the late 1990s. Argentina crashed in 2001, but so has every Latin American or Asian Tiger at one time or another.

People hunt in packs, and most end up as sheep following the leader. The first ones in, and the first ones out tend to win. Those who linger too long find themselves having to pay for the drinks at the party while the more savvy guests have already left.[9]

Operational risk management trains you to think and act positively. Not doing anything to combat risk threats becomes an active way of attracting harm. In emerging markets you have to be doubly careful when you deal with the thorny issue of operational risk.

Once again, the main impediment in risk management, to prevent *damage to image* mentioned at the beginning of this chapter, remains paramount. Reputation risk is everything. No investor will confess that they have fallen victim to such an obvious and outrageous 419 scam. The registration of the bank, fund or financial adviser with the SEC or FSA is taken by some to imply that investment schemes are approved by the regulator. Under such circumstances, many people will fall victim, much money will be lost and no one will go to jail. Sounds outrageous? Believe it.

UNINTENTIONAL DAMAGE

CASE STUDY: SPLIT CAPITAL INVESTMENT FUNDS

There are often unintentional and legitimate outcomes that can cause far greater damage than outright fraud. One such ongoing case is that of the Split Capital Investment Trusts – the "splits", listed on the London Stock Exchange. A split capital trust consists of several types of shares and bonds, e.g. dividend shares, capital shares, preference shares, zero-coupons and such like. These splits have taken off over the past six years, commanding assets once valued at £12 billion. Although the risks of such investments were earlier brought into question, little was effectively done to prevent them continuing to be such a

---

[8] *Risk Management in Russia and the Baltic States*, Financial Times Publications, Y.Y. Chong, 1998.
[9] Professor Avinash Persaud, Gresham College and Managing Director, State Street Bank, London, 3 October 2002.

popular purchase.[10] See Table 8.2 for an example. Just like the "tulip mania", the splits' bubble burst and what is left is not worth more than air.

Some splits were initially marketed as a suitable and safe investment option for those who want fund growth with a relatively assured fixed return. Furthermore, many splits offered tax advantages by operating offshore. They are high-risk closed-ended funds that are not backed with security, nor do they offer swift recourse in event of failure.

Split-capital trust funds were estimated to have caused losses to some 50 000 investors in the UK. These instruments were often marketed as market risk-free instruments. Some split funds are in danger of joining the 90 % club, having lost their investors 90 % of peak value. No split fund manager ever wanted to lose their customers 90 % of their money, but the damage was real and legitimate. Private investors have lost millions due to the fall in value of the split capital funds, which were marketed as safe investments.[11]

There were also allegations of collusion by a group of funds referred to as "the magic circle", which bought stakes in each other's fund, a move that amplified the fall in values when markets turned downward.

The splits invest in other funds or splits, and also allow them to borrow in a high gearing ratio. This means that there is a "magic circle" whereby funds can hold shares in one other, and the risk exposure is localised. Thus, Fund A holds a share of Fund B; Fund B bought a share of Fund C; Fund C possesses a share of Fund A; and so on. This raises overall risk to a dangerous level, especially during a market downturn.

A Financial Services Authority (FSA) survey on a sample of splits found that they had total holdings in other splits amounting to 17 % of their gross assets. The funds with high total holdings in other splits tend also to have high levels of gearing (gross asset to debt ratio of 2.88). This left them vulnerable to adverse market movements while their level of debt remained high.[12] When markets fell down, the losses were magnified. A report noted that there were 120 splits on the London Stock Exchange, of which 40 were in financial difficulties.[13]

Splits in trouble have tended to use a complex cross-holding structure that internalises the risk exposure. When one sector collapses, it has a wide impact upon the whole fund sector. This concentrated the risks similar to the 1980s' Lloyds reinsurance failure. Investments and nepotistic risk exposure were packed in the Lloyds Names' reinsurance within the same underwriter groups syndicates. The main aim of reinsurance is to spread the risk exposure, not centralise it. Thus, a large loss event only affects many parties, and each of them to a limited and bearable extent.

Unfortunately, when the large loss risk events occur (such as Exxon Valdez sinking or Hurricane Andrew), then the exposure borne by any one party can be huge and damaging to the point of bankruptcy. These risks were not fully understood at the time, but we should have been better prepared to avoid the splits problem occurring years later.

Sadly, the likelihood is that these problematic funds or investment vehicles will continue to be offered to the public in some form or another. The regulator has downplayed the splits problem somewhat; it has reminded companies and clients that funds and advisers

---

[10] "FSA 'sat on' early alarm over £12 billion scandal", *Independent*, 11 October 2002.
[11] "Split trust lifeboat only 10 % funded", *Financial Times*, 3 May 2003.
[12] "FSA seeks views on regulation of Split Capital Investments", FSA/PN/169/2001.
[13] "Aberdeen Asset Management", *The Times Business*, 30 April 2002.

are required to comply with the FSA's Principles for Businesses, of which Principle 1 is "Integrity".[14] Ironically, this is almost identical to the primary motive for instigating risk management, namely limiting *"damage to image"*. A PR drive can move you to carry out cosmetic changes rather than to address the fundamental root causes of the problem.

The last line of caution against the 419 carries the financial health warning that could apply equally to split capital funds:

"NEVER rely on YOUR Government to bail you out."[15]

It is quite worrying that most private investors think that market regulators are here to protect them against such frauds, and that most of their money will be safe. We sometimes get more return from the Tooth Fairy.

Table 8.2   A typical 419-type fund operating in the West

National advertisement		Notes
"A WONDERFUL SAVINGS PLAN FOR THE FUTURE."	1	Another big come-on.
Dear Investor,	2	Big upside lure.
Take advantage of big end of tax year savings from our fund. Beat the tax man and cash in on tax-free good returns		
We are xxx Split Capital Fund. We have discovered new ways to invest your money in a secure and tax-efficient manner.	3	Invitation to safe collaboration.
Our fund offers tax-free accounts which are managed by our team of professionals. We invest them in a wide portfolio of fund investments to keep up the value of your money.	4	There is little or no downside risk. Reiterate the big ££ gain.
We offer you a chance to transfer your money into xxx Fund account at an introductory rate 2 %, plus 0.5 % management fee p.a.	5	Your part in the legal investment.
Xxx Fund only invests in secure allocation of investments to preserve the value of our portfolio. Our 1999 performance showed a fund growth of 25 % over the previous year.	6	Calming reassurance. It's a sure-fire investment scheme.
To start your account, you only need from £100 in the account listed below. So please reply before the end of tax year!	7	A small realistic sum to get the investors into the net.
We are a City-based company with offshore operations and we manage £x billions of investor funds.	8	The come-on: good reputation and performance
Our team of professionals will be happy to speak to you and handle your queries in confidence on our Freephone 0800 TRUST-US.	9	Reassurance again.
Xxx Fund is regulated by the Financial Services Authority.	10	Assurance of operational propriety.
Note: Shares can go up as well as down. Previous performance is no guarantee . . .	11	Caveat: Your cut of the profits (or losses).
We welcome you to take part in the security of our investment fund. Xxx Split Capital Investments	12	Final assurance and contact details.

[14] "Split capital problems confined to a minority, says FSA", FSA/PN/053/2002, 16 May 2002.
[14] The 419 Coalition, Harrisonburg, VA, 22802, USA, http://home.rica.net.

Rogue staff

Fraud or theft at banks, pension funds, offices, stores and warehouses can be rife. It is not something that any company would like to talk about much. In fact, many companies are happier to sweep it under the carpet (see: Reputation risk).

> *Not uncommon are cases when theft is committed by the personnel. Foreign businesses do not often do special pre-screening of their personnel before hiring them. They do not always keep records of the personnel's passport details, or their residential addresses – which complicates the search for thieves.*
>
> *Swindling is also a common crime. . . . Even though there may be a court judgement, it still does not facilitate the recovery of money or assets stolen through swindling.*[16]

While modern businesses are swift to criticise the harshness of the Russian mafia threat, there has been little advance on handling fraud loss in the West itself. The problem is worse when the theft or misappropriation of funds is done at the top of the management hierarchy. One extreme example is the Enron case where parties at the top managed to effect a large-scale fraud on a business that was worth only a fraction of its stated worth while it was operating. At its demise, Enron's net worth became negative – a monumental example of reputation risk.

Exposure to fraud at the top

The operational room for fraud and loss becomes larger as the responsibility rises. Thus, top managers dealing with larger departments or huge budgets are not necessarily scrutinised more thoroughly per se. There is some degree of scrutiny over the CV and a large dependency on the outcome of the job interview, but deeper checks into the CV and character references are perfunctory in many cases.[17]

This is ghastly news because staff recruitment is key to development of a company.

> *Effective personnel selection for hiring and promotion is critical for the management of the most important risks faced in many financial services organisations, the risk of poor work performance, staff turnover, and employee fraud.*[18]

Risk monitoring and risk management should be conducted deeper, more frequently and also reach to the top.

> *The board of directors should ensure that the bank's operational risk management framework is subject to effective and comprehensive internal audit by operationally independent, appropriately trained and competent staff. The internal audit function should not be responsible for operational risk management.*[19]

The game is lost already if the regulator does not impose punitive damages on top management. Thus, everyone else in the corporate elite will take it as a clear sign that a rap on the knuckles is worth the risk of high stakes in crooked profit.

---

[16] *Risk Management in Russia and the Baltic States*, Y.Y. Chong, Financial Times Publications, 1998.

[17] "Veritas CFO resigns after lying about MBA degree", *Associated Press Business*, 3 October, 2002.

[18] "*Measuring and Managing Operational Risk in Financial Institutions*", C. Marshall, Wiley, 2001.

[19] *Sound Practices for the Management and Supervision of Operational Risk*, Bank of International Settlements, July 2002.

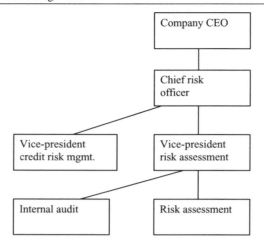

Figure 8.2   Risk-managed organisational structure (extract)
Source: "GARP Risk Review", Global Association of Risk Professionals, March–April 2002.

Think of restructuring the company remuneration system so that it does not reward losing shareholders' value. Otherwise, instead of paying key staff a large salary, consider "locking" them in through:

• Payment in shares of company, as a risk burden (if it is a dud company, they get paid in dud shares).
• Pay in part- or phased payment by performance hurdles.
• Lock in service for years, i.e. impose corporate contractual "handcuffs".

Nevertheless, despite these precautions, staff errors do arise. For example, a key staff member loses a lap-top with crucial data, or leaves for a rival company – neither is a criminal act. There is, as yet, no effective legislative countermeasure. Destroying a company's value through the poor decisions of directors and CEOs falls in this category.

How to incriminate the culprit directors and CEOs? One improvement since the pre-Enron days is that regulators now seek greater protection for evidence and whistle-blowers. An external audit or an oversight committee did not help control WorldCom since most of the errors originated at the top of the hierarchy. A stronger control structure could have possibly exercised more restraint (see: Risk-managed organisational structure).[20] Yet, we are unsure of true risk management effectiveness where this is a purely superficial or corporate PR feature.

Corporate America has been quick to portray the oversight or internal audit committee as a panacea for curing the operational risk ills of an insider job. Seeing that the CEO has unsurpassed decision-making powers over the chief risk officer (see Figure 8.2), we must conclude that this leader must direct risk management with sincerity and effectiveness. Otherwise, the oversight committee and risk management exercises become mere rubber-stamps for the CEO's decisions.

The Enron catastrophe illustrated the authority of the CEO above all risk officers. Until the Enron case is resolved in full, it is unclear whether the law courts will decide that it was

---

[20] Securities and Exchange Commission, Litigation Release No. 17588, 27 June 2002.

an example of fraud on a huge scale, or corporate misrepresentation. The shades of grey in between are blurred by the imagination of company executives. One of the best barometers for checking the patient's financial health is the examination of the annual accounting report. This is the remit of the auditor.

Accounts are prone to misrepresentation if the corporate environment is lax. Legal flexibility permits annual reports to be cosmetically amended. It is easy enough to draw up an audit that is deemed to give a "fair and accurate view" of a corporation's financial health at any given point in time. Booking sales in a convenient time period, or valuing assets leave a lot of leeway. Even the "best" accounting firm can make huge mistakes. Currently, there is a major lawsuit in different parts of the world against most of the Big Four accounting firms.[21]

The possibility of companies failing completely after receiving good pictures of health in audited accounts is now very real. It need not be an accountant's criminal activity or conspiracy for two reasons:

1) The auditing company wants to get repeat business to conduct the accounts examination the following year, so it gives a more glowing picture than prudent. Most audits are labour-intensive exercises that have a low profit margin.
2) The company being audited may wish to withhold or misrepresent some data for the accountant. This can be done easily because everyone knows the date when accounts have to be filed and the format in which they need to be presented. Even the most diligent auditor may be caught off-guard.

It is a good training exercise for staff in risk management to log errors and losses. Formulate, or refer to these previous auditing mistakes and fraud incidents in a loss database. These can serve as alarm bells for systemic error or fraud. The line between fraud and misbehaviour relies on the burden of proof. When fraud risk is involved, the burden of proof is likely to be more difficult to define than for underperformance.

Exposure to fraud lower down the rung

We have discussed in the previous cases, organisational errors at Barings and AIB providing fertile ground for operational risk long before the star dealers became "rogue traders". The structure of the banks was a ready-made breeding ground for such errant behaviour. Rogue trading is a high-profile risk, but it is much less prevalent than other errors within the organisation, such as the usual back-office mistakes.

Yet look at the most developed Western banks, where the "superstar" recruitment system exists. It was apparent from the Barings, Deutsche Morgan Grenfell or AIB that there are occasional shortfalls between one's claimed trading profits and the real trading positions. Nick Leeson took over control of Barings Singapore, even with no real experience in trading. While he was head of both front-office trading and back-office accounts, the profits kept rolling in. You can shut your eyes to risks you have decided you do not want to see. The reputation of Barings, known before as the bank of kings and queens, sank almost without trace. Sadly, reputation is no guarantee of risk-managed performance.

---

[21] *The Times*, Business, 16 April 2002.

CASE STUDY: DEUTSCHE MORGAN-GRENFELL, 1996

In September 1996, irregularities were discovered in the management of the funds of the Morgan Grenfell subgroup of Deutsche bank in the UK. From 1994, the funds had become more concentrated in risky investments of unlisted securities, despite anti-concentration financial regulations. Rules were circumvented by Peter Young, who set up holding companies to hide his tracks. These companies took over the troubled securities of the fund and hid them. Peter Young was accused of setting up false Luxembourg-based accounts as a special-purpose vehicle (SPV) to hide these losses.[22]

SPVs can prove useful, but they are also open to abuse. Enron used the same tactic with SPVs years later. SPVs will recur in some future investment disasters because they are difficult to legislate against.

The real barrier to enforcing effective control over the complex myriad of financial threats is a knowledgeable and proactive management. This ranges from high-fliers in treasury or mergers and acquisitions to the secretarial pool. Such is the concept of "enterprise-wide risk management" (ERM).[23]

A risk-conscious organisation should actively inculcate key risk management competencies, tips and skills across all departments, not just a few high-profile areas. This fundamental business culture mitigates against risk. A lax business environment is replete with various risk-ignorant platitudes, such as:

- "Not my problem".
- "Don't bother me now, my annual bonus is up next month".
- "Pay back-office peanuts because they don't make us profits".

But, if an organisation wants to create an effective management system team, it requires an adequate business culture as opposed to a group of selfish actors in a comedy. This effective culture rests loosely on informal risk management guidelines. Formal measures for developing risk-conscious staff need much more planning and investment.[24] Unfortunately, it is a labour-intensive and potentially costly enterprise-wide activity that is most likely to be scaled-down during a poor economic cycle.

Thus, risk management applies to the whole organisation, not just the trading room. Effective management guidelines within the company team structure are more effective than throwing money, technology or an internal police force to control the risk problem.[25] These risk guidelines have to be tailored in the modern commercial world. There is no adequate "one-size-fits-all" rule for dealing with operational risk.

AN OPERATIONAL RISK PERSPECTIVE

The investment errors from taking a wrong bet on interest rates, Forex and other price movements were lumped together under the convenient opt-out label of "market risk". The market

---

[22] "Night of the regulators," *Global Custodian*, spring 1997.
[23] *"How Safe is Safe Enough"*, ch.8, Institute of Actuaries, 12 June 2001.
[24] "Finding the truth", Maxima Risk Management, www.Maxima-group.com.
[25] "Informal risk management guidelines", p. 147, in *Measuring and Managing Operational Risk in Financial Institutions*, C. Marshall, Wiley, 2001.

is not a living creature: it is neither malicious nor benevolent. The investment errors are purely the result of human action. Once human control becomes too lax and there is a systemic pattern of errors, then these mistakes can become categorised under corporate operational risk (OpRisk).

Operational risk protection: the "roof"

Finding out who, where, when and how much damage was caused is an expensive and labour-intensive risk management process. Most companies are in a downsizing cycle – paring costs by cutting personnel across the board. By doing so, they may be increasing operational risk while reducing operating costs.[26] Key knowledge workers with crucial client links and process innovators can be lost amongst those trimmed off as obvious corporate "fat". A reduced ability to meet customers face to face, relegating them to voice-mail and websites, can harm customer satisfaction and disrupt the revenue stream.

There is a divorce between risk horizons, cutting operating costs while increasing long-run costs to regain the lost customer base and to recover key staff. A short-run good-risk move becomes a long-term strategic nightmare.

There are many ways of handling this risk. But, this presumes that the company has the risk awareness to want to manage risk at all. One thing to do is to receive the correct market intelligence, which is especially true in developing countries. Damage-limitation, or control against accidents, is essential. In Russia, such protection is often called a "krisha" or roof – a device to ward off unwelcome attention from the Mafia gangs. There will be strong incentives to build a strong "roof" against local anti-social elements – such as the Nigerian 419-scam gang members. The roof protects us from the outside. In the West, most of the damage threat comes from inside.

This is the crux of the problem; most of the roofs are "pointing" the wrong way – they are designed to protect against damage from the external sources. Unfortunately, much of Western mainstream risk management has been trained on deliberate fraud from the outside. The damage coming from inside the company is less acknowledged. That is why we have been slow to focus on investment threats that originate from the CEO and the company leaders.[27]

Furthermore, some company "accidents" have been either unknown or swept under the carpet, so we remain unaware of the business losses.

Under the new Basel II banking regulations, there will be drives to force the company to record the full extent of financial damage within the loss database. The lack of experience of companies and the market watchdogs to process this database comprehensively will continue to be a challenge. There will be obstacles when a company does not have adequately skilled staff, or the board of directors remains unwilling to detail the full financial losses. Further design and documentation problems remain for this valuable information.[28] The board has to act positively to support risk management initiatives if it is to succeed.

This power of the board to create corporate wealth, and also to cause damage is a forceful factor to concentrate the investor's mind. Shareholders have concentrated on the leaders' wealth-creation abilities, less on their risk management prowess.

---

[26] "Managing people costs", Towers-Perrin Insurance, www.towers.com, 2002.
[27] "Can auditors detect fraud: a review of the research evidence", C. Albrecht, W. Albrecht and J. Dunn, *Journal of Forensic Accounting*, Vol.2, 2001.
[28] "Overcoming the practical challenges of implementing an Integrated Loss Database", ABN AMRO, Infoline Conference, London, 5 June 2003.

... clear strategies and oversight by the board of directors and senior management, an operational risk culture and internal control culture (including, among other things, clear lines of responsibility and segregation of duties), effective internal reporting and contingency planning are all crucial components of an effective operational risk management framework.[29]

While the board of directors continues to act selfishly to feather its nest, it has also been under spotlight of new corporate governance measures. Underperforming company leaders have to be tracked and reprimanded. Use of organic risk management procedures focus upon the real added-value (or Alpha factor) from a company's leaders.

One step has been to monitor the financial news and to use all avenues of public expression. Shareholders have finally started to show their dissatisfaction by actively voting against the party line at the company AGM. Investor inertia has been shrugged off eventually in the GSK (GlaxoSmithKline) case, and the shareholders voted in the majority against the generous remuneration package of Jean-Pierre Garnier, estimated at $35 million in event of a pay-off for a lost job.[30]

Investors are now looking for Alpha, or the company manager's contribution to the value of the firm. The quest for Alpha is detailed at the end of this chapter, together with control structures for maintaining performance. The days of a carte blanche for the CEO continue, but they are numbered while shareholders look out for freeriders.

INVESTMENT PROJECT GROWTH

The crux of the matter is that most projects run in a cycle (Figure 8.3) that stems from the initial love affair with those controlling the investment. The life cycle of an investment project often runs in an unpredictable manner. As we have seen, RAMP (risk analysis and management

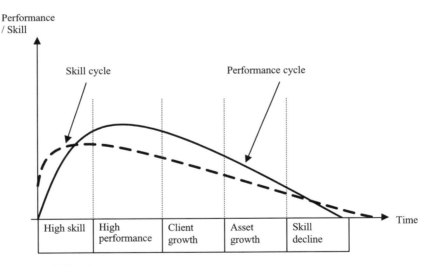

Figure 8.3   The skill cycle
Source: *Concept of Investment Efficiency*, Institute of Actuaries, p. 52, 28 February 2001.

---

[29] *Sound Practices for the Management and Supervision of Operational Risk*, Bank of International Settlements, February 2003.
[30] "Pay deal question goes to the heart of capitalism", *Financial Times*, 21 May 2003.

for projects) is one methodology that seeks to put a control structure around such a project.[31] Arthur Andersen was often enthusiastic in pushing its view of this progression within a "journey management" philosophy. The journey runs a perilous course across twin rocks of company failure and false protection of reputational hubris.

Some call this business cycle inevitable, but investors keep being caught out by the downturn. The investment honeymoon seems to be over.

Phase 1: High skill

This is generally the hard-slog period when the business grows through sheer sweat and toil. Self-doubt crops up, partial failures happen, but the idea eventually grows into a success. "Things can only get better" was chanted by the UK Labour Party during the 2001 elections.

Every company that is drilling for natural resources, or seeking the Midas touch in biotechnology, runs upon this attitude. There is a goodwill asset, or hope capital, that is limited. The investor needs a cautious optimism, tempered with a stiff dose of realism.

Phase 2: High performance

The company displays confident growth and has already gained an impressive reputation in the market.

The company success empowers the CEO to take fairly major corporate decisions without effective control under such an aura of personal infallibility. But, leadership turnover at CEO level in the FTSE and S&P 500 firms shows that such a honeymoon phase is short and transient. The UK tenure for big firm CEOs is typically becoming a one-year contract. The American average is often three years. Such short contracts may well encourage the bosses to squeeze the most compensation from the company before making an early exit.

A sense of proportion is the first casualty during the early weeks of corporate bliss. Further good returns gloss over the risks that accumulate *sub rosa*. The company key sponsors reach for higher profits, and the CEO is generally keen to promise them.

Phase 3: Client growth

A company boasts an excellent track record performance during its previous phases, and emphasising its impeccable credentials. Thus, as an enterprise that could not fail, LTCM (Long-Term Capital Management) won respectability by having a Nobel prize-winner on the board, while relegating corporate governance and transparency to the side-lines.

Similarly, the UK property boom (1998–2002) followed in the same pattern: over-indebtedness, aggravated by excessive leverage on mortgages. The UK household sector debt-to-income ratio rose to a record 1.20 during 2002.[32] Corporate debt-profit ratios rose to record levels as UK companies were betting in similar games. Gambling on continuing rises in property prices by the public are funded by the banks. When the real estate bubble bursts, there is a rush for the door at the same time. Exit prices for assets collapse. Eventually, the market returns to fundamental valuations after retreating from this unstable buying mania.

---

[31] *Risk Analysis and Management for Projects*, Thomas Telford, 1998.
[32] "UK corporate debt-to-profits and household sector debt-to-income ratio", Chart O, *Financial Stability Review*, Bank of England, June 2002.

Another parallel can be drawn with the inertia of governments and companies regarding pension provisions. The matter is very politically complex, and a clear-cut picture is not yet discernible. Yet, corporate pensions costs continue to rise while contributions become ever more inadequate to fund them.[33] People still pile in and hope for fundamental problems to solve themselves.

Phase 4: Asset growth

This phase signals the prickly problem of matching over-expansion against performance. Management egos grow until the first cracks appear.

CASE STUDY: SOROS QUANTUM FUND AND BUFFETT'S BERKSHIRE HATHAWAY

These funds handled some of the biggest budgets anywhere in financial world. Unfortunately, having stalled in performance against key benchmarked funds, many investors started to feel that the fund management was being too cautious or had lost its "star picking" gifts. Some investment pickers performed better at this time, including many of the dot-com pushers.

Both Soros and Buffett grew to the point where their funds were becoming somewhat unmanageable, and their footprints were too big. Hunting a top "star" pick is fine in the heydays, but not when all other investors are hearing your footfall a mile off. Soros' Quantum Fund and Berkshire Hathaway grew rapidly, but were not returning good profits. Some fund investors decided it was time to get out of cycle before the stampeding herd.

It is ironic that Warren Buffett was proven correct in his gut-reaction not to trust the company PR and spin, and to focus upon its leaders and product. Unfortunately, we live in a modern age where corporate image is used as a substitute for risk management. Thus, Martha Stewart rose to dizzy heights and wealth with her Omnimedia company. Her indictment by the SEC has caused considerable damage to her reputation and company share price.[34] Image is everything, and damage to image is the worst sin of all.

Phase 5: Skill decline

"TBTF" (too big to fail) is often heard in this phase to dismiss lingering doubts. It is a mantra to invoke some sort of investor protection. Companies can outlive their usefulness and profitability for years. Institutionalised ideas can survive as old habits die hard. Middle-office analysts and auditors who keep a pessimistic eye are still unpopular up to this point. Risk management, like auditing, is viewed as a boring exercise and an unnecessary cost, so we have to keep down costs.

The wealth may have been built up by many, but it can also be eroded by a few leaders. The main investors and the public remain blissfully ignorant of deeper problems within this asymmetry of information. The accumulated goodwill, the company reputation, is the anchor upon which the ship is securely moored.

---

[33] "Corporate pensions – nest eggs without the yolk: can employers be trusted to provide for our old age?", *The Economist*, 10 May 2003.
[34] "Martha Stewart: it's not a good thing", *The Economist*, 7 June 2003.

It is almost impossible to face up to the need to write off your hard-won personal and financial investment, especially your reputation. Ebner at WorldCom, Skilling at Enron had brilliant reputations – theirs was the business model to follow. Some very capable and honest staff worked at Enron and Worldcom, they become tarred with the same brush. These people need to be separated from the dross in organic risk management through proper interviewing and screening.[35]

INVESTOR RISK SKILLS

Investors can learn risk awareness by following a logical series of business procedures under organic risk management.

- Pre-screening key insider staff and implementing tough recruitment procedures.
- Pre-screening counter-parties with a proper due diligence, not a quick once-over or a nod and a wink.
- Proper due diligence in new business areas, e.g. emerging markets or emerging technologies such as biotechnology or Internet start-ups.
- Practising adequate mandate-risk management – keeping up to date with risk studies. Logging breaches of fiduciary duty and complying with new guidelines for corporate governance.
- Locking investment parties using cash-shells instead of fully fledged IPOs for companies.
- Locking in key personnel in the company's service through staged payments for challenging performance-related pay.

Investment management skills in the market

The single biggest source of business failure is the people involved in the process. Organic risk management recognises that people are our greatest asset, but also our biggest threat. Going with the investment "professionals" is not a risk-averse action because many of these "experts" are offering a veneer of good reputation. Furthermore, the inability of the regulators to enforce effective punishment means that we have to educate the investor and the risk manager to recognise the inept professional.

Warren Buffett tends to shy away from the advice of "professionals" who have vested interests at stake. This is the first phase or analytical stage of organic risk management. This is based upon the fundamental worth of the company's product of service.

Buffett proposes a slimmed-down due-diligence process, not the heavy-weight, inept and expensive process favoured by the "professionals". This is the second stage of organic risk management where deeper checking or forensic investigation is carried out. Face-to-face questioning gives a better judgement than the outsourced assessment or telephone discussion. He feels that this is a better way to sort out the wheat from the chaff – to remove those capable business managers from the misleading background noise of corporate PR and misrepresentation. There is no secret to Warren Buffett's time-honoured value investing – he does not look for the quick speculative gain on a "sexy" stock, just an undervalued one.

---

[35] "Finding the truth", Maxima Risk Management, www.Maxima-group.com.

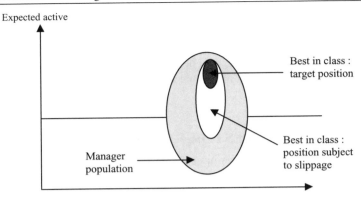

Figure 8.4   Investment manager universe
Source: *Concept of Investment Efficiency*, Institute of Actuaries, p. 57, 28 February 2001.

Hiring star managers and CEOs

Warren Buffett shuns paying large fees or "golden hellos" to attract the best individual manager – certainly if they appear only for a short-term service. Yet, this is what many banks do when they routinely poach other bank's key stars. This just increases the operating costs of the company and depresses the annual return to the shareholders. Yes, there is an extremely narrow distribution of investment skills (see Figure 8.4) worth recruiting, but many of these skills are transient and not innate. Figure 8.4 shows us empirically what is true – Lady Luck (and fundamental investment skill) comes only to a few.

There is a rare investor animal that is innately a very good fund manager or CEO. But, they are confused with a secondary layer of managers who are also perceived as "best in the class". The problem with this secondary tier is that of "slippage" where after a stellar year of success, another year's performance falls below the performance benchmark set. Furthermore, high welcoming pay encourages the unhealthy notion that a "star" can drop in and suddenly drop out with profitable consequences for that person, and damaging results for the company.

Maturing and taking a realistic market view is a valuable asset as Buffett has found. One pitfall is the self-delusion that many investors carry; they aim at outperforming within a market through leverage. It is easy to forget that leverage can only be justified by having better skills than the average market player. Otherwise, we take unacceptably high risks. A profit obtained by leverage is only due to the loss of other market participants. The self-styled winning trader who conceals losses (like Leeson, Hamanaka or Rusnak) defers being found out for the time being. They go deeper into "double-or-quits" gambling to hide or recoup their losses. As we have argued, these egregious risk-seeking punts will continue so long as banks operate a "star" trader system.[36]

Investment managers and governance

The investment managers and governance bodies seek to put an ongoing control structure for a fund to make self-sustaining returns. An investment governance structure that manages risk as an ongoing process is shown in Figure 8.5.

---

[36] *The Management of Risks in Banking*, J.N. Allan et al., Institute of Actuaries, 23 February 1998.

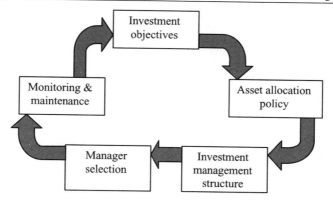

Figure 8.5   Asset planning cycle
Source: *Concept of Investment Efficiency*, Institute of Actuaries, p. 7, 28 February 2001.

This management format gets us past misleading background noise and self-publicity. Furthermore, we can use the concept of diversification to hire a pool of managers so that some will still remain stars, even through difficult years. The research findings are:

> When grouped in a portfolio, uncorrelated, high-performing, risky managers can result in a high return, low risk layer.[37]

So, some banks and funds have been on the wrong track racing to recruit the single "best" type of winning trader. It would be better to hire a mix of dealers. You can hire tiger investors to mix in a fund manager pool, and end up with wise owl profits. This can accompany comparatively low or acceptable risk levels. Mixing the different investor animals can create a better recipe for success.

Creating a winning fund management team

The star system of hiring the best trading staff has been called into question. This is because the star system is focused upon perceived reputation and Alpha α (the net fund return minus benchmark return). Forward-looking companies recognise the defects of the star system, so they are adopting more holistic (i.e. organic) views of risk.[38]

Thus, they also include the wider risk factor analysis of:

- standard deviation of Alpha α (tracking error).
- Theta θ (non-financial factors).

Theta takes behavioural (organic risk management) themes for investment managers to include:

- **SleepWell** – benefits for the investment manager's trustee to have a comfortable knowledge that risk is not too much, and that the investment manager is not unsuitable.
- **SeemsGood** – peer view of the investment manager's profits; these may be based on unsound knowledge or bias that leads to manager's underperforming returns.

---

[37] *Concept of Investment Efficiency*, p. 66, Institute of Actuaries, 28 February 2001.
[38] *"Structured Alpha: A Practical Application for Institutional Funds"*, Watson Wyatt, December 1999.

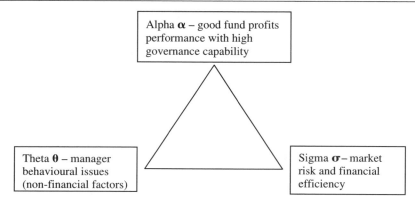

Figure 8.6   Integrating investment risk with return

Influential players like Warren Buffett seek the fundamental SleepWell qualities of fund management. When companies are not performing, he can utilise his Kalashknikov pen and paper to fire off vitriolic correspondence to effect higher standards of corporate governance and higher returns.

Unfortunately, many of the perceived wonder capabilities of top management are predicated upon the more ephemeral SeemsGood corporate leadership skills. Separate the true star managers from the also-rans. A quest for true investment style over perceived image is another way of expressing this is discrimination. Therefore, a suitable investment style derives consistent returns, even in difficult markets.

> A fund manager may have the highest calibre staff, the best computer systems and an honest approach to clients. But if they have not had the right style approach over the past few years, all the technical expertise in the world will not have helped their performance.[39]

So, we have an integrated organic map for the investment manager's risk-return characteristics (Figure 8.6). This is not too different from the Basel II "Three Pillars" structure for viewing risk-facing banks.

Building for investment resilience

A strong business system is built on solid foundations, the first being good staff. Theta, the manager behavioural skills that are not expressable in the company balance-sheet, needs to be hired – this is the role for organic risk management. This requires the identification of the skilled manager that we want – instead of hiring the manager who SeemsGood. See Table 8.3.

Moving ahead from the investment herd

Investment orthodoxy and traditional risk management in MBA courses often do not work well in practice. This is clearly seen when handling new financial instruments, or dealing with emerging market risk. Promised returns meet real uncertainties full-on despite the wealth of academic knowledge from the experts. Financial experts who trumpet their own skills from the

---

[39] "Investment strategy: getting the right style approach", *Financial Times*, 21 May 2003.

Table 8.3   Fund management control

Governance model	Features	Likely manager
Investment sub-committee and executive	Well resourced Focus on performance Capacity to select a large number of managers	All manager types can be used
Investment committee	Reasonably resourced Focus on performance and safety Capacity to select and monitor a few managers	Passive and active fund manager core
Single group or boards of trustees	Limited time resources Focus on safety and due diligence Capacity to select and monitor a small number of managers	Passive and active fund manager core

Source: *Structured Alpha: A Practical Application for Institutional Funds*, Watson Wyatt, December 1999.

roof-tops soon fail to maintain their reputation. Good investigative organic risk management can remove their undeserved reputation. Finding out the investor's active return, or alpha, is one good method to temper their ploy. Pursuing alpha is better than the current investment orthodoxy that is "gold-plating". Launching an IPO, a new bond issue, or conducting a company due diligence along orthodox lines includes:

- Hiring the "best" investment bank to lead the project.
- Buying the "best" and most expensive management consultancy for their excellent technical advice.
- Engaging the top law firm to negotiate and draft contracts.
- Picking the top accountants to examine the books and financial numbers.
- . . . .and so on.

This "best of breed" business philosophy is merely gold-plating the expenses bill. It's time to herd up our lost sheep, for we have lost sight of what risk management truly involves.

RECAP ON OPERATIONAL RISK

There are several risks that face any company, and mainstream risk management up to now has focused on market risk and credit risk. These have not necessarily been the most important risk factors that have caused us the most problems or financial damage within recent corporate history. Two problems associated with OpRisk management were a lack of a standard business definition for operational risk, and an absence of an industry standard for its risk management.

Yet, leaders of the risk management pack have given a wake-up call for the business community signalling recognition of the importance or staff recruitment and training. Basel II regulations even provides financial incentives to improve a company's OpRisk management. Basel II offers guidelines for greater publication of company's performance and relative operating risk level, plus driving for market transparency. This moves us closer to equalising the asymmetric distribution of corporate information, from the company leaders to the investors.

Thus, outsiders (including the shareholders) do not agree that hiring a star fund manager is a safe decision only to be made by the committee of old boys. Neither is finding a suitable CEO and drafting appropriate remuneration packages a mere task reserved for those in the "know". Some CEO remunerative packages are obscure and are a deliberate move against corporate transparency.[40] The search for real leadership value, or Alpha, has already started in many shareholder initiatives.

Within operational risk, there is a large area for handling the hazards presented by the behaviour and decisions of humans – dealt by organic risk management. Organic risk management and its forensic investigation component zeroes in on the desired human skill elements to derive true value for what you pay for. This operational risk management screening process guides you to separate the true financial skills from the background noise, and to distinguish the specious SeemsGood management abilities from those skills that enable the investor to SleepWell at night.

Operational risk management involves identifying the relevant risk factors, and deploying the appropriate risk countermeasures. It never includes writing a blank cheque for the most expensive services. Fraud from external sources may once have been perceived as the main threat. Now, we see that some of the biggest threats to business are committed by "our own side", and these damages may not even be deemed criminal.

Organic risk management is expressively for assessing and controlling the business hazards posed by human beings. Recognising these risks, we stand a much better chance of spotting the real business dangers ahead.

---

[40] "Stock option accounting can be materially misleading", D. Crumbley and N. Apostolou, *Journal of Forensic Accounting*, Vol.3, 2002.

9

The Basel II Banking Regulations

CURRENT BANKING PROBLEMS

The banking system comprises a set of vulnerable processes. The most frequently cited weaknesses in banks in one example included:[1]

- non-existent, weak or waived covenants;
- indefinite or over liberal payment terms;
- inadequate financial analysis;
- insufficient collateral support;
- elevated leverage ratios;
- repayment dependent on highly optimistic or undemonstrated cash flows.

The resulting credit risk manifested itself when 59 % of poorly rated loans had been rated as approved in the previous year. Furthermore, 14 % of the negatively rated loans were initially approved to new borrowers. This means that banks are taking on new loans without proper risk analysis to check credit suitability. These inadequate procedures will come back to haunt the bank, its investors and regulators.

The current Basel I banking regulations are criticised as operating too inflexibly in the one-size-fits-all fashion. An across-the-board 8 % capital adequacy ratio makes no discrimination between a well risk-managed bank and one that is not. The areas of banking vulnerability outlined above are not addressed adequately by Basel I. How is the new Basel II going to tackle these weaknesses?

BASEL II – A BRIEF OVERVIEW

The new Basel Capital Accord rules are commonly known as "Basel II" after their author – the Basel Committee for Banking Supervision (BCBS). These rules are designed ensure that the world financial markets operate properly with a good level of risk management. The Basel Capital Accord rules for capital adequacy assist all financial bodies to manage financial risks – market, credit and operational risks, see Figure 9.1. Basel II does not change the handling of market risk substantially; it makes considerable amendments in the treatment of credit risk; it creates a completely new inclusion for the management of operational risk. We focus on operational risk.

National regulators, EU and financial agencies such as the UK FSA will use the Basel II guidelines to formulate their own financial laws. Only 20 internationally active US banks will operate along Basel II rules. Basel II will enable financial regulators to monitor and intervene so that the procedural weaknesses do not cause the banks to become terminal cases.

The latest rules will change management of capital and risk within financial institutions. There will be an immediate need to create new business processes, training and IT systems.

---

[1] "Lending and Credit Risk Management Conference", J. L. Williams, Office of the Comptroller of the Currency, 5 October 1999.

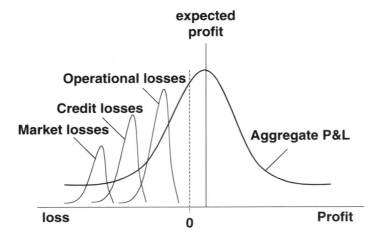

Figure 9.1   Market, Credit and Operational risk losses

These will be driven by three sets of directives or "Three Pillars". We can think of Basel II as a three-legged stool where all regulatory pillars are linked as shown in Figure 9.2.

1. Pillar one: capital requirements

The first pillar is the capital adequacy ratio (CAR) of capital that *all* the private banks must hold in reserve. Just like the high-street retail store, a bank has to keep reserves in order to cover future losses. This capital is often regarded by many banks as idle or "dead" capital – it could be making profits elsewhere.

The Basel Committee is now reluctant to adhere to any "one size fits all" scenario in risk management. The uniform 8 % CAR for all banks is dropped by Basel. This 8 % is still kept for banks and funds that do not want to want to move from the lowest level of risk management at the basic level. It permits them to remain with the old Basel I rules.

There is the potential discouragement of increased CAR for non-compliant banks, backed up with the incentive of lower CAR for those achieving the higher risk management levels of Basel II. The Basel Committee reverses the direction of development from the former decrees of Basel I. Thus, it gives the chance for banks to prove that they are more risk-compliant by allowing them to develop their own mathematically based financial models.

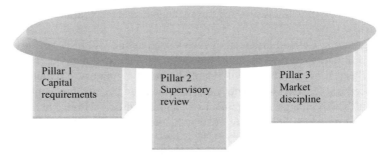

Figure 9.2   Basel II structure – the Three Pillars

Table 9.1   Levels of risk management

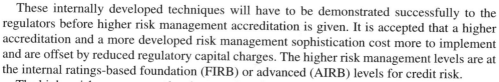

	Low development	Average development	High development
Credit risk	Standardised	FIRB	AIRB
Operational risk	Basic	Standard	Advanced

Risk management sophistication

These internally developed techniques will have to be demonstrated successfully to the regulators before higher risk management accreditation is given. It is accepted that a higher accreditation and a more developed risk management sophistication cost more to implement and are offset by reduced regulatory capital charges. The higher risk management levels are at the internal ratings-based foundation (FIRB) or advanced (AIRB) levels for credit risk.

The higher risk management levels are at the advanced measurement approach (AMA) level for operational risk.

A financial institution can choose to progress to the levels of risk management that it aims for. See Table 9.1.

The new capital requirements will differ greatly between industries and also between companies. The IRB-advanced approach uses a summation of all the constituent risks throughout the business lines.

$$\text{Capital requirement } (K) = \text{Sum } [\text{Exposure indicator } (EI) \times \text{Probability of default } (PD)$$
$$\times \text{ Loss given default } (LGD)] \text{ for all business lines}$$

Basel II intends this contingency risk capital in the CAR to be granular, i.e. proportional to the bank's evaluated risk rating. Thus, the bank's handling of credit and market risk must satisfy the regulators to put a commensurate amount of capital in reserve. "Risky" banks must leave more capital assets in reserve. There are going to be obvious areas of argument for banks that feel hard done by an excessive *EI*, *PD* or *LGD* that is given by the supervisor. It will be the beginning of a long train of negotiation with the supervisor as to what these ratios should be.

2. Pillar two: supervisory review

Banks must meet the new Basel-recommended operational risk (OpRisk) requirements that have been tailored by the host country. There is an OpRisk capital increase and market risk charge for "risky" banks. The banks with lower OpRisk ratings will have lower insurance premiums. It is just like any car driver with a better road record – a "bad" driver has to pay more insurance premium.

Conversely, a better risk-managed bank that conforms to IRB Advanced level can benefit from a −2 % reduction in its overall capital requirement, see Figure 9.3.[2]

A supervisor may feel that, after risk review, the bank should allocate more capital in reserve under Pillar One. The regulator can enforce sanctions where necessary to cajole the bank into adopting stronger OpRisk management procedures. The supervisor should not have to, but it could revoke the banking licence as the ultimate sanction when there is no attempt at improvement. The better risk-managed banks will have major competitive advantages over rivals.

---

[2] 'Supplementary Information on QIS3', Basel Committee on Banking Supervision, 27 May 2003.

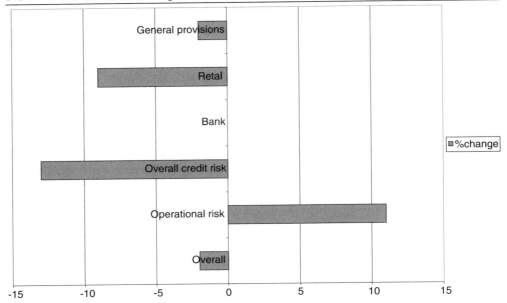

Figure 9.3   Changes to capital requirements at IRB Advanced

3. Pillar three: market discipline

Banks must fulfil the Basel requirements for disclosing company data in a strategic move to ensure greater market transparency. The banks will have to reveal more information of the sources of their profits and losses. A supervisor may recommend that the bank's weak P&L account indicates a need for more capital allocation under Pillar One.

This analysis creates increased disclosure of banks' capital structure and risk exposures. External analysts, insurance companies and credit-rating agencies will have more information to evaluate. A resultant product within the more advanced risk-managed banks and funds will be the Loss Database. This database would be useful to the bank for reducing potential losses.

We take a different standpoint from Basel II, and we try to go farther than their OpRisk guidelines within some areas. Our view of the business environment is shown in Figure 11.2.

The goal is to come up with a more flexible OpRisk methodology that has applications from the narrower remit of managing banking risk. One of the problems of coping with risk is that many companies and organisations are unbalanced in operational standards. For example, a bank may have a great front office that is selling stocks and bonds very well. But its middle office risk management department can be sleepy or ineffective, while its back office may be swamped and unable to process buy/sell orders. We investigate this subject later in section: **Balanced organisation**.

COST-BENEFITS UNDER BASEL II

Banks and funds should already be developing more sophisticated risk analysis and more effective risk management. Creating risk profiles for the bank's counter-parties in the manner of a murder investigation may sound sinister. This process operates within CRM (credit risk management) where risk probabilities, default exposures and customers' records are logged. A detailed risk map of the customer's current risk position, plus probabilistic directions, should be drafted for banks.

Business counter-party profiling takes in the whole range of risk appetites, from the conservative to the wildly speculative. Another CRM (customer relationship management) or a detailed KYC (know-your-customer) process will further spotlight the customer's track performance. Basel II offers incentives for identifying losses and knowing your wise owl to the thieving magpie. Profiling of past risk events will form part of the loss database under Basel II to offer forecasting potential. This is similar to the VaR principle of using a historic dataset to predict the future. The Basel II Accord assumes that in operational risk, past errors and losses can be a guide to the future using the loss database. History repeats itself.

No standard set of business scenarios will fit the bill for any one institution. There will be different reasons why banks lose money. Furthermore, there will most likely be different categorisation money for the same case of why a bank lost. Standardisation will be tough to enforce across all banks, but the regulators will try to advise.

Compliance with regulation has now become more worthwhile. Basel estimates a 6 % drop in capital reserves for a large EU bank that wishes to manage its credit risk at the advanced AIRB level. A similar large EU bank aiming to achieve the lower standardised level on its core portfolios will most likely pay an additional 6 % capital charge.[3]

Nevertheless, there will be some groups who will feel aggrieved that Basel II punishes them unfairly. For example, the EU leasing industry is probably faced with a 6 % capital requirement, derived from a gamma (γ) risk weight of 75 % multiplied by the 8 % capital ratio. The Basel II documentation implies a probability of default (PD) in the 5 % to 25 % region, which is particularly high. The empirical research by the leasing industry indicates that the PD is realistically nearer 3 %.

This is because physical collateral assets such as real estate, cars, trucks and plant machinery have a long-established time-series for developing financial control skills. Understanding of the specific industrial sector, plus the option for securing the lessor's assets through repossession, means that default risk is low. External banking regulators have given little consideration for these risk mitigation factors, so the leasing industry becomes harshly treated.[4]

The regulator's seal of good housekeeping is worth winning under the new rules. The Basel II Accord recognises that levels of risk management skills should rise commensurately with lowering capital reserve limits as an encouragement. Fines and punishment of higher capital limits rise to the tipping point of where the pain becomes overbearing. Thus, the probability of being detected by better supervision and monitoring, together with the financial fines impact, make compliance an activity that creates return on investment.[5]

Basel II has to be well designed for every bank so that regulatory capital will be commensurate with their risks. The worst-case scenario is that Basel II will misallocate capital and increase regulatory reporting constraints. Market risk and credit risk may demand more regulatory capital, but more administrative aggravation will hinder current business lines within some banks. Local supervisors would have to be more cognisant of specific industrial needs before applying capital charges in full.

---

[3] *Quantitative Impact Study 3*, Basel Committee on Banking Supervision, 5 May 2003.
[4] *Joint Position Paper*, Leaseurope, June 2003.
[5] *Quantitative Impact Study QIS 2.5*, Basel Committee on Banking Supervision, 2002.

Basel II rules will be applied in the UK by the FSA. There will be some input from the European Commission in Brussels. Some quarters have argued for an EU "super regulator" to coordinate the migration towards Basel II and to standardise EU standards for open financial markets. It would be desirable to have an effective form of Basel II coordination and supervision to monitor the complex migration process. This financial super-cop is unlikely to come about soon given the political and economic diversity within the EU, and the potential conflict between the numerous stakeholder groups.[6]

The USA prefers to adopt a more laissez-faire attitude, where only their globally active major banks will be in the vanguard of Basel II adoption. These top 20 US international banks will have to comply with Basel II with the rest of the European rivals, but not the US domestic banks.

The FSA and SEC can move around banks during supervisory visits with a check-list for Basel II framework and other compliance controls. These have performance bands based upon aggregate data for similar banks in their banking sector. It is rather akin to the IRS or Inland Revenue tax authorities audit checks. A potential disadvantage of this check-list method is that financial supervisors may have less time to evaluate the banks' financial modelling thoroughly. Just ticking off a check-list makes it simpler to hide errors and pass off riskier banks with advanced IRB and AMA risk management certification.

RISK FOR FINANCIAL INSTITUTIONS AND INSURANCE

The convergence of banking and insurance business interests has led to M&A across the industry. Banks in Europe have recognised the benefits of M&A for banks with insurance companies. Cross-selling and strengthening the capital base and skills base. The new business model was clearly aimed at selling insurance products through the bank's network, so increasing synergistic revenue. This will satisfy a larger proportion of customer service needs through a one-stop shop.

Risk management methods of both professions must cross-fertilise each other. This has been expected to happen quicker than both professions can imagine, but already we have many situations where big insurance companies, e.g. SwissRe, MunichRe, AON, AIG lend money to business. The Prudential Assurance owns Egg Bank in the UK, while Lloyds-TSB Bank owns four insurance companies including Scottish Widows. Which major bank does not own an insurance company? They perform corporate and trade finance functions in the same manner as banks.

It becomes difficult to manage the different enterprise cultures required in one new organisation. Change management and a modified *Weltanschauung* (world view) are needed for the merged entity, especially if your bosses have been changed. Furthermore, financial structures will change and the ground can shift under your feet. Insurance companies used to rely on a steady and relatively predictable revenue stream from customers' premiums. They have found that new income volatility from the investment banking side had a damaging effect on their retail market financial health.

Risk structures and risk appetites may change in the merged corporation, so organic risk management should analyse the likely behaviour of this new investor animal. Insurers' initial risk perception was more optimistic than it should have been. Some of this stems from the

---

[6] *Supervising the European Financial System*, K. Lanoo, Discussion Paper SP137, Financial Markets Group, London School of Economics, 2003.

positive risk outlook from marrying a prestigious investment bank. Similarly, the big four UK clearing banks in 1986 tried to nurture an investment bank for their retail banking business. All four have retreated from this ambitious business strategy to various degrees. They should have put pessimistic scenario into their risk plan. Risk has a price, and many merged bancassurance companies initially had a rough ride.

Nevertheless, insurance offers significant contributions to banking, both in terms of cross-selling and tapping a skills base. Basel II sees that insurance will become more closely linked to banking and fund management as the finance industry develops. Credit-ratings agencies and insurance companies will be inextricably tied to banks and funds because market transparency means that relative rankings of company "risk" become public. These directly influence in-surance policy costs and, more indirectly, how customers view the reputation of these rated companies.

It is great news for consumers to see that this market combines insurance and banking to offer more choice of financing. Stress tests have so far proved that the market has enough resilience to withstand more competition. Yet, new entrants and new products will put a strain upon revenue streams and profit margins.

Research indicates that the opening of the EU financial markets, and the impact of e-banking on traditional bank business lines, will cause likely profit margin erosion. These range from savings/deposits, mortgages, mutual funds and on brokerage. The different risk and business profiles of European banks make it hard to derive general estimates of this impact. Nevertheless, a fall in profitability from margin erosion has been suggested in the range of -10% to -25% for most banks.[7] Banks would do well to assess their risk profiles in response to the changing market drivers.

Another issue is how the broad spectrum of banks, insurance companies and finance houses can be strongly monitored in the market by regulators who traditionally concentrate on banks. The FSA and Basel II are well geared to supervise banks offering traditional products, but they may be less prepared for non-banks providing the same banking products.

The Basel Committee has had to adopt a wider context of what is a bank and what is not. Furthermore, it took a narrow view of banking risk as a combination of the three factors – market, credit and operational risk. This is often too limited and we should consider in addition:

- structural risks
- strategic risks
- reputational risks.

It may appear that these Basel pillars are independent and stand alone. This is the concept of the risk silos (Figure 9.4). Basel II concentrates on the three types of risk – credit, market and operational risk. Investors could be led to believe that these are the major risk types, and the only ones that matter. Or worse, these are the only business risks that exist.

Banks may feel that risk is not contagious so long as risks are hedged between its divisions, i.e. risk localisation or damage control. But, sources of risk are related and interlinked, and a culture of lax risk awareness can be pervasive throughout the entire bank. Some banks have been more eager to adopt an enterprise risk management view.

This wider risk view permits the integration of risk management across silos to protect businesses adequately. Basel II recognises this principle and goes part way in linking the

---

[7] *The Regulatory Environment for a Changing World*, Howard Davies, FSA, 1 September 2000.

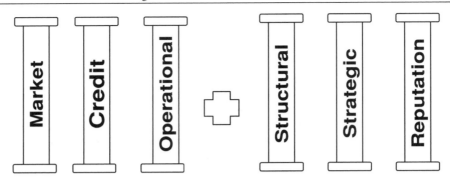

Figure 9.4   Separate risk silos/risk pillars

pillars in a mutually supportive fashion. Basel links the Three Pillars together, partly with supervisory visits and the imposition of regulatory capital. The explicit Basel II doctrine is that you buy all Three Pillars together in a job-lot; you cannot choose not to comply with any one of the Pillars.

The Basel II major progress has been to integrate some of the split risk silos. It will combine market, credit and operational risk within the combined Basel II operating framework. That is not to say that Basel II has its limits or its detractors.

Instruments such as popularly traded bonds will have a credit rating; other obscure bonds may not. There is a default bond rating, and if the bond is inherently risky or unsafe, then it may not benefit the bank trader to get the bond rated especially if the default rating is more lenient than a fair rating. This is not likely to be a loop-hole that will be closed as it is unlikely that any regulator can force all banks to get external credit ratings for their entire bond portfolio. Leeway for local supervisor judgement and initiative will continue to exist.

One factor also lies in the self-certification of risk. Banks at the outset will be presenting their validated risk management models. They know that they will receive regulatory benefits if they can present a good model. It is not in the interests to be forthright with regulators to admit that they have a bad risk management system. Banks are given regulatory capital incentives to validate their risk management models, even when these embed realistic assumptions and inherent weaknesses.

Regulators have to establish consistent standards for comparing across banks and across risk management models. Otherwise, banks will win with the greatest presentations and "sales job" on the regulators. There will be a learning curve for both sides as the banks try to develop ever more sophisticated models, while the regulators gather enough survey data to sniff out who has developed good risk management practices and models. Conversely, this will also lead the supervisors to deduce what constitutes a poor model and risk management practice for Basel II.

THE BASEL II OPRISK PRINCIPLES

The new mix of banking principles has opened up new opportunities, together with potential technical problems over implementation of risk management systems. The clash of political agenda and issues will, doubtless, arise in many financial institutions over the implementation

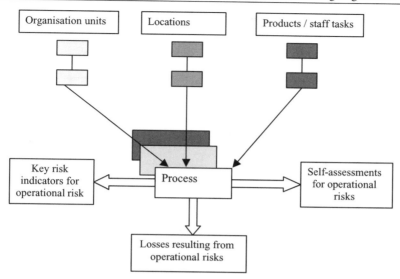

Figure 9.5   Attributed losses to processes
Source: Adapted from "A risk scorecard approach", U. Anders and M. Sandstedt, *Risk*, January 2003.

of Basel II. However, the recognition of the importance of OpRisk is a sure start to opening the Pandora's Box of risk management.

Loss database

This Loss database is the first step to detailing the losses or leakage that are parallel to the leakage and pilfering in the high-street stores. Operational risk is with us to stay, admitted or otherwise, in the banking and investment fields. It has been with us to stay in most other professions since their start. Creating a loss database in some ways is just catching up with standard retail industry practice.

OpRisk analysis, certainly under Basel II advanced standards, will eventually lead us to link the role of the investment parties with their associated losses. See Figures 9.5 and 9.6.

Furthermore, the database is compiled in the hope that we can link the internally manageable risks to establish lines of causality. One example has been to create a relation between the number of failed trades and the ratio of settlements processed per employee, plus to factor in the staff quality.[8] More sophisticated regression analysis and other techniques such as Bayesian probability or neural networks hold some hope for connecting causal lines between losses. Doing it successfully will assist companies to improve their business processes. Good management demands that weak process areas must be found, and that means pinpointing who is responsible. Laying the blame for losses squarely at someone's door is likely to be one of the less universally acceptable tasks initiated by loss database analysis.

The Basel II Accord stems from the tremendous increase in financial leverage under a global market and the rising sophistication of the risk management activities. The new financial regulations have been introduced partly to integrate more forms of risk and to improve the

[8] 'Forecasting from Loss-Events', Z. Molla, Investec, London, 5–6 June 2003.

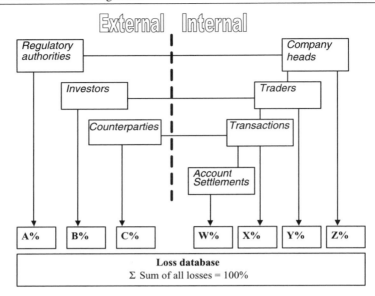

Figure 9.6   Investment project parties and associated losses

reputation of national financial systems following recent infamous financial failures. But, the potential of risk management monitoring has to meet the abilities of the internal management corporate skills. Where these levels remain low, then there will be difficulty for the bank to effect constructive change.

Financial statements and operational risk variance and exceptions will be noted and reported. Further supervisory visits are likely when the deviance cannot be initially explained. Further investigation may then cause additional regulatory capital to be demanded. Written warnings are then issued. Finally, if the miscreant bank does not comply, the last resort is the withdrawal of the banking licence. So, logical progression of the regulator's bark to bite:

1. Check-list performance bands.
2. Variance and exceptions report.
3. Further supervisory visits.
4. Additional regulatory capital.
5. Warnings.
6. Withdrawal of banking licence.

Loss database drawbacks

The loss database has a business case justification going for it. But, it is battling against the banking status quo of how things are traditionally done. One of the main reasons for data losses will come from the difficulty in reconciling all the composite dealing and accounting systems from the bank to derive a consolidated loss figure. Lack of IT systems integration will cause some data accuracy to be lost. Loss of control over the input and collation of the data will also increase the room for error. Data input by manual means also increases the room for data error. Some banks and funds will not have the data internally for developing the Loss Database. See Table 9.2.

Table 9.2   Data capture for loss database

Data source	% of sample respondents
Manual process	58
Vendor system	10
In-house system	32

Source: *Reporting and Forecasting Operational Risk: An FSA Perspective*, F. Shah, 5 June 2003.

Another factor is the lack of granularity. System design constraints to keep the database implemented on time and on budget will cause some data to be omitted. So, a cut-off limit of losses over $10 million could be made. This means that those losses not meeting this threshold will be omitted; these errors that almost happened or were rectified, will not be classified at all. These near-misses will not be entered, so we will not learn from this unrecorded experience until the near-miss becomes a real registered loss. The data loss becomes greater once the cut-off limit is raised. Thus, Standard & Poors sells a database history of US corporate losses where the threshold limit of losses is over $50 million. You will lose on data granularity.[9]

Another data loss will come from a haphazard classification of risks. A dealer makes a trading error of an overpayment, and it becomes queried by treasury. It is likely to be classified as a counter-party error, especially where the counter-party is weaker, so as to push the blame on someone else. The loss database will record it as an error initiated by the external party, even though the root cause was made internally by the trader.

Internal documentation risk events may be booked as a credit risk even though it stemmed from an internal operational risk error. Corporate standards must exist for interpreting and classifying losses. Otherwise, we end up with arbitrarily grouped losses with no discernible pattern to link them.

Many financial institutions driven by the call for Basel II compliance may plan for a linear progression in seven project stages 1–7 (Figure 9.7: straight diagonal line). However, it is quite

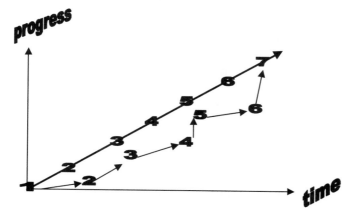

Figure 9.7   Possible Basel II project progression

[9] Standard & Poors, www.SP.com, 2002.

Table 9.3   Loss database project progress

Project progress	% of sample respondents
No plan	0
Planned	9
Developing or implementing	67
Near completion	24

conceivable that the resultant progress will be more haphazard, in going from stage 1 to 7 in fits and starts (Figure 9.5: zig-zag lines).[10]

Project stage 1 – "We are already a good compliant bank".
Project stage 2 – "We will examine Basel II when the industry is ready".
Project stage 3 – "We are prepared to install compliant risk management systems".
Project stage 4 – "The team is working. Basel II regulations are not yet set in stone".
Project stage 5 – "We met the board. We have bought Basel II project components".
Project stage 6 – "All Basel II components are ready for testing".
Project stage 7 – "All Basel II business functions approved".

The importance of using the loss database for meeting Basel II compliance standards has not been missed by many major banks and funds. A survey showed that most are in the process of developing or implementing a system.[11] See Table 9.3.

SCENARIOS FOR BASEL II OPRISK

The global effects that Basle II will have are not yet clear-cut. Side effects are unknown. However, a two-tier banking world is likely to emerge from the Basel II banking regulations, where there will be those who are in the fast-track for Basel compliance (more regulation and lower risk), versus those banks in the slow lane of compliance. These "slower" banks will have less regulation but more risk, even if they are guarded by more regulatory capital.

This is the possible outcome that there will be a two-tier banking system in the Basel domain:

- **Fast-track**: Advanced banks doing well with lower capital requirements, excellent risk management and risk reporting systems. They will thrive in the new markets.
- **Slow-track**: Other banks, slightly paralysed by higher capital reserves and regulatory requirements, will need to install more sophisticated risk management and risk reporting systems. The market perception of them can be negative (i.e. more risky banks or funds), so they can be doubly penalised by lower credit ratings /raised insurance premiums and lower customer respect.

More likely, there will be a large middle ground of banks and funds that are muddling along, not excelling themselves in advanced Basel II risk classifications, trying to find a niche.

NEXT STEPS: AFTER BASEL

The Basel II banking regulations will encourage willing financial institutions to focus on handling more diverse sources of risk. High-street stores try to meet more diverse risks because

---

[10] "Rolling out risk management", ERisk Report, www.Erisk.com , June 2002.
[11] *Reporting and Forecasting Operational Risk: An FSA Perspective*, F. Shah, 5 June 2003.

they recognise that just focusing on one risk (shoplifting) will lower returns at the margin on risk management efforts. Similarly, RAROC analysis shows that we gain through diversification, and that the areas for new investment can be identified profitably.

Rapid progress has been made in analysing market risk; value at risk and its variations still lead the way. Yet, we still have to recognise the correlation between different risks of which market risk is only one. The risk factors are combinative and not mutually exclusive. Loss data will only be useful when the theme of causality is tackled. Then regulators will truly have a safer banking system.

Basel II, under Pillar 3, will force banks to become more transparent as they will disclose more information. The Basel II regulations contain some of our *organic* risk management themes to treat companies as changing dynamic entities, rather than on a static one-size-fits-all basis. Organic risk management techniques complement and build upon components present in Basel II. Organic risk management and Basel II are part of the road for developing more amenable structures for corporate governance and risk-balanced companies.

The Basel and regulatory clout upon the financial institutions means that the banking and funds industry is forced to meet the new Basel II-based guidelines. How they meet the regulatory authorities' demands in practice is another question.

The Basel II project will most likely cost ten of millions US dollars for large global banks. This will include major changes in bank business and accounting procedures. Staff training, specialist consultancy time and new IT systems will add to the costs. Guesstimates are already flying around. One figure of $50 million has been given for Basel II standard certification, while $150 million has been banded around for a large global bank aiming for the highest advanced certification. How these costs can be expected to compare with business benefits will be a matter for strategic planning and effective project implementation to resolve.

Many banks are unhappy with the high costs of Basel II project implementation. They are still unsure as to the exact reduction in capital charges in some cases. Some banks are unwilling to go for the "Big Bang" for Basel II. They will choose to adopt a migration from standard to advanced level. Other banks may opt for taking a combination of risk management levels. One can pick advanced AIRB credit risk management level on its mortgage loan portfolio because it is a highly volatile and high value business line, while selecting standard operational risk management level on its asset management business line, which is lower volatility and value. Banks have really begun to splinter into different strategy groups.

Banks seeking to implement the Basel loss database have to think of the business rationale in the first place. We are discussing whether it is sensible to think of operational risk in terms of the questions: "Where did go wrong? How much did it cost us? How can we avoid or mitigate it?"

Not all banks will choose to adopt the loss database. Used properly, a loss database can encourage companies to think usefully about the nature or causes of operational risk. It offers three advantages towards building an understanding of risk.

1) Initially, we can think of operational risk in terms of risk events. The loss database matrix in this raw form is not yet detailed enough to be of use for risk management purposes. We need causal modelling, where an incident has a concomitant in a cause-effect relation.
2) The second phase is to link events with their causes. The matrix is just a set of boxes, where to put an initial incident and link it to a subsequent result. This cause-effect relationship is sometimes known as 'forward chaining' in knowledge management. Yet, we have yet to see substantial evidence that such data-mapping exercises create real value-added.

3) It will be likely to be compromised by budget and personnel limits that prevent scaling upwards into appropriate corporate action. The loss database is also backward-looking as long as it does not support an active loss prediction strategy.

The loss database will most likely reach its full potential when used in connection with a balanced risk scorecard to effect constructive changes in business processes. Scorecards are used for schoolchildren to monitor educational progress, but some companies have been slow

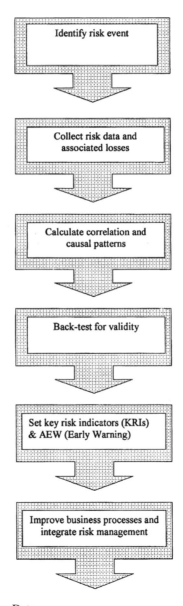

Figure 9.8   Benefiting from Loss Data

to take up this most fundamental procedure. The balanced risk scorecard establishes a standard questionnaire, with graded answers, to derive a weighted score of how well the company has translated business vision into reality. This score can be used at the initial period to set up a starting performance benchmark, and used to monitor progress thereafter, see Figure 9.8.

These techniques rest upon successful balanced growth models in most corporate environments, not only banking situations.[12] Balanced sustainable growth is possible for companies if the organisations are risk-managed at the top management level (strategic risk) and the tactical (operational risk) level. An operational risk scorecard has been used at Dresdner Bank to complement the drive for Basel II compliance.[13] This scorecard product has several objectives, among them:

1. Assess the level of current operational risk within the organisation.
2. Analyse where the risk comes from, and what connections to other departments and risk factors exist.
3. Determine the likely causes of the operational risk, explaining the reason for the high score and what actions can reduce it.
4. Concentrate the focus of top management to act constructively in selected business areas to mitigate risk.

Basel II compliance will require a massive allocation of resources coordinated in a skilled project management method. The potential benefits have to be seized by company directors to form the business case for project initiation. Only some firms will act to walk the talk at advanced Basel II risk-management levels successfully. All the project risk lies in getting there.

---

[12] *"The Balanced Scorecard: Translating Strategy into Action"*, R. Kaplan and D. Norton, Harvard Business School Press, 1996.
[13] "A risk scorecard approach", U. Anders and M. Sandstedt, *Risk*, January 2003.

10

Future-Proofing Against Risk

We first look at risk detection, then focus on risk countermeasures. Some elements resemble a risk attack, and we detail a hunt for evidence to be used against target parties in court cases. We also examine the techniques of insurance and how they cover executive actions. A look at fraud, corruption and whistle-blowing is made to see how we can cut crime. There is a study of forensic accounting and choosing an appropriate governance and risk management structure.

MORAL HAZARD

Investor risk is perceived as fear or underperformance, notably in losing the value of the original investment. Substantial benchmarking occurs, notably in the comparison of returns against inflation, stock-market and other industrial yardsticks. Similar executive peer-group pressure and benchmarking lead them to see who gained the highest award from the remuneration committee. Not all CEOs are intent on removing value from the company, a fine minority contribute by increasing investor wealth whether in share price or earnings per share.

The hazard remains that many CEOs are executive recruitment failures. They create negative shareholder return and blacken the name of the company. Reputational risk emerges as one of the more obscure risks, while being costly too. An incompetent executive seems to be excusable in the markets, certainly if we believe the newspaper accounts; being crooked is not. Either way, CEO tenure is usually short term, so CEOs may adopt the attitude: "Better clean up the company assets before they boot me out."

We have seen that the Board of Directors is not always an adequate counter to the ego of the CEO and the wish for more M&A and self-aggrandisement. Non-executive directors, who are enlisted in a cabal to add to the existing yes-men on the Board, can never serve to deter the company from embarking on an unacceptably risky course. We need an essential set of conditions for successful corporate guidance.[1]

- An appropriate range of multidisciplinary skills
- Power to ensure effective implementation of decisions
- Ability to undertake effective assessments of the soundness of decisions associated with projects
- Suitably qualified and dedicated support staff for the collection and analysis of data

Otherwise, we are condemned with the dire corporate leadership that has steered so many companies on the rocks.

An incompetent or crooked CEO underperforms colleagues and rivals. The bottom line is either the profit level or the share price. They fail on both scores. Failure should destroy their reputation in the industry. While the CEO can inflict great damage upon the company, reputational risk decrees that the executive can be punished with the embarrassment of being summarily ejected. By then it may be too late. There are two subrisks operating here – stemming from:

---

[1] 'The Philosophy of Risk', ch.9 'Assessment of risk acceptability', Chicken J. & Posner T., Thomas Telford books, 1998.

- an inept executive;
- a crooked executive.

What to do? Risk management becomes an empirical business study in corporate control. We have seen how risk comprises:

- hazard;
- catalyst;
- result.

We come back to the risk of a shark attack at the beginning of this book. The shark has a large dorsal fin that alerts us to its impending attack. We have already detailed an AEW warning system to alert us to the adverse CEO choice.

There are various risk management techniques to shed light upon a dark corporate operational area. These can include more effective interviewing to bring unsuitable executive candidates under the spotlight.[2] Another is to undertake a management review of the control structure for recruiting key staff.[3] Redesign the audit processes to block potential fraudulent financial statements passing the accounting process.[4]

Compare this risk management arsenal against the risk of a fraudulent CEO. Fraud needs conditions:

1. motivation;
2. opportunity;
3. rationalisation.[5]

We deploy risk countermeasures:

1. Anti-fraud motivation measures – better training of staff and recruitment, screening and interviewing of new applicants, monitor HR performance at work plus instigate an effective ethics programmes.
2. Anti-fraud opportunity measures – better staff monitoring, accounts screening, external audits, limit IT systems access and raise security physical access limits.
3. Anti-fraud rationalisation measures – raise chances of detection, raise punishment levels to act as deterrent, lower expectations of profit.

Risk management is really about a logical sequence of tasks to protect the business investment. The enterprise risk management strategy or life-cycle could be outlined as the series of tasks.

I. Risk detection.
II. Risk countermeasures.
III. Risk monitoring.

RISK DETECTION

This is the risk radar that investors switch off when they buy a company based on perceived reputation. Reputation is used instead as the proxy for risk management. Thus, many investors went into Enron, Worldcom or Equitable Life because they were regarded as good pedigree

---

[2] "Interviewing as a forensic-type procedure", T. Buckhoff and J. Hansen, *Journal of Forensic Accounting*, vol.3, 2002.
[3] "Avoiding Disappointment in Investment Manager Selection", R. Urwin, paper to International Association of Consulting Actuaries, March 1998.
[4] "The perceived occurrence and acceptance of dysfunctional audit behavior", D. Donelly, D. O'Bryan and J. Quirin, *Journal of Forensic Accounting*, vol.3, 2002.
[5] "Forensic expert classification of management fraud risk factors", B. Apostolou, J.M. Hassell and S.A. Webber, *Journal of Forensic Accounting*, vol.1, 2000.

Table 10.1   Marconi premises and checks

Premise	Checks
Telecoms market booming.	Forecast how long boom will continue. Are your forecasts reliable? What is the downside?
US company assets look cheap.	How valid is the valuation report? Run simulations and alternatives.
Companies fit into Marconi strategic needs.	Are you sure? Re-cast simulation of US companies within Marconi to check if balanced fit.
Marconi assets and cash are substantial.	For how long? Run cash projections. Consider issuing bonds or shares to fund take-over. What asset safeguards?
We have regulatory compliance.	What would shareholders and company investors say?
No fraud spotted on horizon.	How valid is the due diligence? Who conducted it? How deep did they delve?
Marconi business continuity and expansion are safeguarded.	How? Under what assumptions? Are these assumptions realistic? What if these assumptions do not hold? What do we do then?
There is no viable alternatives.	Are there?

companies. Long-Term Capital Management, adorned with a Nobel prize-winner on board, had a total market exposure estimated at $1250 billion against its capital of $800 million.[6]

Many people just want rapid profit, but they do not have a clue about real risk management. Setting an investment project goal with a risk limit is essential; it is not an optional extra. A predefined project by RAMP methodology has goals, expected performance and variance reporting. This puts adverse CEO spotting back on the project agenda.

CASE STUDY: MARCONI[7]

We can think of Marconi as an investment vehicle that was nearly "totalled" by bad driving from its directors. A proud company that was once valued at £6 billion is now fighting for survival and trying to rise from the ashes of its market cap of £50 million in September 2002. Shareholders were bought out by the bond-holders of banks and other lenders, and they were left with a paltry 0.5 % of equity. It is a reminder that equity takes second place over debt in the order of who is paid first.

Lord Simpson was credited with having turned Marconi into something sexier from the legacy of his predecessor, a somewhat dour-looking Arnold Weinstock of the old GEC days. The cult of personality would propel the company forward into the future. Over a cliff.

Marconi moved into the US telecoms market just before the TMT crash, using cash to fund take-overs of their investment targets. It was suckered into the M&A craze even though the chances of success are not too high. The objective was to take over US telecoms firms for Marconi expansion. Table 10.1 shows a list of Marconi premises and checks.

Compare with the risk map that we outlined earlier. The risk map identifies potential hazards; it also gives us a start point of where we are in relation to the risk and where we are heading. It is a potential reality check upon the mad mania of M&A. Another way we could look at the familiar take-over/merger scenario is to recap our risk-map knowledge. M&A is just not about cash; it is about taking on people and that is where the greatest wealth lies.[8] See Table 10.2.

---

[6] The Rise and Fall of Long-Term Capital Management, Roger, Lowenstein, 1998.
[7] "Troubled telecoms giant face grillings from angry investors", *Daily Telegraph*, 19 July 2001; AFX news, 16 December 2002.
[8] "The role of human capital in M&A", Towers-Perrin, November 2002.

Table 10.2 Evaluating the merger/acquisition risks

Objective	Evaluation
Take-over US telecoms firms for Marconi expansion.	
Venture risk rating	High
Target performance indicator (rise in stock price)	Positive
Our knowledge of market	High
Our knowledge of target	Low
Risk transfer or assurance	None
Assurance providers (insurance backing / hedging?)	None
Payment method: cash. Risk burden?	High
Fall-back plans	None
Impact of potential failure	High
Net risk-return view	Pessimistic

Finding the company on our corporate AEW radar can warn us that the company is about to "blow". This organic-based system uses both figures and mathematical techniques, but is more about the manner in which human beings operate. The forensic evidence can be tracked down in audit trails. There are scents given off by CEO sharks associated by red flags alarm signals for indicating weak banks.[9]

There are essential tools to identify weak banks using early warning techniques. This subjects the supervisor's data on the bank to a stress testing process, of the bank's expenses, asset quality of portfolio and their funding. Then we can derive a better risk-discounted picture of the earnings, capital and solvency. This is followed by qualitative (note not quantitative) modelling:

Qualitative data

- Management/board of directors have oversight administration deficiencies; the oversight committee may not be empowered, or it is too chummy with the CEO.
- Risk management has deficiencies in resourcing, empowerment and skills.
- Strategic mistakes have been made by the board into the market.

Quantitative data

- Performance-related rise in declared profits, asset value, sales.
- Aggressive growth and expansion strategies.
- Sudden and major deterioration in earnings.

Basel II recognises that such operational risk weaknesses cause big problems for the investors. Its AEW[10] system also focuses on warning signs in:

- Board management quality.
- Effectiveness of policies, procedures and planning.
- Execution of risk management controls and audits.
- Quality of MIS systems and reporting processes.

---

[9] "Early warning analysis & stress testing", Association of Supervisors of Banks of the Americas V Annual Assembly, May 2002.
[10] Sound practices for the management and supervision of operational risk, Basel Committee for Banking Supervision, July 2002.

RISK COUNTERMEASURES

Once detecting operational risk conditions is in existence, we can think about deploying risk countermeasures. Could any CEO shark engineer himself some huge pay-off based on undisclosed benchmarks?

Frankly, yes and no. Yes, they could get away with it easily in the old days. General Motors was a classic example where the head of a modern corporation could do what he liked in the era of Roger Smith. Pressure from the board, CalPers and H. Ross Perrot eventually forced him out. More recently, NYSE chairman Richard Grasso was pressured into resigning after the resultant furore that erupted when his $140m pay package was made public. Was this a case of Kalashnikov risk management used successfully? Some would say with justification that the aggrieved Western shareholders are amateurish when it comes to reining in the wayward behaviour of boards and CEOs. The professionals in the Japanese mafia do it so much better.

CASE STUDY: THE YAKUZA AND SHAREHOLDER MEETINGS[11]

The Japanese mafia (Yakuza) has a branch of corporate relations or *sōkaiya* activities that is very effective. They appear at the shareholder meeting where they can attack or protect the corporation. They can pass through a company's resolutions on a nod and a wink, or block motions completely through obstructive debate or physical attacks upon individuals present at the annual general meeting (AGM).

Shooting deeper, challenging and potentially embarrassing questions at the directors can have strong effects. The Yakuza in Japan are masters of this craft honed over the years at the AGMs, so that many directors are willing to do almost anything for them to desist. Many Japanese companies defer to the Yakuza and pay them to avoid trouble.

Western shareholders could well adopt this tactic as a last resort. The UK GSK and the US GM meetings do not even compare in skill. This is one of the positive role models of the Yakuza systematically ignored in the Western world. They could teach shareholders how to level the corporate playing field by disrupting the AGM. If they get continually fobbed off, then they could always shoot the directors one supposes.

Badgering and damaging leaders' reputation certainly can have effect. Corporate governance is coming along slowly. It would arrive faster if we could borrow some of the Yakuza's tactics in Western companies. In the meantime, we have the regulatory cogs slowly grinding around the Combined Code, Higgs Report and Sarbanes–Oxley to protect us.

The covering up of negative financial reports and losses are examples of corporate misgovernance to head off risk of reputation damage.[12] The eventual cost on ongoing business may be greater where the fundamental causes of the original loss have not been remedied, but merely swept under the carpet until recurring later.

This behavioural trend increases systemic risk where greater eventual damage is vested upon the wider industry. We have already seen this in Lloyds insurance, where a nepotistic code of doing business with "our sort of chaps" represents a sclerosis risk that nearly blew the UK insurance industry. The more we ignore it, the more it can blow up in our faces.

---

[11] *Sōkaiya: Extortion, Protection, and the Japanese Corporation*, K. Szymkowiak and M.E. Sharpe, 2002.
[12] "Implicit claim incentives on the accounting choices of troubled companies", D. Peltier-Rivest, *Journal of Forensic Accounting*, vol.3, 2002.

These hidden losses and weaknesses make it more difficult to value a company and its assets. The persistent ramping of a company's value, and the love of M&A to increase company size instantly, creates additional problems for investors in Western firms. It is a problem rooted in the modern business culture, much influenced by the USA.

The weaknesses inherent in embedded value methods are repeated and added to in US GAAP reporting. These need to be anticipated, adjusted for and fully understood before reliance should be placed on the results.[13]

How to discourage the executives from acting in an irresponsible fashion?

RISK FIREPOWER

We use the Kalashknikov as a metaphor to demonstrate the power of corporate risk management. We need to question how more effective our risk firepower would be if we could deploy the right firepower upon the company's leaders.

CASE STUDY: HUNTINGDON LIFE SCIENCES (HLS)[14]

While shareholders have been ineffective against the stonewalling and visionary promises of executives, animal rights activists have led their to victory to show what is achievable when you seriously want to take on the board of directors. A five-year protest that was marred by occasional violence, street protest, verbal threats and intimidation proved that determined individuals can force corporate leaders to change their decisions dramatically.

Executives were cowed by a vehement campaign that included physical attacks against managers, including the mailing of a suspected letter bomb. The HLS managing director was attacked by a gang of animal activists armed with baseball bats. If only we could harness their anger and considerable determination on the fraudsters at Enron and similar executives?

Banks refused to offer facilities to HLS in fear of suffering physical damage or being hounded. It showed that there are activists who will observe no limits in order to change company executive decisions. The activists nearly drove HLS out of business.

Executives and CEOs have been fortunate, up to now, that shareholders have been patient. AGMs have been peaceful, but it is only a question of time before avaricious CEOs suffer the full force of fate. Although HLS was an unpleasant case to observe, it does demonstrate that investors have not even come close to the full extent of venting their spleen.

This has clouded the corporate bottom line in many cases. So, we have to look through the fog. One thing we need to change is auditors' attitude and professional execution of the job. They must pay more attention and exercise own professional judgement to prevent or detect fraud. All professions are waking up to the dangers of fraud. Sleeping through the investment crises, or passing the buck is not a risk option anymore.

Professional exams now check whether students have grasped the value of corporate ethics. The Association of Investment and Management Research (AIMR) formulate the Chartered Financial Analyst (CFA) exams. Whereas professional exams may have included little on ethics before, the CFA curriculum has changed with time. The Level I 2003 exam has a 15 % topic

---

[13] "US GAAP reporting", R. Houghton, *Insurance and Financial Services Review*, February 2002.
[14] "Huntingdon: hounded out of existence", *The Scotsman*, 10 November 2002.

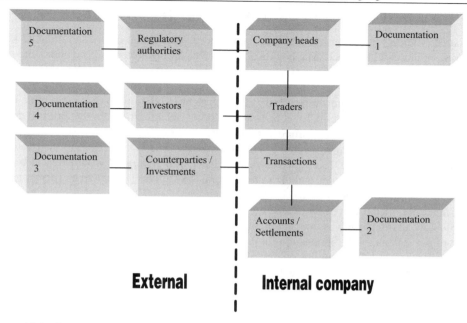

Figure 10.1   Investment project parties and incriminating documentation storage

weight for Ethics and Professional Standards, and a 30 % weight for Asset Valuation.[15] There is real hope that these can safeguard against some of the flagrant corporate excesses committed recently.

Graduates and auditors are also more familiar with IT systems and technology. They understand the principles of IT operations, including off-site storage and backup facilities. This means that they are able to consult with others to rebuild an incriminating audit trail of evidence against directors who have committed serious corporate errors.[16] One infamous example was the Enron–Andersen shredding of vital documents. Another case was New York attorney Eliot Spitzer successful action against Merrill Lynch and CSFB for their part in "ramping" worthless dot-com shares during the TMT craze. All these are possible with technology to reconstruct shredded statements or deleted emails. These audit trails can sift through the archives in the documentation storage points 1, 2, 3, 4, 5, shown in Figure 10.1.

The successful litigation against Merrill Lynch and CSFB shows that punitive action can be effectively taken despite attempts to obstruct it, or to destroy vital evidence. A business tradition was to take risk as an inevitable part of life, callously saying: "Leave losses to be recovered from insurance or law-suits."

This does not add to corporate profits, but detracts from it, once the final bills have been calculated. The litigation against the culprits of the Barings and other banking and fund fiascos still continues, and there seems little net compensation for the losers, after accountants and lawyers have deducted their fees. Insurers are not mugs, and they are reluctant to pay for someone else's errors, especially when they stem from a risk-seeking or risk-ignorant attitude.

---

[15] www.AIMR.org.

[16] "Black tech forensics: collection and control of electronic evidence", G. Stevenson Smith, *Journal of Forensic Accounting*, Vol.1, 2000.

INSURANCE: THE BUCK USED TO STOP HERE

Executive scandals in corporate America continue to disgust shareholders and to incite vocal opposition, but to what effect? Maybe one player is whispering softly and carrying a big stick over errant companies. This move might be a more effective persuasion to clean up corporate accounting and malpractice.[17]

The insurance industry now emerges as a key enforcer in refusing to cover corporate executives, or to cancel current policies if executives do not open their company books to deeper scrutiny. Insurance providers of directors and officers (D&O) liability coverage have been less willing to pamper company clients. The risks were formerly passed on to the insurance companies who wrote the D&O policies. Incompetence or malfeasance would have to be paid for by the insurance companies and the shareholders – executives go scot-free. This no longer seems an acceptable business model for risk management.

Furthermore, the burden of proof is being passed back to the executives under examination. The previous assumption was that a company was clean unless there was overwhelming evidence to prove fraud. The "innocent until proven guilty" principle worked well in law courts for individuals, but when you are talking about potential damage to thousands of investors, this get-out clause seems inadequate. CEOs and executives have such remunerative incentives to cover up company bad news that an auditor is battling uphill. Shifting the burden of proof upon the client executives becomes an effective way of concentrating the mind upon finding all evidence. This is the well-known scientific technique of "null hypothesis" where it is easier to disprove a theory by finding exceptional data, rather than proving a hypothesis.

Countermeasures against errant executives are already in place. There has been a flurry of shareholder-initiated lawsuits, possibly empowered as US senior company officers are forced to swear to the accuracy of their financial statements. Punishment terms up to 10 years' jail are on the scoreboards just to keep CEOs on the righteous path.

Marsh, AON, Chubb and AIG in the USA control most of the US underwriting business, including D&O coverage. Insurance companies are shoring up the ramparts by hiring more forensic accounting staff. More exacting financial data are requested from clients, followed by questioning top executives on their corporate performance and knowledge of the reports stated. A proper due diligence examining current management practices, accounting standards and board skills means that this procedure is no longer a rubber-stamp for the client.

The big stick waved by the insurer comprises demanding higher D&O premiums or refusing coverage. Former risk game rules permitted corporations to pay a few hundred thousand dollars for annual D&O coverage against litigation. The same policy will cost more than $1 million. There are additional deductibles running into millions of dollars that force companies to shoulder a large part of the cost of any litigant's claim. Companies are given incentives to reduce the element of doubt in the insurer's eyes by furnishing detailed proof of innocence.

Insurers are not suckers who are going to soak up the risks of "moral hazard" originating from immoral CEOs. Some insurers are rejecting coverage for clients that are judged to have questionable accounting and management practices because of the considerable downside risks. The insurers are faced with:

- huge potential pay-outs for the D&O policies;
- the regulator imposing strict penalties;
- threat of shareholder lawsuits;
- the reputation risk from underwriting fraudulent accounts.

---

[17] "Insurers demand full disclosure", *Business Week*, 13 August 2002.

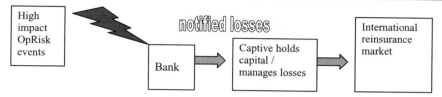

Figure 10.2   Tools of the trade – insurance captives

The investor public wants to know that corporate cleanliness is next to godliness. Only sound corporate management practices, instigated by a determined and ethical board, can provide it. Where the board feel that the operational loss events can have such high impact as to endanger the continuing business of the bank, then they may seek to insure against the severe loss. This brings in the role of "captives" within the financial markets. Banks may feel confident enough to take on, or self-insure (SIR) themselves for a part of the operational risk damage estimated. The captive can take or reinsure the rest in excess of the SIR. Captives may offer more cover than is readily available in the open market, they will go to the international market to reinsure their portfolio. The reinsurers will also want to avoid the "moral hazard" risk posed by inept or corrupt CEOs of the client bank.[18] See Figure 10.2.

Nevertheless, the insurance sector can provide a very useful foundation for enterprises trying to negotiate the modern risk conditions and a new raft of regulations. One is the use of risk financing using contingent capital. This offers some mitigation against severe operational risk events. Clients can sign up by paying a stream of premiums known as "commitment fees" that have some analogous points to options or warrants. It enables the substitution of on-balance sheet economic capital for contingent capital provided by the insurer. The purposes are limited only for operational loss events affecting the bank.

The contingent capital can only be unlocked or exercised when a major operational risk event triggers or breaks the agreed limit. Thus, the insurer can agree to provide cover for major risk impacts by providing contingent capital when the operational risk event is $50 million damage. This triggers the release of capital for covering damage. There is no cover for P&L damage or for protecting directors against the moral hazard of their own mistakes.[19]

RISK MONITORING

Risk management has suffered from various forms of opposition from top management. Something along the lines of:

- Expensive – the IT systems and the rocket-scientists are all too much to pay.
- Slow – risk groups will never deliver on time.
- Naive expectations – the risks will never hit us.
- Weak management – let's talk about this sometime (procrastination).
- Unrealistic – we'll get the insurers and lawyers to get us out of the jam.

Once we convince top management that there is a justifiable business case for risk management, then we can deploy a full range of countermeasures. We still have to be alert to market

[18] *Insurance in the Management of Financial Institutions*, T. Leddy, Swiss Re, London 12 June 2003.
[19] *Insurance in the Management of Financial Institutions*, T. Leddy, Swiss Re, London 12 June 2003.

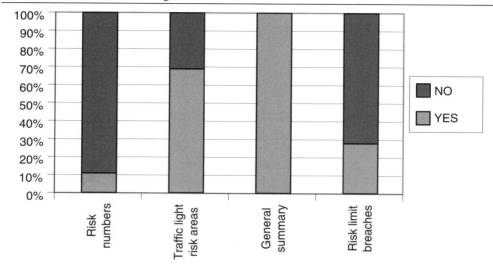

Figure 10.3   What information is included in the Board report?

changes, but risk management gives us a safety buffer. Everyone is trying to move ahead of the investment pack. Given so much ego and PR, there is a crying need to compare performance. There are various forms of benchmark, e.g. against the previous year's performance, whole industry or the top rival in the sector, etc.

Benchmarks are used to handle trickier points of detecting operational risk within a company. Fine corporate PR and good-looking financial statements could have been ripped apart by organic risk red flags. One of the problems may be that the risk management reports sent to the board do not have the right information, a suitable format to understand, or the board may not have the skills to understand. See Figure 10.3.

We have already detailed the Barings, Enron–Andersen, Worldcom incidents of the ships that sank. What can we say of the boats that stay afloat? MCI floats on, after its previous incarnation, WorldCom, sank.

CASE STUDY: WORLDCOM

There can be fewer corporate PR campaigns that have inculcated a greater unfounded sense of security or value than at WorldCom. The opening of holes in the company accounts eventually led the SEC to charge the WorldCom board with committing a $3.8 billion fraud. SEC sought financial punishment of directors, while prohibiting destruction of case documents and evidence (see: Whistle-blowing).

SEC alleged that WorldCom fraudulently overstated its income and falsely portrayed itself as a profitable business. WorldCom did so by capitalising expenses of $3.8 billion of its costs, added to capital accounts in violation of generally accepted accounting principles (GAAP).

Some of these bizarre book-keeping techniques are analogous to a householder counting gas, utility and repair bills as income. These misled investors and manipulated WorldCom's earnings to keep them in line with estimates by Wall Street analysts. The fraud came from the inside, ably assisted by the financial experts on the Street.

> The SEC charged WorldCom with violating various anti-fraud legislation in June 2002. The court orders sought against WorldCom prohibited it and its directors from destroying valuable evidence and relevant case documents. The IT records cannot be destroyed if the investigation is to have a good chance of success. All incriminating email letters should be able to be tracked down or reconstituted.
>
> WorldCom funds were frozen, especially more generous payments to its directors or employees that might have been enjoined to destroy evidence. Regulators have to protect the data, whistle-blowers and then hunt for the key culprits.

What we need to do is to examine the living corpse that is the company CEO before they cause damage. This process may reduce or even prevent financial losses that have caused major shareholder grief in recent years. We have to conduct an adequate due diligence before the company falls apart with us locked into the investment. Part of this process comes under the investigation comprising forensic accounting.

Forensic accounting

Forensic accounting is a potentially rich source of value-added in financial environments. Part of forensic accountancy is an art, part science and the rest is detective work. There are three ways in which it can provide a valuable service in organisations:

1. Investigate a case post facto to see where a loss has occurred within the investment environment; sniff out the cause or possible rats, then set up the enquiry for full regulatory/judicial process and compensation/redress where possible.
2. Examine a business to spot current areas of weaknesses that may cause future losses. Shore up, fire, retrain or recruit staff to reinforce the system.
3. Compile a list of weaknesses within the organisation and detail reasons for investment loss. This exercise is a training tool for auditing and back-office staff. Such forensic investigations must feed active front-office trading personnel, compelling them to document significant risk events for the benefit of the back office.

There is more incentive to promote this type of procedure under Basel II regulations for market transparency and discipline. Part of the Basel II philosophy of risk is predicated on the notion that top management want to grasp the nettle and actively manage OpRisk. The first thing forensic accounting can provide is a corporate health check or a company risk audit. They may use a variety of techniques to derive this audit:

- Self-assessment of risk areas – running a checklist audit or workshop to identify the strengths and weaknesses of the company's business environment, especially against potential stakeholder lawsuits.[20]
- Risk mapping – diagramming the various constituent business units and process flows. Each area and its associated risk are identified and documented, then the follow-up risk management action recommended. Risk mapping can be used within functional areas for key risk indicators (KRIs). Departments can define operational limit bands of functionality like a risk thermometer. Crossing these limits (e.g. asset-liability gaps) shows the company's risk

---

[20] "Forensic risk management – a sharpened fraud focus reduces litigation risk", D.O. Burgess and C. Pacini, *Journal of Forensic Accounting*, Vol.1, 2000.

exposure here is "hot". The responsible party or group designated with the risk origination can also be flagged, and the risk management group alerted.[21]

- Business scorecards – these build on Kaplan and Norton's seminal work in measuring and quantifying the performance of corporations.[22] These are qualitative performance levels, but the resulting scorecard can identify areas of weakness that may be reinforced with additional capital and training.
- Loss database – this keeps a historical log of above-threshold value financial losses. Statistically significant losses or high damages can be highlighted automatically for the attention of senior management.[23]

We have developed advanced tools and techniques for:

- Corporate governance.
- Benchmarking and measuring performance.
- Identifying areas of risk or weakness.

The problem is that an investor is an irrational animal and other influences often take over the driver's seat. This is certainly true at the top executive level, and OpRisk groups have less to say about how strategic decisions are made.

The two main risk horizons remain for financial institutions.

- Strategic policy risk – the fundamental asset allocation and performance benchmark design. This has been the subject of much research, but behavioural factors do exert a strong influence. Strategic policy risk has the greatest influence upon bank and fund success. Governance and trustee defined roles working under a multilayered control hierarchy can keep a better link between declared corporate objectives and the actions of managers.[24]
- Tactical implementation risk – investment manager structure and manager selection. Investment managers are generally recruited from a narrow band of skills and social backgrounds, so they can develop a tendency to socialise and to invest as a herd. This leads to a restricted range of assets chosen for investment. Careful interviewing and screening of recruits can reduce undesired wayward behaviour.[25]

APPROPRIATE RISK MANAGEMENT STRUCTURE

Effective counter-measures have to be put in place and tested. We have outlined some of the Basel II guidelines for effective risk management. The trouble is: "Do you have the corporate influence and the budget to get the proper risk management in place?"

Where advice and plans fall on deaf management ears, nothing concrete is likely to be done. Budgetary constraint, as an opponent, is no stranger to the champion of risk management.

The financial world is set on cutting costs and automating business processes; risk management systems are just one facet of this drive. Yet, the quest for lower costs and automation can blind us to the fundamental areas for error. Human intervention and room for exercise of staff initiative can become stifled.

[21] *OpRiskVision – Misys*, Amelia systems, UK, January 2002.
[22] "The balanced scorecard", Kaplan R and Norton D, *Harvard Business Review*, 1996.
[23] "*Sound Practices for the Management and Supervision of Operational Risk*", Basel Committee for Banking Supervision, July 2002.
[24] *Structured Alpha: A Practical Application for Institution Funds*, Watson Wyatt, December 1999.
[25] *Avoiding Disappointment in Investment Manager Selection*, R. Urwin, paper to International Association of Consulting Actuaries, March 1998.

This is partly why human error is cited as the source of most operational failures. However, this is often just an excuse for poor management and badly designed systems and processes that remove checks and controls in an effort to improve efficiency by lowering costs.[26]

Much of this corporate culture against disclosing the truth stems from the top of the financial institutions. Switzerland, for example, makes whistle-blowing a crime. Therefore, unfavourable financial assessments can remain hidden from the investors. Whistle-blowing really saves investors money in the long run. It pinpoints the perpetrators of economic crimes and reduces the period during which they could be removing or destroying economic capital of the company and its shareholders. Whistle-blowing reduces the time-lag after which auditors and investigators can look for relevant evidence.

CASE STUDY: BCCI BANK

Regulators worked apart, rather than together, on this case. It led to calls establishing supranational regulators; yet no world-wide "super regulator" exists anywhere. This disjointed investigation enabled BCCI to continue its fraudulent operations. Yet, central bankers and regulators preferred sealed lips for so long until all authorities could muster up enough evidence and courage to act.

When BCCI closed in 1991, about one million depositors around the world lost their money. The larger depositors included central banks and governments in major countries around the world. BCCI had a cult of anonymity and banking secrecy for its customers.

BCCI systematically money-laundered around the world, supporting some unsavoury regimes. It bribed and peddled influence systematically to foster extensive relationships with prominent business, political and military figures in most of the 73 countries where it operated.

The case demonstrates:

1. The value of business influence in protecting a financial institution for a long time.
2. The value of prestige in "short-circuiting" investor common-sense.
3. The slowness and fragmented process of central banking and regulation.

By the late stage when BCCI was stopped, a lot of innocent people had been defrauded. Once again, it had the elements of TBTF, reputation risk and corruption at the very core of the top executives.[27]

Whistle-blowing works on a raising series of red flags. When there is no visible recourse, or for major crimes, resort to an escalation of whistle-blowing. Alert the press and media, then report to regulators, police and other supervisory authorities. A proper whistle-blowing methodology can be set within the staff contract to lift the lid on fraud and crime. For minor transgressions: keep the dissent internal initially and keep an account of all errors, crimes and relevant data. Consult the ombudsman or newspaper if the company refuses to act.

Whistle-blowers must be protected and encouraged. Right now, the downside risk is being fired or shunned in the professional for "squealing" on the company or colleagues, while the upside potential is not much. Immediate risk is being questioned for technical competence, political competence, sanity, naiveté; onus is on the whistle-blower to understand the

---

[26] *Measuring and Managing Operational Risk*, p.13, C. Marshall, Wiley, 2001.
[27] *The Insolvency Liquidation of a Multinational Bank*, Bank of International Settlements, December 1992.

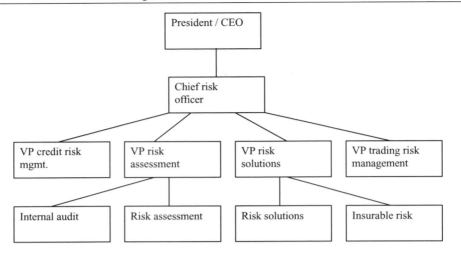

Figure 10.4 Risk organisation chart
Source: Global Association of Risk Professionals, *GARP Risk Review*, Mar–Apr 2002.

whole of the story; first managerial reaction is often "you do not have a view on the whole picture".

Many corporations do not encourage whistle-blowing. Certainly, discouraging the leaks of information is an overt attempt to block all events that present a corporate reputation risk. Enron did not support whistle-blowing, but preferred to hide or shred the facts. Fraud and concealment of the truth were deep-rooted in the structure of the company. Worse, the fraud was perpetrated at the top. A company has to have a structure that is rooted in business and risk management. See Figure 10.4.

Risk ignorance does not work, especially if the top management is ignorant or crooked. What an open risk-managed structure does is to open the corporation to the control function of the risk managers. They actively let the company be open to the idea that "squealers" can inform on the company if something wrong or fraudulent is suspected.

An internal company "fraud hotline" should be set up, where anonymous whistle-blowing can be channelled and processed for action. Nowadays, whistle-blowing is possibly anonymously through setting up temporary email accounts that access the regulatory website.[28]

A US survey concluded that 6 % of business revenue or $400 billion is lost within the UK economy as a result of fraud, and a most of this loss comes from internal staff. Furthermore, KPMG estimated that only 4 % of these fraud incidents were spotted during external audit. The reasons for this huge damage comes from a lack of internal corporate controls and poor stock-control/accounting.[29]

Many shareholder interest groups exist to protect the rights of the smaller investor. Grouped together, they command a huge pension fund and influential voice. Calpers, Teachers, NAPF and PIRC are among many. PIRC (Pensions and Investment Research Consultants) was vocal in its criticism of arrogant boards that do not press forward to embrace corporate governance recommendations.[30] PIRC has called for more transparent and accountable directorships to

---

[28] e.g. www.fsa.gov.uk, www.SEC.gov, www.FBI.gov etc.
[29] "Interviewing as a forensic-type procedure", *Journal of Forensic Accounting*, vol.3, 2002.
[30] "The effective non-executive director", PIRC, www.PIRC.org.uk, 28 June 2002.

make UK boards more geared towards increasing shareholder value and socially responsible investment.

PIRC is an agency committed to SRI (socially responsible investment). It encourages investors to monitor how companies are managing their stakeholder relationships. One byproduct is FTSE4Good as an index of SRI stocks that such investors can choose from. PIRC gives investors relevant information and SRI advice, particularly on corporate governance, including:

- shareholder rights
- best practice compliance
- suitable board structures
- remuneration schemes
- investor relations.

PIRC has called for a series of changes to make UK board of directors more effective.

- Encouraging more boards to have more non-executive directors than executives.
- Making sure non-executives are genuinely independent rather than chums of the chief executive. PIRC says only 20% of FTSE 100 boards have a majority of independent non-executives.[31]
- Independent appraisal of board members.
- A widening of the pool of non-executives. Companies could advertise for new recruits.
- Better resources for non-execs, including secretaries and researchers as well as access to independent research and advice.
- More contact between non-execs and shareholders.

NAPF (National Association of Pension Funds) operates with a similar mission. Its priority is to ensure an efficiently regulated market for the provision of employer-sponsored pensions. It advocates sound governance of pension fund assets as NAPF represents pension funds that cover about 10 million UK employees. These funds control 20% of the shares of the London Stock Market. NAPF also opines that independent directors articulate the wishes of their investors, while the non-executive directors fully understand the shareholders' expectations of them. One role could be for them to exercise effective restraint over the sympathetic remuneration committees that are inclined to pay the top executives too much ("fat cats").[32]

Fat cats are blamed for skimming off the cream from the corporate milk, so impoverishing their investors. Executives have to be charged with the duties of wealth creation and safeguarding it through risk management, not for sleeping on the job. The risk management directors' duty is listed in the Basel II banking document that prescribes a healthy environment for business. It states that the function of risk management should go all the way to the top:

The board of directors should be aware of the major aspects of the bank's operational risks as a risk category that should be managed, and it should approve and periodically review the bank's operational risk management framework. The framework should provide a firm-wide definition of operational risk and lay down the principles of how operational risk is to be identified, assessed, monitored and controlled/mitigated.[33]

---

[31] PIRC, www.Pirc.org.uk.
[32] www.NAPF.org.uk.
[33] *Sound Practices for the Management and Supervision of Operational Risk*, Bank of International Settlements, July 2002.

Invest within companies where there is a culture of openness and risk management. The new Basel II banking regulations encourages corporate transparency. One's conscience is better put at rest than by a superficial report that white-washes the remaining dangers.

We have looked at sensing for top management errors and lack of ethics deep down the company – see AEW: advanced early warning.

Your sixth sense can save you a lot of money!

FACTS, NOT FIGURES

Corporate cover up works most of the times. When it does not, it boosts the impact. Covering up transforms a high-probability low-impact risk into a low-probability high-impact risk. Accounting analysis is generally the prior step before making the investment. Other proposals are to invest where:[34]

1. Accounting standards are strong enough to link reporting to reality.
2. Accounting statements from publicly quoted companies are accurate and timely, and a regulatory framework exists to enforce the accounting principles.

There are other tell-tale signs to spot within the increasing onslaught of corporate PR and white-wash:[35]

- Too optimistic sales forecasts – take your risk analytical Kalashknikov and shoot the balance sheet apart.
- Does the overall balance sheet "feel" right – too rapid a turnaround?
- If the balance sheet is that good – then why are directors dumping their shares?
- Do we have a good balance of voices on the board, or are they all in unison trying to get into some scam?
- Were there a few too many "balancing items"?
- Which period were the majority of revenues booked and received (no receipt means no revenue).
- What sort of products and services were called revenue-producing?
- Are they disposing of a lot of assets from the group?
- Is the auditor also employed in another fee-paying activity within the company?

Another view for detecting cooked accounting books:[36]

1) Record revenue too fast or too much.
2) Registering false revenue.
3) Increasing income with once-off gains.
4) Shifting expenses back or forwards into another period.
5) Reducing liabilities or completely omitting them.
6) Shifting current revenue forwards into a future period.
7) Shifting future expenses back or forwards into another period.

---

[34] "Renewing confidence in the markets", D. Tweedie, *Bank of England Financial Stability Review*, December 2002.
[35] "Cook the books and you will go directly to jail without passing go", D.L. Crumbley and N. Apostolou, *Journal of Forensic Accounting*, Vol.2, 2001.
[36] *Financial Shenanigans*, Howard Schilit, McGraw-Hill Education, 2002.

How long can this go on? It is not acceptable corporate behaviour, but if we are to believe the regulators, it will continue as long as companies grow or change.

In each of the cases involving banks, management seemed to be content with the loss of vigor in the process and the external auditor was apparently satisfied to simple collect a fee. This is totally unacceptable. Further, as the organization evolves by offering new products, changing processes, outsourcing services, complying with the new regulations, or growing through mergers, the controls need to be modified to reflect the changes in risks. In some case, the controls failed with respect to the newer risk exposures that were not identified, or growth put strains on existing control processes that were not suitable for a larger organization.[37]

Risk management means not sleeping on the job.

NEW RISK FOCUS

Risk management is a sequential series of tasks: analyse, forecast, investigate and mitigate against risk. Risk reporting alone is just fine for appearance – this is where many lax financial companies ran into trouble in recent years. Any reaction to a threat in such firms is likely to be ineffective because the risk management function will be underfunded and understaffed. Lack of training and proper risk management procedures result in a haphazard counter-attack against risk. Organic risk management takes the human and team factors into account to build a risk-managed corporation. This means an active risk outlook, not a passive one.

RAMP is a project methodology that has in-built self-checks to counter bias or project deviation. It should be considered for managing financial projects.[38] This way we can have a real audit check that goes beyond simple numbers on the balance sheet, towards monitoring the fundamental sources of business risk. RAMP provides a design template for implementing a project. A brief extract of this process is shown in Figure 10.5:

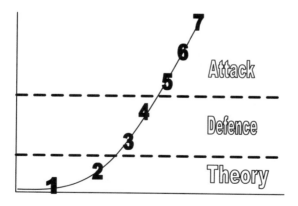

Figure 10.5   Risk management project cycle

---

[37] 'Strengthening compliance through effective corporate governance', Susan Bies, Board of Governors, US Federal Reserve System. 11 June 2003.
[38] *Managing Project Risk*, Y.Y. Chong, Financial Times Management, 2000.

1. Create liabilities and threats risk map.
2. Model long-term investment horizon plan.
3. Structure management control mechanism and project staff.
4. Set budget for risk management process.
5. Determine performance benchmarks.
6. Monitor active returns and performance; amend where needed.
7. Review results against plan and action.

The new focus is to provide concrete business benefits through integrated risk management. This progresses along a defined risk management project cycle.

11

Integrated Risk Management

We examine the risks that exist for the investor. We look initially at promising developments in the financial risk management, some of the leads that Basel II and RAMP offer. We then complement this study with contributions from organic risk management (ORM). ORM offers us some light into the continuing loss of control over miscreant CEOs, partly by separating perceived reputation from reality. Ways of identifying deceit by forensic accounting and interviewing are proposed. Unorthodox methods of hitting back at underperforming CEOs are examined under the "Kalashnikov" school of risk management. We take a look at integrating market, credit, operational and reputational risk views and how this can help meet business challenges of the future.

DEVELOPMENTS IN THE FINANCE SECTOR

Risk is an everyday hazard that faces banks, funds and insurers. It can usually be mitigated, but it is rarely eliminated completely. There are some cases where a positive "hazard" is a very good thing to have – each business faces a risk or probability of making profits. Millions of people buy lottery tickets each day facing the small risk that they will become instant multimillionaries. Business always encounters some form of risk.

It is good that we recognise that operational risks are present in our company. It is better when we can predict the risk event that will happen. It is best when we have reinforced the general resilience of our system through risk management countermeasures. The business operational risk shock is going to be absorbed by our company, so the company has to respond.

Not all banks have put operational risk firmly on their corporate radar. Few banks seem to have detailed an operational risk map by making provisions for expected operational risk. Basel surveyed 89 banks, and only 33 had designated expected operational risk loss measures. The actions varied – see Table 11.1.

Therefore, we need a management structure to plan the continuing and increasing system resilience of the company.

Doing risk management, rather than merely talking about it, will separate the banks from the boys for Basel II implementation. The measures of pricing, reserving and expensing for OpRisk are already one significant step ahead of risk managers simply answering:

We are risk-compliant because we have already submitted the Risk Compliance Report.

This reporting for the sake of reporting is a risk-ignorant form of control activity in a mindless ticking of boxes in a questionnaire. Will reporting and complying with the regulations catch out the next Enron?

The above techniques get us closer, may be, to a real-life model of risk management that we call 'organic'. Basel II reaches for some risk silo integration, but real life is messier. Messy problems can be handled in a project management control structure, such as RAMP.

An investment company, with its people and processes, its clients and their investment needs and preferences, is like a living organism. It can encompass every type of business risk, instead

Table 11.1   Number of banks that use expected operational losses

		Number of banks using expected operational losses for:		
Business line	Number of banks responding	Pricing	Reserving	Expensing
Entire bank	33	13	14	19

From *2002 Loss Data Collection Exercise for Operational Risk*, Basel Committee for Banking Supervision, March 2003, Table 22.

of just the ones we would like to handle. We see that there are many organic risk stakeholders at play in the market. See Figure 11.1.

ORGANIC RISK MANAGEMENT

Organic risk management (ORM) aims at improving the lack of progress made in four investment areas within the modern corporation:

- Corporate responsibility
- Command-control
- Accountability
- Corporate transparency.

This ORM control issue has already been addressed in part by integrating the investment manager selection factors of: alpha, sigma and theta.[1]

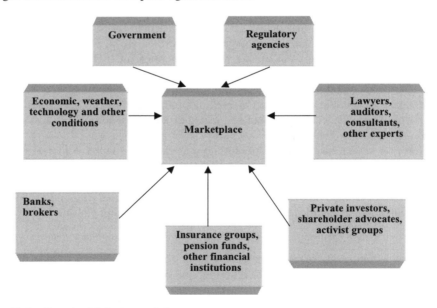

Figure 11.1   Organic risk factors and players

---

[1] "Avoiding disappointment in investment manager selection", R. Urwin, paper to International Association of Consulting Actuaries, March 1998.

Table 11.2   Risk-return, linking product and customer

Investment managers' Alpha target (basis points over benchmark)	Product sold	Customer targeted
100–150	Conservative	Cautious
250–350	Regular risk	Average
500–750	Aggressive	Tiger

- Alpha is the active return contribution by the manager.
- Sigma has been defined as the tracking error of performance, using the standard deviation of alpha.
- Theta are the non-financial behavioural factors that contribute to the resultant manager selection and control structure.

Too few companies are focused only on alpha; fewer still manage to link all three contributing factors together to derive optimal manager performance.

ORM recognises that people at work present risks of their own, and the drive to create wealth brings risk catalysts into play. Business processes need people to work together in an orderly and predictable fashion. The Basel II view of OpRisk is very focused upon banks, omitting the significant role on OpRisk played by insurance or non-bank financial companies. It is ironic since non-bank institutions compete by providing core banking services and products.

Another way to design ORM structures is to link risk-return offer with risk-return demand or appetite. See Table 11.2

Therefore, the ORM approach is focused on integrating operational risk from different areas, rather than concentrating upon risk silos only within banks. This separation is spurious as operational risk stems from the business processes that connect different groups. The Loss Database has to face this tough fact. Extensive research from Basel bears this out.[2]

The most frequent combinations of two business lines contributing to a single loss event were:

- Retail banking/Corporate banking.
- Retail banking/Asset management.

The most frequent combination of three business lines contributing to a single loss event was:

- Retail banking, commercial banking and Asset management.

ORM takes a more integrated and holistic view of the corporation. Forensic accounting provides benefit within ORM by checking the likely truth content of a target individual, and to map his probable value to the company. The media have often concentrated upon the actions of a person within the company, namely the CEO. But, this individual was hired by the company structure. A single person damages the whole company because the corporate structure is fundamentally risk seeking. Few companies take the trouble and expense to run full ORM background checks on the job applicant. This lax staff-screening process transforms the entire company into an entity with medium-probability events that have high negative-impact results.

Organic risk management attempts to examine and conduct damage limitation to stop one infected part hurting the whole corporate entity. There are no Lazarus come-backs for a dead company.

---

[2] "2002 Loss data collection exercise for operational risk", Basel Committee for Banking Supervision, March 2003, Table 11.

Table 11.3   Risks and ORM: an overview

	Organic risk
Main risks	• Corporate responsibility – underperformance • Command-control features – e.g. fraud • Accountability – lack of transparency • Organic personal risks – e.g. risk seeking
Type of review	• Corporate health check for operational risk gaps • Forensic accounting of financial health • Organic screening of company's leaders
Risk warnings	Where we are now? – OpRisk scorecard Where we are going? Risk Map Loss database (organic causal model) Who? What? When? How much?
Actions and threats for compensation	Traditional: Lawsuit Insurance claims Financial regulator Professional guild ombudsman Shareholders' advocacy groups e.g. CalPers, PIRC Unorthodox: "Kalashknikov" risk management Destruction of offender's reputation Internet bulletin-board cyber-smear Disruption of AGM (Yakuza–Sokaiya) Street protests Vandalism Arson

Risk management is not a pure defence mechanism, it allows an individual or an institution to meet risk threats by taking offensive action. See Table 11.3.

SEPARATING REPUTATION FROM RISK MANAGEMENT

One problem in detailing reputational risk within the financial industry is that many cases are still unknown or unpublicised. We are subject to the dissemination of cleaned-up annual reports, and a charm offensive from the investor relations department. Many corporations do not encourage the bad news regarding adverse financial or operational conditions, even less so to lay the blame at their own door.

Reputational risk is the risk that the public image of the firm will suffer damage in the eyes of stakeholders, resulting in a lower credit standing. Any CEO faced with this risk event will meet more difficult conditions, and will be tempted to cover up embarrassing facts and figures.[3] Another desire is to preserve their marketability for the next executive job.

---

[3] "Implicit claim incentives on the accounting choices of troubled companies", D. Peltier-Rivest, *Journal of Forensic Accounting*, vol.3, 2002.

Reputational risk has more in common with burglary risk, when your organic risk management countermeasures prevent the hiring of a magpie CEO, he enters another company as a hallowed saviour. Reputational risk analysis, coupled with "Kalashnikov" organic risk management, can put the company shoe on the other foot.

Reputation analysis can successfully be carried out by good old-fashioned interviewing techniques. Too few people at the top of the corporate pyramid are either adept or trained for this task. Our experience with the FBI, KGB, police and security firms shows that there is an untapped resource waiting to be utilised by the hiring and remuneration committees. One tough and structured interview can solve future large-scale company executive problems.

> *One powerful forensic-type procedure available to those responsible for detecting fraudulent activity is interviewing. Effective interviewing is a function of both a well-prepared interviewer and a well-structured interview. Successful interviewers typically have extensive interviewing experience and are proficient in identifying the verbal and nonverbal cues of deception.*[4]

Thus, a top executive level calculus of risk will be made: cover up or not to cover up. If the deceit fails, the total risk impact will double, added by the embarrassment of the subsequent cover-up breaking. If not, then the CEO may just get away with a handsome pay-off and a pension.

The traditional corporate excesses came about because CEOs and top executives had to keep their reputations and their jobs. We saw in the beginning of this book that the top business security driver was to prevent "damage to image". Doing so would give them enough time and prestige to get as much pay and benefits from the company before the inevitable departure in a few years. Their reputation risk management was to go after big mergers and acquistons (M&A).

The bigger you are, the better you are. Actually, the bigger the company, the larger the salary bonus for the CEO who now takes a percentage cut of a much expanded revenue base under an M&A mania. Corporate public relations have been going into overdrive in recent years, expressing clichés including a combination of the two phrases: "synergistic benefits" or "win-win".

Corporate prestige is an age-old selling line that is based on the traditional elitism. Hence: "snob value = quality". "The bigger company = a better reputation". You cannot question a company with good credentials and a top reputation. Like Enron.

CASE STUDY: ENRON[5]

The complex fraud at Enron showed massive deception of asset values, coupled with executive greed. All without paying any tax to the government despite earning billions of dollars in stated profits. Enron deliberately used fake transactions and SPVs that were partly owned or controlled by the officers themselves for deception and self-enrichment. These used the Midas touch to change profits into losses, and taxes into tax shelters.

The top 200 executives of the company received $1.4 billion (£864 million) in salary, bonuses, and share options in 2000, before the largest corporate bankruptcy in the USA. The clearest evidence of dubious practices in the report concerns the way the top executives were rewarded, even as the company was hurtling towards disaster.

---

[4] "Interviewing as a forensic-type procedure", T. Buckhoff and J. Hansen, *Journal of Forensic Accounting*, vol.3, 2002.
[5] "Enron's trail of deception", BBC News, 13 February 2003.

Top 200 Enron executives' pay
1998: $193 million
1999: $401 million
2000: $1.4 billion

Most of the pay consisted of stock options, which increased from $60 million to $1 billion, explaining why Enron was so desperate to keep ramping its share price and keep executives in power.

Controls on this pay-out craze were weak or non-existent. The board's compensation committee never questioned a single pay award. The company did not have to keep adequate records of some of the questionable transactions. This can be partly limited by legislation – for example, by the ban on loans by companies to their executives in the Sarbanes–Oxley Act. Other deeper defects require a change in current corporate practices amid rising shareholder anger. Investigators and investors were appalled by professionals (lawyers, accountants and bankers) pretending that all details were in order, in return for the $87 million in fees they earned from creating the tax shelters for Enron.

There is no magical "silver bullet" that would stop such future corporate abuse. Large corporations determined to use complexity to confuse shareholders and taxpayers will still continue to look for get-outs. The legal changes alone will not change company behaviour. Rather, a potentially hostile investment climate with forensic accounting procedures, armed by vitriolic publicity, will help prevent another Enron. But current corporate practice is still way off this mark.

The depth and truth of risk management systems and operational procedures may not be consonant with this risk-ignorant arrogance. Traffic lights indicating company green, amber or red status are better forms of evaluating the company's vulnerability to business stress or risk. We have highlighted these risk triggers or forensic accounting "red lights" in Table 11.4.

Company structure is an operational risk organism, in which animals interact, the success of one part is taken as the success of the whole. A company is a creature that breeds (merges) and seeks risk.

Unfortunately, many companies (creatures) do not improve their risk-return structure within their selection of projects in its business portfolio – many projects or products are just 'inherited' and continue to consume labour and resources. A review across the corporation's projects of the value-added and risk in a Balanced Scorecard is often not done, mainly for historical or political reasons. When conducted properly, a Balanced Scorecard offers great benefits for the corporation. See Table 11.5.

Table 11.5   Corporate Balanced Scorecard

Department	Project	Goal 1 contribution %	Goal 2 contribution %	Goal 3 contribution %	Value-added (€ m)	Risk warning light
Finance	A	25	0	12	€ 23	Green
	B	20	5	0	€ 19	Green
	C	0	3	−2	€ 1	Amber
IT	J	13	0	1	€ 5	Green
	K	3	−2	3	€ 0	Amber
	L	2	0	−3	−€ 2	Red

(Compare against: "Portfolio management: Delivering business strategy through doing the right projects", T. Cooke-Davies, Project Manager Today, Feb. 2002.)

Table 11.4 Organic risk management – an example diagnosis

Organic risk management		Medical diagnosis	
Is the trading going fine?	No, not well.	How are you feeling today?	Doctor, I am feeling ill.
How is it performing, then?	We are losing money.	How are the symptoms?	I have a strong pain.
Where are you losing money?	We lost it in asset management.	Where is the pain?	In the head.
How much money has been lost?	$26 million over the past 12 months.	What is the temperature?	39.5°C (thermometer).
How much money was lost in the previous year?	$14.5 million over the year before that according to the Loss Database.	That's high. What is your normal temperature?	38.4°C the last time you gave me a check-up.
What else has changed since the previous year?	We appointed a new trader.	What has changed in your life?	I was appointed to a new job.
Maybe he is not a good trader. Could he be linked to the losses?	Impossible. His, performance in his previous company was stellar.	What does this new job entail?	More responsibility, travel, socialising and drinking with clients.
What does his job reference say?	Said he was an excellent worker with a good pick of bonds and equities.	It is cold outside. What if going out gives you a head cold?	Could do, but I have to travel a lot.
Who wrote it?	His previous company boss.	How much do you drink in the evenings?	About one bottle of wine a day.
Maybe they were trying to get rid of him. Have you run a personal reference check through your own contacts, rather than his own?	Maybe, but I think it's highly unlikely. I don't think I could spy on the man – I trust him.	The alcohol makes your blood vessels dilate. This will be bad in cold weather. It can also damage your kidneys. Do you get pain there?	Well, actually, I also get pain around the side of my stomach area.
If you have not checked him yourself, can your company have let him slip through proper screening?	It is possible.	Then maybe you are drinking too much. Do you vomit as well?	Yes, sometimes during the end of the week.
Would you consider letting him go?	Yes, if it can stop us losing this much money.	Would you consider giving up, or severely cutting down, your alcohol intake?	Yes, if it can get rid of my illness.

FUTURE FOR RISK MANAGEMENT

The future for financial risk management looks bright with every additional market shock. When these business shocks are high impact, or the directors' risk precautions have been poor, then the hazard can get uncontrollable. This means that risk management experts will be hastily called in post facto, and that can only be good for their fees.

There seems genuine surprise when another bank or fund loses large sums from an error. This can only help the industry where it provides an essential risk catalyst for instigating effective risk management. Basel II has been another catalyst to spark life into risk-ignorant dodos. If the reality check is soon forgotten, then our misjudged investor perceptions remain unchanged. Risk management is a continuous process.

Successful risk management is predicated upon:

1. Appropriate investor perception, especially at top management strategic level.
2. Mandate for board level commitment of resources.
3. Accurate risk analysis.
4. Appropriate risk management implementation.
5. Follow-up and continuous monitoring.

RAMP is one management methodology that structures these steps in great detail. It could bind the complex mix of people, their skills, finance and technology into a successful risk management project. Regulatory compliance and the craze for mathematical modelling in risk management has led to a burgeoning supply of technology in the middle office. The Basel II Loss Database is just one example. Introducing new risk management technology backed with large-scale funding does not guarantee a successful project.

THE CASE FOR ORGANIC RISK MANAGEMENT

The process flow outlined in RAMP above is only a small part of the risk management methodology:

1. Analyse
2. Understand
3. Report
4. Mitigate or implement countermeasures
5. Follow up.

Directors of companies fundamentally break companies, not rogue traders or Nigerian fraudsters on a 419 scam.

The market disasters have come about partly as a mismatch between investors' bid for an investment that is incongruent with their risk appetite. Investor disillusionment continues. We are likely to have more faith by asking a crystal ball than consulting the investment "experts" for financial advice.

Shareholders in companies hope for the best when they invest. But, it often turns out that there is more to choosing a firm's equity than mere external market fundamentals: maybe weighted 25 % fundamentals and 75 % good internal management. A study of 1357 companies in seven countries showed UK productivity was critically hampered by inefficient management in comparison to its international rivals. UK workforce days are wasted in nearly 50 %

Table 11.6   Reasons for failures in productivity in the UK

Reasons	% of sample
Insufficient planning and control	43
Inadequate management	23
Poor work morale	12
Lack of skills and qualifications	8
IT-related problems	7
Ineffective communication	7

of the working year (see Table 11.6). This is a waste that is valued at £111 billion in the year 2001.[6]

Therefore, a good guess is that the success of a corporation depends upon good steering and leadership skills of the board of directors. This makes it a major factor in determining the success of your investment's value. Selfish executive action can break shareholder value quicker than it takes a business guru to lecture on "Dow Jones 36 000".

The fear Enron and Worldcom sank was that the CEO and board of directors will attempt to fleece the investors with the benediction of modern corporate capitalism. The losers are many:

- fund managers
- banks that lent the CEOs their money
- company shareholders
- pensioners who put their savings for old age *et al*.

The company leaders need to be checked by ORM investigations. Such checks have usually been unprofessional and shallow up to now. Forensic accounting holds hope for finding truthful information. We take an organic risk management view of this loss among the participant stakeholders. CEO applicants can lie or mislead, that is why we need deeper and more professional interviews.[7]

If we are to hire the best company leader or manager, then we ought to think outside the box and select them based upon their abilities, not their appearance or sales spiel. Closed recruitment can mean a locked mindset that is unreceptive to new ideas. Modern management methods may be one of the casualties. A major survey of corporate respondents shows that UK senior management in companies needs to be good at taking risk and introducing structural corporate improvement. These skills cannot be assumed as given[8]. See Table 11.7.

Table 11.7   UK senior management skills in companies

Management skill	% responding
Risk taking	70
Implementing major change	60
Forward planning	50
Effective leadership	50
Strategic thinking	42

---

[6] "Untapped potential: barriers to optimum corporate productivity", Proudfoot Consulting, 2002.
[7] "Interviewing as a forensic-type procedure", T. Buckhoff and J. Hansen, *Journal of Forensic Accounting*, vol.3, 2000.
[8] "The 2002 Challenge of Change" survey, www.changemanagementonline.co.uk.

Over half of major change projects are actively managed by the board. With companies typically undertaking 2,666 such projects per year (averaging three major change projects per annum per company) this means that a massive 35 % of senior management and director time is spend managing change.

Not all top-management investment styles work. Certainly, no single one works all the time in all circumstances. It is true that the investment posture has to be tailored to fit the market situation. Modern investment history is littered with the corpses of banks and investment funds that have not succeeded in handling change management. Twenty-first century profitability means being both:

- risk conscious
- risk managed.

The Barings, Sumitomo, AIB banks after their disasters clearly showed the risk-ignorant facet of management creeping up again. Does your top management fit your risk appetite? Thus, from a risk management viewpoint, it would do well to conduct a corporate command and control analysis. Where investor style and management style do not meet, this mismatch means trouble.

There is little come-back for someone who gambles much-needed money in extremely risky "investments" or scams. Like the "419s" scams, it happens all the time. The large trading profits at Barings or Enron or AIB were eventually exposed as false – these were 419s in all but name. There will be more investors who fail because they falsely believe themselves to be less risk-seeking or more informed than they really are.

There are many companies that consider themselves, or advertise themselves as, well risk managed. While banks and insurance companies may feel that they are already adequately risk managed, one can find that many corporate left-hands do not know what their right-hand is doing. HR investment and training are examples where companies put money in, but do not know exactly what they get out of it. The balanced scorecard is a cost-effective progress snapshot analysis. Operational risk assessment can also be conducted using a scorecard to identify corporate areas of weakness by department and by business process. One of the fundamental considerations of integrated risk management is to examine in depth how linked risk initiatives are in reality. Enterprise risk management (ERM) scorecards have been proposed for handling operational risk in Dresdner bank.[9]

We have talked about corrupt CEOs, we have pinpointed examples when executives have lied or misled. There are now two questions:

- How to know?
- What to do?

Forensic accounting can be a way through the fog. Either employ an investigator or do it yourself. Apply for a job in the target under an assumed name with some inconsistencies or lies. Even hiring a John Smith with a criminal record who lists "No previous convictions" in the company application form is one tactic. If he gets through, then it seems that anyone of questionable credentials can get into the company because it has a lax risk management culture. Tabloid newspapers revel in this type of scoop.

---

[9] "An operational risk scorecard", U. Anders and M. Sanstedt, *Risk*, January 2003.

CASE STUDY: HUNTING FOR STAFF DECEIT[10]

Hunting for an audit trail of previous deals, comments and work experience of key staff becomes a necessity of our modern employment environment. Digging up previous convictions is generally unlikely, but sackings, bad debts and fines are more probable. Keeping an ear out and an open eye are ways to detect interviewee key risk indicators.

Prospective employers are changing their risk perspective to take a proactive stance and sniff the Internet for a scent that candidates are lying behind a wide smile. The PR image embellished in CVs and interviews begins to crack when employers find incriminating evidence left on websites. One employee called her boss a "bitch from hell". A job applicant admitted "lying through his teeth" at the hiring interview. Another confessed that his CV was "a masterpiece of fiction".

These deceitful job candidates were rejected after prospective employers discovered their true outpourings on the Internet. It is cost-effective forensic cybersurfing.

There is the checking of previous jobs, professional and academic qualifications. Other character references not on the CV would be worth contacting too. Based on all this accumulated forensic data, you should be in a position to make a better-informed decision on how to proceed. Otherwise, you could be hiring or handing over your investment mandate blindly.

Many companies do not bother undertaking all this workload. Those that do may wish to take a more jaundiced eye when it comes to examining sparkling accounts or glowing CVs and job applications. A healthy dose of cynicism is good for the corporate soul.[11]

Our operational risk management is composed of more flexible techniques that are designed to be balanced and achievable. It explicitly takes business processes data as being subjective and open to machinations and poor performance of human beings. We call this methodology "organic risk management". See Table 11.8 for an overview. Figure 11.2 provides an overview of the "risk universe".

Let us examine organic risk management in more depth. We have seen how the wish to limit damage to public prestige is the great industrial motivator. There are two forms of corporate damage that hurt investors:

- unintentional (ostensibly) and legal
- intentional and illegal.

Unintentional (ostensibly) and legal

The short-term nature of a CEO's tenure is a driver for leaders in the modern economy to remove as much value from the company for themselves rapidly. Executives have been adept at this collusion because regulators and investors have been slow to monitor the company distress, and weak when handing out punishment. Knowing that there are lots of assets to strip, and there is less chance of being caught, serves as a risk catalyst to create the risk-loss event. This will be less likely when regulators implement new warning mechanisms and impose tougher

---

[10] "Bitch boss remark no way to win job", Reuters, London, 20 June 2003.
[11] "Conducting a pro-active fraud audit", C. Albrecht, W.S. Albrecht and J.G. Dunn, *Journal of Forensic Accounting*, vol.2, 2000.

Table 11.8   Organic risk management overview

Organic risk	Traditional risk elements
Corporate responsibility Command-control features Accountability	Market risk Interest rate risk Currency risk Asset-liability management
Organic risk management Mandate risk Flexible due diligence "Kalashnikov" risk management	Operational risk management in organisation Basel II banking regulations
Corporate/organic health-check Intuitive inspection of corporate health Personal background screening Risk Countermeasures	Basel II financial health-check Pillar 1 Pillar 2 Pillar 3
Loss database (causal model) Who? What? When? How much?	Rules for participation Regulatory capital Supervisory review and checks Disclosure and transparency of operations
Punitive action or threat Destruction of offender's reputation Recovery of assets	Documentation and threat of revoking banking licence Increase regulatory capital

Figure 11.2   The risk universe

penalties. The investors should not be left out of the investigative process, but should include ORM and forensic accounting measures within their arsenal.

Intentional and illegal

There are many ways to cause damage or steal from the company. Fraud, rogue trading, arson and theft remain the ones that are best known. Increased monitoring raises the likelihood of catching the criminals, while severe penalties and jail terms serve as some deterrent. The public often focuses a lot of attention on these root causes, but ORM should also point staff to intentional threats originating from within their company.

Whatever the extent of danger (risk events) that we face in the business, risk management is a journey on a potentially rocky road. It needs a good road map. See Figure 11.3.

THE REIGNING INVESTMENT IDEOLOGY

All the above risks manifest themselves in various manners, mostly as corporate financial losses or, worst, bankruptcy. The losses that have occurred within the corporate jungle during 2000–2002 cannot be said to be novel losses. But, investors and financial experts keep being surprised. During 1980–99 there have been large monthly losses greater than 5 % on several times (see Table 11.9).

These corporate losses can be entered in a log or loss database under the appropriate category. This has been defined as one element within the new Basel II banking regulation rules. Thus, from Table 11.10 at the most generic level.

Or, you could face corporate losses shown in Table 11.11.

This is the top-level view of risk. It also gives the underlying reasons for the losses. These can be deduced from detailed analysis of the loss database. But, industrial logic engines are not currently developed enough in the majority of cases to derive such rapid and succinct conclusions from the masses of data.

Total risk also depends upon which investment vehicles and business lines that you choose. See Table 11.12.

The financial institutions have concentrated on credit risk and market risk. There are two reasons given.

Table 11.9   Occurrences of large monthly movements

Decade	Large losses > 5 % on S&P	Moves > 5 % on gold
1980s	9	41
1990s	5	18

"Fallacies about the effects of market risk management systems", P. Jorion, *Bank of England Financial Stability Review*, December 2002.

Table 11.10   Corporate losses at the generic level

	Credit risk	Liquidity risk	Market risk	Operational risk	Total
Losses (%)	28	8	32	22	100

Goals (destination)
Give the best return for shareholders and staff at acceptable risk.
High corporate responsibility in line with defined governance measures.
Accountability to shareholders and other stakeholders.
Dedication, reward and training for staff to maintain standards and profitability.

Tactics (vehicle)
Integrated risk management methodology.
Operational risk management for managers.
Position-keeping portfolio value.
Control of customer service quality.
Training: check risk-awareness standards of enterprise-wide staff.
Check CVs and backgrounds of executives, managers and line staff.

Procedural controls (road-signs and milestones)
Check cash, capital and asset levels.
Monitor sales, cash-flow and other accounting targets.
Obtain current customer service feedback.
Benchmark monitoring.
Mathematical models to detect variance.
Loss database analysis.

Standard of staff performance (gasoline)
Corporate health-check 1 – what were the financial (alpha) returns?
Corporate health-check 2 – what are the company non-financial (theta) factors ?
Individual health-check – what were the previous companies of job applicant really like?
    What was their performance there?
Physical appearance: check with curriculum vitae (CV) with a structured, forensic-type
    interview.

Risk threats (dangers on the road)
Legal: low staff dedication (job-hopping), sloppy work and attention to detail, low quality
    of customer and work relations, non-delivery of promised performance targets, lost
    profits, other damage to company.
Illegal: fraud, arson, theft, breach of contractual employee relations.

Normal countermeasures
Court action and seek legal damages.
Recovery of goods or damages in court or through other repossession channel.
Prohibition from working through the industry regulator.

Unorthodox "Kalashnikov" risk management
Use industry personal contacts to get CV corroborated.
Hire independent investigators to conduct background check.
Publicise errors or crimes in industrial media.
Disrupt the AGM (Yakuza).
Street protest (GSK).
Destroy guilty party's reputation on Internet (cybersmear).
Personal attacks on the individual (HLS).

Figure 11.3 Risk management road map

Table 11.11   Corporate losses

	Credit risk	Liquidity risk	Market risk	Operational risk	Total
Losses (%) of total annual loss.	32	13	20	35	100
Underlying cause	Inadequate screening of customers. Poor loan officer training.	Treasury has poor asset-liquidity-management. Accounts not coordinated with treasury.	Limits system not working. Mark-to-market is slow and inaccurate.	Management not understanding OpRisk. Poor pool of in-house skills.	

Table 11.12   A simplified view of the main risks

Fixed income	Equities	Commodities	Derivatives
Credit risk + interest rate risk + OpRisk	Valuation risk + market risk + OpRisk	Market risk + OpRisk	Market risk + credit risk + interest rate risk + OpRisk i.e. combination of the underlying asset classes

- It is because these are the risk factors where they have greatest experience. It does not mean that operational risk constitutes a minor threat or causes less damage.
- Risk experts are unsure how risk factors combine to result in loss.

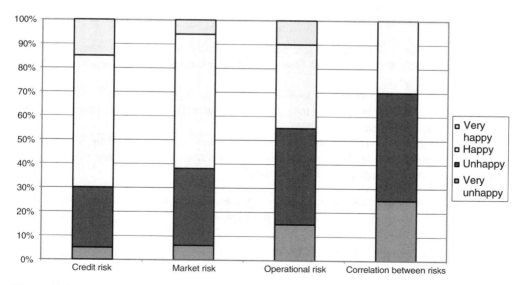

Figure 11.4   "How satisfied are insurers with their risk quantification methods?"

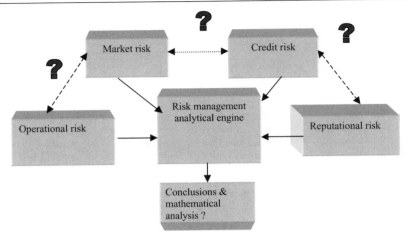

Figure 11.5   Risk interaction

Many risk professionals prefer to enumerate the risk hazards and use quantitative analysis to study them in depth. But, there is considerable unease as to the success of these techniques.[12] See Figure 11.4.

A key business factor must be to understand what business you are in, what risks you face and what sort of risk appetite you have to meet these risks. "What risk percentages do you face; how do these risks combine to hurt you?"

Given that even the experts are unsure about risk quantification and risk interaction, there must be room for doubt in the minds of investors. See Figure 11.5. We need more light in this risk management dark area.

Work goes on at a furious pace to evaluate the nature and extent of these linked risk factors, some of them are:

- The scorecard work done at Dresdner bank for logically connecting [business units with location and staff] → [processes] → [key risk indicators, assessment of operational risk and losses] so links can be evaluated.[13]
- Loss database causality modelling to connect risk causes with risk events and the eventual consequences. Loss events are tied to key risk indicators (KRIs) so that benchmarks can be set as early warning alerts.[14]
- Business process analysis standpoint with workflows moving between entities and business actors.[15] A good case for business process reengineering (BPR) is made to handle risk management requirements, especially for Basel II.

The salient points are that business processes are a collaborative effort by various staff from different work groups. These business participants create a dynamic workflow that has

---

[12] "How satisfied are insurers with their risk quantification methods?", Watson Wyatt, *Insurance and Financial Services Review*, February 2002.
[13] "An operational risk scorecard", U. Anders and M. Sanstedt, *Risk*, January 2003.
[14] "Forecasting from loss-events", Z. Molla, *Investec*, London, 5–6 June 2003.
[15] "Analysing business processes", J. Palm, *Risk*, March 2003.

inherent risk elements. Mathematical modelling and audit control focused upon risk elements within traditional workflows that we believed were well understood, i.e. market and credit risk. Basel II, loss database, operational risk analysis, balanced scorecards and risk maps shed light on other areas that were hitherto rarely emphasised.

Our understanding in this area has improved and it has definitely become more interwoven or holistic since the Basel II initiatives. These encourage a wider enterprise risk management (ERM) view and not a closed one. A lot of good risk management work has been done so far, but much more needs to be achieved.

12

Summary and Conclusions

SUMMARY OF RISK MANAGEMENT

Risk management has run part of its course from haphazard gut-feeling to deeply scientific. Some have realised recently that there is too much extraneous data and statistics, and too little accurate business information. Investors are now demanding the basic truthful information needed for forming proper decisions. Much past "investment analysis" has been exposed as PR and corporate puff masquerading as professional advice. Legal and industry supervisors have cracked down upon professional misconduct. We used to look in the wrong places or the ask the wrong people to help us. The finance industry has to move forward.

Recent "pump and dump" schemes by the professional financial staff have proven the extent of self-interests within the industry. The focus has turned away from blaming the market to targeting the actions of individuals. This has been part of the realisation that operational risk, the hazards posed by human elements, can pose a bigger threat than traditional risk elements. The new Basel II banking regulations are geared towards combining traditional risk management elements of market and credit risk to connect operational risk.[1]

IDENTIFY STAKEHOLDERS AND INTERESTS

Operational risk involves the actions of many business groups, so mapping out the investors and stakeholders is an organic process and a complex one. PRINCE 2 and RAMP are examples of two methodologies that place stakeholders and expected returns on paper. We can deploy risk analytical tools. Returning to our shark attack example at the beginning of the book, we can consider poor company performance or financial loss as a **hazard** requiring detailed risk analysis. The causal element or **risk catalyst** stems from unsuitable leaders or inadequate investment managers leading to a fall in earnings and damage to business reputation. The dreaded result is the **risk event**, such as the adverse effect of a start-up investment loss or disastrous M&A decision. We can set the threat versus the risk management in Table 12.1. Analyse the subjective worth of the company heads – determine the value-added (positive or negative) that can be ascribed to the top management. One effective method is to interview then face to face to find the truth.[2] Already, regulators are expanding and are on the war path gearing up for getting tough on criminal activity by corporate management.

> The UK's chief financial regulator is lobbying the government for the same powers as its US counterpart to stamp out accounting abuses by companies and guard against Enron-style business scandals. . . . . It would amount to the biggest shake-up of corporate accounts policing since scandals such as Maxwell and Polly Peck. Under the plan, the FSA would resemble the Securities and Exchange Commission . . .[3]

---

[1] *Operational Risk Capital Allocation and the Integration of Risks*, E. Medova, Judge Institute, October 2001.
[2] *"Interviewing as a forensic-type procedure"*, T. Buckhoff and J. Hansen, *Journal of Forensic Accounting*, vol.3, 2002.
[3] "FSA seeks to extend powers", *Financial Times*, 16 January 2003.

Table 12.1   Risk managing the investment hazard

Hazard	Catalyst	Event	Techniques	Stakeholders involved	Action
Bad company annual results	Unsuitable leader for company	Appalling PR skills. Disastrous M&A decision.	AEW system. Forensic accounting of CV and job history. Chart CEO valueadded in Balanced Scorecard.	All staff, investors, suppliers and clients	Convene Shareholder group representatives to appoint qualified, independent Remuneration and Selection Board.
Financial loss for fund	Unsuitable investment managers	Investment loss for portfolio.	Examine relevant entries in Loss Database. Analyse benchmarks for Alpha against current portfolio.	Line manager, Department head, Actuary, MD, Trustees from investor pension fund mandate.	Set out target benchmarks for Alpha. Interview job applicants in depth for Sigma and Theta characteristics.

The widening definition of crime, e.g. to include false accounts and money-laundering, mean that command-control must be established within an organisation. Some of these can be monitored automatically using computer software with AI logic. Companies that provide a rosy interpretation of balance sheets for the public need a more thorough grilling by the auditors, who are now more alert to their duty.[4] The investors and auditors are on the offensive against fraud.[5] The corporate barriers against truthful information for investors are being attacked, led by funds, shareholder advocacy groups and regulatory authorities.

MATCH RISK APPETITES

The media headlines tend to focus upon the wrong targets. These focus upon criminal managers' activity, or rogue traders. But, most company underperformance or losses are the result of those innocent errors – operational risk and strategic risk. That means that a single top-level planning fault, or a dozen daily back-office errors, will often add up to much more damage than a single rogue trade or fraudulent activity.

We need to re-assess our risk-return appetite against the likely returns in the quagmire of mixed competencies and unrealistic expectations. Risk appetite must match the risk offer. The investor must meet the company, in person or by telecommunications, and grill it with questions:

- "Is the CEO innocent but incompetent; or much worse?"
- "What was his previous record?"
- "How can I get past the PR to track him down?"

---

[4] "An empirical analysis of the role of fraud in client firm market reaction to auditor lawsuits", D. Sinason and C. Pacini, *Journal of Forensic Accounting*, vol.1, 2000.
[5] "Forensic risk management – A sharpened fraud focus reduces litigation risk", D. Burgess and C. Pacini, *Journal of Forensic Accounting*, vol.1, 2000.

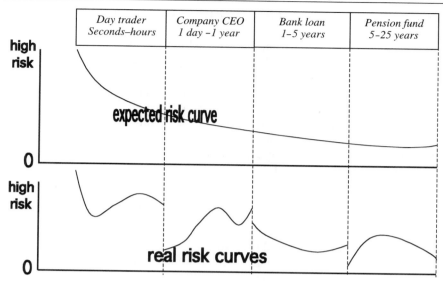

Day trader *Seconds–hours*	Company CEO *1 day –1 year*	Bank loan *1–5 years*	Pension fund *5-25 years*

Figure 12.1 Investor and stakeholder risk time horizons

One of the potential hazards is that CEOs and CFOs are advertising the value of one asset – their innate management skill. This only enrichens their bonus pay, pension and stock options.[6] Where the investor is faced with an unfamiliar company executive or a novel asset, then a risk management methodology such as RAMP may offer much benefit. A risk review by unbiased parties using forensic investigative techniques can provide a lot of benefit. A risk-mapping analysis by impartial experts can be obtained in a Delphi-group risk-reward analytical process.

MATCH RISK TIME HORIZONS

No professional football player wants to stick his neck out, or his health, for more than the designated 90 minutes. Some companies are already playing close to their limits in extra time. Investors' risk time horizons should match the risk scenario. See Figure 12.1.

The sophisticated investor is already aware of these potential cash-flow problems. What is rather more galling is when cash is running dangerously short, despite all prognostications. Companies play out favourable scenarios with dwindling assets or cash. The complication arises from the chain of market players all with different risk time horizons. Everyone wants a cut or return at different times. Because investors have different entry times and various time horizons, it is no longer fitting to state as gospel truth that all long-hold investment decisions are correct. The real risk curve will change along time and market conditions; this can be startling to learn.

It is also important to recognise that the available data and the criteria for judging acceptability may change with time so that what might have been acceptable when a project was initially proposed may no longer be so several years on . . . Thus, the acceptability of the

---

[6] "Stock option accounting can be materially misleading", D. Crumbley and N. Apostolou, *Journal of Forensic Accounting*, vol.3, 2002.

risks associated with a project must be kept under constant review throughout the life of a project.[7]

The real risk curve will differ from the expected risk curve; sometimes, even the most respected pension fund or venerated CEO will fail hugely. An eternal buy-and-hold strategy may no longer be suitable in the modern market. Reputation risk management means that we have to separate deserved prestige from the veneer of respectability and corporate performance. CEO worship is no longer worth the votive candles burnt. The truth may be more along the lines of a real risk curve laid out for the sake of discussion. See Figure 12.1. Unfortunately, the time horizon of a CEO is usually in months and not years – this creates the need to maximise the most that can be wrung out of the firm. Thus, balance sheets can be cosmetically made up for a smoke-screen, not for the benefit of investors.

ORGANIC DUE DILIGENCE

Everyone wants profit on their investment, but we all invest different amounts of resources in research. A modern bank or fund would be happy to invest $50 million into a venture and to spend $500 000 on a due diligence with lawyers. It would be unwilling to fork out $5000 on discreet enquiries and a chat with detectives in the FBI, Russian FSB, City of London Fraud Squad or similar. Due diligence has become ossified in its own rigorous blinkered thinking.

Fallacy: only banks, insurers, lawyers and accountants have the monopoly in professional investment knowledge.

Private investigators, from AON, Marsh, Control Risks Group, Pinkertons and Wackenhut all offer potential corporate added-value here. They also operate under the forensic accounting banner to undertake deep financial and behavioural analysis. A proper due diligence can win through more flexibility and discretion. One such due diligence by Dynegy on Enron made the correct call on risk hazard and called off the merger. It saved an unbelievable fortune.[8]

Basel II enables Moodys and Standard & Poors, plus the corporations themselves, to certify the level of operational risk. Some groups will have become disposed towards offering a more tailored or sympathetic risk assessment. The traditional credit-rating visit cannot be so highly valued seeing that the target company has lots of advance warning. To paraphrase Heisenberg's principle of uncertainty:

You can never be sure of the direction or health of a target company, because these are directly affected by the means you use to observe them.

Newer aspects of this investigative process show that company data are more accurate and accountable when the target is completely unaware of the observation carried out by snooping.[9] Forensic accounting comes in useful; it is more akin to industrial espionage, but the data is less likely to be compromised by a public relations exercise. These forensic agents can be employed to separate performance from ill-deserved reputation. They can take the subtle, covert observation of the subject to get closer to the truth.

Then, they can get the metaphysical corporate handcuffs on the risk-offering crook. More flexible analytical activity clearly complements the bank's own analysts and traditional due

---

[7] 'The Philosophy of Risk', ch.10, Chicken J. & Posner T., Thomas Telford books, 1998.
[8] "Risk Detectives", L., Eakins *GARP Risk Review*, September–October 2002.
[9] "Black tech forensics – Collection and control of electronic evidence", G. Stevenson Smith, *Journal of Forensic Accounting*, vol.1, 2000.

diligence process. Forensic accounting comes in to provide a deeper investigation. Otherwise, banks and financial companies suffer when they are still locked in a narrow corporate group-think.

VALUE FOR MONEY

Shop around for the best service or risk-return offer. Get the most suitable value for money plus caution-danger calculus for you. Because an investment is a labour project, keep a proper log of time worked on your behalf and materials used by contractors. A bank or fund should use people like hiring a plumber. Employing a star trader without value for money or risk considerations is a recipe for disaster. The cross-reference table of staff selection based upon return (alpha), risk (sigma) and behavioural (theta) factors brings a more organic and profitable view of risk management.

Fund management has had to become more compliant with additional regulations. Funds are recognising the value of focusing on consistent return, not on reputation of individual staff deemed as "stars". Alpha, the active return, is a better and consistent profit compared to the ephemeral advantage of trader's luck, or fraud. This screening of investors and diversification of assets helps us to separate the real stars from the also-rans in the surrounding satellite performers.

Similarly, capital expenditure projects should be assessed for cost benefits rather than simply high profile. Most of the financial dealing systems we have worked on rely on a higher expenditure and publicity for the glamorous front-office dealing end. The drab back-office and accounts side was largely side-lined by comparison. This attitude can have a serious, unintended cost.

> *Had Barings purchased a system that enabled the settlements department in London to reconcile trades made in any part of the world with clients' orders . . . . Leeson's fraudulent of the 88888 account would have been exposed within months, if not weeks. Such a system, known as BRAINS, would have cost about £10 million.*[10]

The resulting fraud by Leeson was estimated at £800 million.

REPUTATION RISK

A move from living off yesterday's reputation is gradually taking over the market. One failure has come from the "best of breed" philosophy for hiring the best and paying the most. This attitude has been severely tested in an era of underperformance and corporate cost-cutting.

People are trying hard to forget the reputations of the prestigious accountants and the "best" investment banks. The fines against Wall Street and the investigations of Jack Grubman, Frank Quattrone, Martha Stewart *et al.* showed a belated attempt to rein in the corporate excesses. Should culprits try to destroy incriminating electronic evidence, then data recovery procedures will be able to retrieve much of the destroyed evidence. Email audit trails in forensic accounting procedures will find them out.[11]

A star fund manager is no longer accorded the status, but earns it. Disappointing performance drops them into the satellite group of also-rans. The research done by actuaries,

---

[10] *"The Collapse of Barings"*, p. 268, Stephen Fay, Wiley, 1996.
[11] "Black tech forensics – Collection and control of electronic evidence", G. Stevenson Smith, *Journal of Forensic Accounting*, vol.1, 2000.

forensic accountants and other financial analysts offers sound ground for assessing staff se-lection. Background checks for finding real suitability, rather than professional skill listed in a glossy CV can find out the sad truth.[12] Otherwise, risk and return appetites become more estranged.

Similarly, the reputation of a "top" services company can be just as short-lived and cheap as a bacon-lettuce-tomato sandwich. Go for performance delivered. Give them a check-list or interview to see if they can show results and sincerity.

THE CORPORATE GOVERNANCE MODEL

Corporate governance has moved forward from earlier carte blanche control structures. Dif-ferent management structures have been examined, and changes will be inevitable through regulation or internal pressures for reform. Mandating the money immediately without control or lien is a bad idea and one that has fallen out of favour in fund management. Control by a more proactive group of trustees, an elected board of non-executive directors and more effec-tive risk-burden sharing is on the cards. Tie everyone in and knot tightly to secure corporate loyalty and performance.

Governance capability levels show some ways in which we can exercise more control over the CEO and investment manager. '. . . the Sarbanes-Oxley Act is a call to get back to the basics that we have been discussing. Simply stated, the current status quo for corporate governance is unacceptable and must change. . . . The message for chief executive and chief financial officers and senior management is: Uphold your responsibility to maintain effective financial reporting and disclosure controls and adhere to high ethical standards. This requires meaningful certifications, code of ethics, and conduct for insiders that, if violated, will result in fines and criminal penalties, including imprisonment.'[13] We have shown some of the models for reforming and monitoring the fiduciary duty of the board of directors and investment managers. Organic risk management plays a valuable role here by asking what is the value of leadership – i.e. stripping away performance from perceived reputation. These models have the potential to move us into the light rather than signing your money away and being left in the dark.

HITTING BACK

Place less reliance on the legal system for redress – it is often too slow and expensive. There are cheaper and faster industrial arbitrators. You can create your own insurance protection. Then, there is the more constructive financing and hedging role being offered by traditional insurance companies and captives to handle your operational risk loss. Make necessary variations and amendments to take into account local risk practices, e.g. in an emerging market. You should have thought about it beforehand, not afterwards.

The Kalashnikov school of risk management is a frivolous thought at first sight. But occasionally, you have to show the potential or intent to injure a counterparty, even if it means a non-violent sense of destroying their reputation. New York Attorney General Eliot Spitzer's investigation and fines on Wall Street, the shareholders' revolt against executive pay at GlaxoSmithKline, freezing the payoff to Messier at Vivendi, the lawsuit against the Equitable

---

[12] "Interview as a forensic-type procedure", T. Buckhoff, J. Hansen, Journal of Forensic Accounting, Vol.3, 2002.
[13] 'Strengthening compliance through effective corporate governance', Susan Bies, Board of Governors, US Federal Reserve System, 11 June 2003.

Life directors are just examples of this vengeful trend. The Russians call this "kompromat". For some companies, their reputation is their livelihood. It can be destroyed.[14]

KEEP YOUR EYES ON THE PRIZE

Evaluate the appropriate monitoring and forecasting techniques for determining corporate risk and profit performance.

Employ the correct mathematical tools for investment modelling, not the jazziest or what experts tell you is in vogue.

Monitor the investment throughout, the annual AGM is just too late. Do not go to sleep for a year and wake up at the AGM. Or, you could send your Yakuza influences to the AGM to exercise your Kalashnikov school of hitting back. Everyone is angry across all age groups and investor categories. See Figure 12.2.

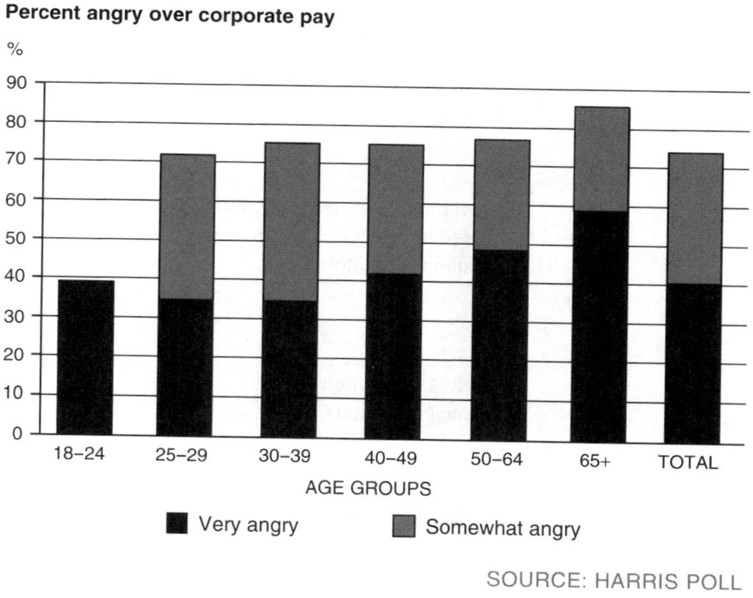

Percent angry over corporate pay

SOURCE: HARRIS POLL

Figure 12.2   Investor angry

What do the other investor advocacy groups, e.g. CalPers, PIRC, say? Establish your sanction mechanisms and keep up to date on developments.

The AEW early warning radar has been described as a way in which we can raise our sensory antennae towards potential corporate risks. There are already alternative radar warning systems for companies.[15] These can take passive or active stances on handling risk. The passive risk posture adopts analysis and reporting as the actions carried out, but it has to be complemented by active risk management. The Enron crash destroyed investor confidence. Yet, there are major lessons from the Enron debacle alone that offer a wealth of investigative knowledge, such as developing an AEW investor warning radar. We need to take it onboard.[16]

---

[14] "The pump-and-dump and cybersmear: An investigation of two cases of internet-based stock price manipulation", A. Cataldo and L. Killough, *Journal of Forensic Accounting*, vol.3, 2002.

[15] An example: "Raft radar" for operational risk management", www.raftinternational.com.

[16] "Forensic risk management – A sharpened focus reduces litigation risk", D. Burgess, C.Pacini, Journal of Forensic Accounting, Vol.1, 2000.

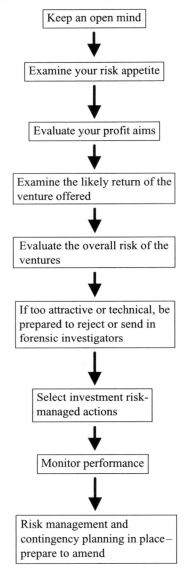

Figure 12.3 Flowchart for organic risk management

The Basel II loss database incorporates a predictive element within the risk-reporting framework for forecasting likely financial damage. It is in its elementary stages of development as a method of judging the future, so greater accuracy will continue to be desired. It is a tool for the operational risk management decision-making process within the company.

Keeping your eye on the prize is all but lost when people equate booked revenue with cash. Managing all business risks does not mean being expert in credit and market risk and letting operational risk hang.[17] The top management and links to auditors are brought to book and

---

[17] *Operational Risk Capital Allocation and the Integration of Risks*, E. Medova, Judge Institute, October 2001.

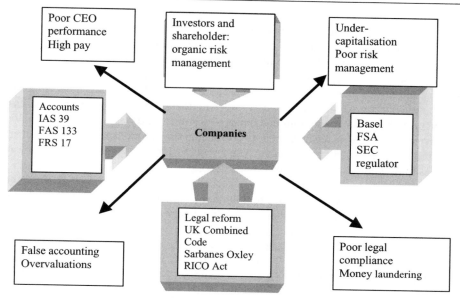

Figure 12.4 Corporate governance net and lost value

examined under the microscope. By doing so, we are looking into operational risk in detail –
the risk that is often the hardest to model.[18] See Figure 12.3.

CONCLUSIONS

Risk management used for too long to be an optional extra, just like a motorcar quad CD
player, it is now a necessity. Much of the business orthodoxy was built when risk management
was a mechanistic afterthought rather than a fundamental constituent of investment. Risk
management based on pure accountancy or IT lines is not only inadequate, but also mind-
closing.

The risk management technology and techniques are being developed. As fast as business
solutions suppliers can develop a "better" risk management system, new financial products and
company disasters inform us that we have to change the model. VaR, Monte Carlo, RAROC,
Loss Database open up some risk vistas, but they are really only tools with limits in the broader
scheme of risk management. Used well within an integrated risk framework, they can offer
real value-added for the company.

It was not rare to consider risk management an orphan or appendage in accounts. Risk
management has become elevated into a department of its own, and split away from accounting
and audit where it usually sits in many banks. Risk management is not just hedging with some
derivative instruments, it is a whole business process. Engineers and actuaries have proposed
RAMP as a risk management methodology, and it is one that is worth considering. Risk
management methodology is worth developing and employing since it loads more of the odds
in your favour when some of the investment playing cards are already stacked against you.

The corporate governance models and associated governance capability levels indicate
some options to exercise more managerial control over the investment trustee. The new IAS

---

[18] www.Erisk.com, January 2002.

accountancy standards will serve as guidelines for regulating company inspection and audit. These should not serve as the sole picture for gauging corporate health. Discreet inspection and company research that borders on espionage will bolster the staid and unwieldy traditional due diligence process. Forensic accounting serves this purpose well.

There is much less room for sitting back and letting rating agencies and others keep watch, regulatory authorities police the companies in a limited way. Risk management is a proactive exercise, not reactive. AEW corporate early warning radar enables us to lift our senses away from perceived industrial reputations and financial scams towards real corporate risks. Various groups, from shareholders, legal, regulatory and accounting sectors are closing the net around the major corporate governance problem. The net is closing slowly, but there will always be loop-holes to lose corporate value (see Figure 12.4).

Kalashknikov risk management understands that an inflexible management may not wish to listen to stakeholders, so you may have to point a (metaphorical) gun to their head. Sufficient opportunities exist for naming and shaming of an unbalanced board of directors, by waging a reputation war.

After looking at the recurring mistakes in recent business history, it is easy to lose all faith and become despondent over the level of impropriety. Yet, we need to build a sound investment methodology, not an ideology. RAMP, IAS accounting, Basel II provide sound outlines for handling investment risk.

The companies are already changing to include a new directorate structure and a clearer risk management function. Regulators are increasing their powers and defining greater punishment. Basel II, the ratings agencies and the insurance companies are offering the carrot, of lower borrowing costs and a higher risk reputation. Companies that choose to maintain a stronger risk-managed enterprise will benefit. Corporate governance and shareholder advocacy groups are already declaring their wish to battle companies that refuse to offer investor value. It is a brighter future under real risk management.

Leaving risk management unsupervised to the experts, and you are ignoring your real risks. Organic risk management re-applies analysis and screening of the human beings who are in charge of our investments. Forensic accounting starts to put more management control over the executives in your hands. Otherwise, it's your money in their hands under a carte blanche mandate. Risk management is your business to be managed proactively. Relying upon reputation is a poor proxy for value of leadership and judgement. The large company is a stubborn beast, driven by its directors not always for the investors' benefit. The company sometimes goes for a wayward walk. Tame the corporate animal.

Index

Index compiled by Annette Musker

RISK

perception

reality
(measured)

hedged
downside
minimized

VALUATION